CONTENTS

4: Processes

5: Non-finite Clauses: Raising and Control

6: Reanalysis: a Problem of Bracketing

7: Levels of Structure

PREFACE

This book is an attempt to incorporate some of the less controversial insights from modern theoretical linguistics into the teaching of English syntax. It seeks to strike a balance between the traditional and structural approaches and transformational generative syntax, which is currently the most consistent and influential linguistic framework.

We take the view that it is important for students of English — whether or not they will go on to specialise in English syntax — to be able to interpret the structure of sentences and their component parts. The practice of syntactic analysis, or 'parsing' as it is traditionally called, will improve students' understanding of the structure of English, it will facilitate their comprehension and production of the language and it will enable them to compare and contrast English structures and to perform syntactic operations on them. The ability to analyse structures in their context is a very useful and important skill for undergraduates to acquire and master. It is a skill which involves familiarity with, amongst other things, the principal categories and functions in English, the main syntactic operations, and the methods of syntactic argumentation.

Although the importance of syntactic analysis is generally recognised, none of the presently available grammars of English provides students with a systematic introduction to the methods of English syntactic analysis. Most of these grammars contain excellent inventories of the facts of English, but fail to show students explicitly how to formulate syntactic arguments, and how to apply relevant objective criteria and syntactic tests in the analysis of sentences. This book is meant to fill this gap. It offers an account of what we consider to be the basic rules and principles of English syntax, and it tries to make students aware of syntactic structures and their relations. It also tries to give some insight into the general methodology of syntactic description.

This coursebook is mainly intended for intermediate students of English at universities or colleges who have done one or more introductory grammar courses, but are not yet ready to enter a specialist course. Since in our experience students need a great deal of systematic guidance and practice in the analysis of sentences, we have provided numerous examples and exercises of different types.

A Modern Course in English Syntax also prepares students for further reading in the literature on English syntax, i.e. both the more 'traditional' accounts and the current transformational analyses. It offers some new ideas and insights, especially from the Extended Standard Theory (EST), which we have here tried to deal with in an informal manner; theory-internal discussions and irrelevant technicalities are generally avoided. We have found that the material of this book can be used profitably in English syntax courses in conjunction with reference grammars such as those by Randolph Quirk and his associates. In an attempt to make this book as self-contained as possible, we have refrained from including references to English grammars or the linguistic literature.

It must be emphasised that it is not the technical terminology or the grammatical labels that are of central importance in this book, but the approach developed for talking about sentences in English. While the book does not go into all the descriptive or theoretical detail of a fully developed syntax, and will therefore leave many issues undiscussed, it is intended to offer students the techniques for going into more complex matters. We expect that the book will sharpen students' observations, and make them aware of what are valid arguments and methods for meaningful analyses.

Parts of the material of this volume have been used in English syntax courses at University College, London (mainly students of English literature and language), at the Universities of Nijmegen and Ghent (Dutch and Belgian students of English), and at a teacher training college in Nijmegen.

In developing this course, we have assumed that the student has some knowledge of English grammar. Exercises are included and integrated into the structure of the book. They are meant to give students insight into the main patterns and problems of English syntax, and to appeal to their own linguistic intuitions and creativity.

Our thanks are due to colleagues in several English departments in England, Belgium and The Netherlands for useful comments on an earlier draft of this work. In particular we would mention Ton Broeders, Alasdair MacDonald, Sidney Greenbaum, Annemoon van Hest, Frits Stuurman and Jan Verdonck, who have given us detailed criticisms and sound advice on how to 'solve' and present certain problems. The book has greatly benefited from their suggestions. Needless to say, we accept full responsibility for the views expressed here and for any shortcomings that remain. We are also grateful to Diane Crook, Mies Faber and Mariette Wauters for their patience in typing successive versions of the manuscript.

THE BACKGROUND

The approach presented here adopts as its main theoretical background the multi-level analysis of the EST-framework, which distinguishes levels of D-structure and S-structure, and levels of Phonetic form and Logical form. D-structure (or, roughly, 'underlying structure') is determined by (a) phrase structure (PS) rules and (b) the Lexicon. PS rules generate the underlying structure of the sentence. The Lexicon contains the store of lexical items of the language, each with a specification of its syntactic category and an insertion frame. Verbs, for example, are specified for the type of complementation they require. Inserting lexical material into the structures derived by the PS rules is restricted by a matching condition: nouns can only be inserted into slots marked N; verbs can only be inserted into V slots, etc. The matching condition has recently been replaced in EST by mechanisms such as Case assignment and the Theta criterion, but these notions are not incorporated into this book. The constituent structure generated by the PS rules and filled in by lexical items gives us the D-structure.

The underlying structures may be affected by operations such as 'passivisation', 'extraposition', etc. Following recent developments in the transformational framework, this book distinguishes between elementary operations on syntactic patterns and the functional effect that is achieved by the operations. The process of *wh*-question formation, for example, is not seen as a single transformation but rather as the compounding of

(a) Subject–Auxiliary Inversion, and
(b) *Wh*-fronting

Hence, the transition from *John saw who* to *Who did John see?* is not a single transformation, but a process involving two transformations. Subject–Auxiliary Inversion and *wh*-fronting may both operate independently in other environments, producing other functional effects. For example:

Not one moment *did he* regret his decision.

The girl *whom* he had invited did not come.

We have also followed the recent trend in EST towards reducing the types of transformations to the single operation of 'movement': movement may be either to the left (for example, *wh*-movement, movement of the Object of passives, and raising) or to the right (as in extraposition). Furthermore, we assume that any moved category leaves behind an empty position. The movement of *who* in *Who did Peter invite* ---?, for example, has left behind an empty Object position marked ---. In current EST this approach is covered by Trace theory.

The various movement transformations referred to above yield S-structures. S-structure is assumed to be the level at which Case is assigned and at which coindexing takes place. Since Case assignment and coindexing are not discussed in this book, D-structure and S-structure will look identical for many sentences.

This is a book about English syntax in the narrow sense of that term, and the levels of Phonetic form and Logical form are referred to only occasionally. The level of Phonetic form, in EST, is that at which a number of additional morphological/phonological changes are performed. For example, the affixing of the ending of the finite verb is assumed to take place at the phonetic level of the grammar rather than at the syntactic level, i.e. after the level of S-structure. The operations performed on S-structures in the Phonetic component lead to surface structures. Although S-structures and surface structures, on the one hand, and D-structures and underlying structures, on the other, are not identical in EST, we shall make no rigid distinction between the two pairs, and mainly deal with surface structures and underlying structures. Logical form, too, is only introduced discursively, with respect to the 'binding' relations in sentences. The notion of binding plays an important part in the treatment of reflexive pronouns, which are usually bound to an antecedent in the same clause. This notion is also used with respect to the linking of relative and interrogative pronouns with the 'gap' at the vacated site. However, the treatment of such interdependencies at the level of Logical form is kept very informal and the standard EST treatment of such links in terms of coindexing is not introduced. By reducing abstract formalisations to a minimum, we focus on English sentences and their analysis rather than on the formal technicalities of the analysis.

In keeping with the basic EST approach of this coursebook, we shall not normally refer to semantics or pragmatics, unless information of this type might clarify the analysis. In this book we have devoted more space to grammatical functions than is customary in the EST tradition, adopting the configurational approach to grammatical functions, which sees notions such as 'Subject', 'Object', etc., not as primitives of syntax, but rather as fully configurationally determined, and thus derivative. This occasionally leads to analyses which deviate from the more traditional descriptive tradition, but we feel that these modern analyses are more illuminating than traditional ones. With respect to the motivation of the analysis of constituent structure and function, we consistently rely on standard arguments of movement, substitution and analogy. Analogy has been used to motivate the presence of empty categories, and it may at least partly be seen as an informal translation of the Projection principle in EST, which states that distributional information encoded in the Lexicon (e.g. subcategorisation frames) must be preserved at each level of structure.

Herman Wekker
Liliane Haegeman
Nijmegen
Geneva

1
AIMS AND METHODS

1.1 WHAT IS SYNTAX?

Syntax, or **syntactic analysis**, may be defined as:

(a) determining the relevant component parts of a sentence

(b) describing these parts grammatically.

The component parts of a sentence are called **constituents**. In other words, syntax involves the two closely related tasks of:

(a) breaking down the sentence into its **constituents**

(b) assigning some grammatical label to each constituent, stating what type of constituent (or **grammatical category**) it is, and what **grammatical function** it has.

This definition of syntax implies that we start from what is regarded as the largest unit of syntactic description — the sentence — and proceed until we arrive at the smallest meaningful unit. This is called a 'top to bottom' analysis. The units smaller than the sentence will be referred to as **clauses**, **phrases**, **words** and **morphemes** respectively. However, instead of saying that a sentence can be broken down into smaller and smaller constituents, we might also look at the sentence the other way round — that is, 'from bottom to top' — and say that constituents at different levels can combine to form increasingly larger units: we proceed then from the morpheme to the sentence as a whole. Constituents are like building blocks which pattern in certain ways to form larger and larger units, the largest unit being the sentence. Each constituent (except the smallest) can be broken down into its component parts. The purpose of doing syntax is to discover the ways in which constituents combine to form the **structure** of sentences.

In this book we adopt the (traditional) hierarchy of sentence constituents, as shown in the following diagram:

SENTENCE ↔ CLAUSE ↔ PHRASE ↔ WORD ↔ MORPHEME

This diagram represents the hierarchical scale of constituents. The four double-pointed arrows in the diagram indicate that it may be read 'from left to right', or 'from right to left.'

The arrows pointing to the right indicate that a sentence may consist of one or more than one clause, that a clause may consist of one or more than one phrase, that a phrase may consist of one or more than one word, and that a word may consist of one or more than one morpheme. Morphemes are the minimal, indivisible units in syntax.

Conversely, as indicated by the arrows pointing to the left, we might also say that one or more than one morpheme may constitute a word, one or more than one word may form a phrase, one or more than one phrase may form a clause, and one or more than one clause may form a sentence.

In what follows we shall also see that a clause may contain one or more constituent clauses, and that a phrase may contain one or more constituent phrases or clauses.

To illustrate the hierarchical structure of sentences, let us consider sentence (1):

(1) The snake killed the rat and swallowed it.

This sentence consists of two **coordinate** clauses, joined together by the **coordinator** *and.* The first clause is: *The snake killed the rat,* and the second is: *swallowed it.* The second clause has a reduced form. Its complete form would be *it swallowed it.*

The first clause in (1) consists of two phrases, and the second, as it stands, consists of only one phrase. The two phrases in the first clause are *The snake* and *killed the rat,* and the phrase in the second clause is *swallowed it.* As we shall see later, *the snake* is a **noun phrase** and *killed the rat* and *swallowed it* are both **verb phrases**.

Each phrase is made up of words. *The snake* consists of two words: *the* and *snake*; *killed the rat* consists of three words, of which the last two (*the* + *rat*) again constitute a noun phrase; and *swallowed it* consists of two words, of which the second in itself constitutes a noun phrase. The constituents *the rat* and *it* are examples of (noun) phrases within (verb) phrases.

Sentence (1) contains eight words, including the coordinator *and.* Each word consists of one or two morphemes: *the, snake, rat, and* and *it* are one-morpheme words, whereas *killed* and *swallowed* are both two-morpheme words. *The, snake, rat,* etc. are full words and morphemes at the same time: the word and morpheme boundaries coincide. The two morphemes of *killed* and *swallowed* are *kill* and *–ed,* and *swallow* and *–ed* (see 1.2.2).

1.2 REPRESENTING SENTENCE STRUCTURE

1.2.1 BRACKETING

The syntactic structure of sentence (1) above may be represented provisionally by marking off each constituent from sentence level to word level by square brackets: [ ]. To simplify matters, we shall ignore the morpheme boundaries here. This convention of **bracketing** yields the following analysis, which looks rather daunting at first sight:

(2) [[[[The] [snake]] [[killed] [[the] [rat]]]]
[and]
[[[swallowed] [[it]]]]]

Analysis (2) is the result of first bracketing the sentence, then the two clauses, then the phrases, and finally the words, as follows:

Sentence:

(3a) [The snake killed the rat and swallowed it]

Clauses:

(3b) [[The snake killed the rat]
and
[swallowed it]]

Phrases:

(3c) [[[The snake] [killed [the rat]]]
and
[[swallowed [it]]]]

Words:

(3d) [[[[The] [snake]] [[killed] [[the] [rat]]]]
[and]
[[[swallowed] [[it]]]]]

Analysis (3d) is of course identical with (2) above.

The bracketing has here been done on a purely intuitive basis. In the following chapters we shall deal with the formal arguments which justify those choices. Check through the above analysis carefully again, and try to bracket the following sentences from sentence level to word level in the same way:

(4) The terrorists assassinated the ambassador.

(5) Her husband is an aristocrat.

(6) He gave his mother a present.

In (2) above we can see that word and morpheme boundaries may coincide: *the*, *snake*, *rat*, etc. are all one word and one morpheme, as opposed to *killed* and *swallowed*, which are words consisting of two morphemes each. Words and phrases may also coincide, as in:

(7) John laughed.

In this sentence *John* is both a phrase (a noun phrase) and a word (a noun); *laughed* is also both a phrase (a verb phrase) and a word (a verb). The units sentence and clause also coincide in (7). Bracketing from sentence level to word level yields (8):

(8) [[[[John]] [[laughed]]]]

Word, phrase, clause and sentence may also coincide, as in:

(9) Run!

The bracketing of sentence (9) is as follows:

(10) [[[[Run]]]]

It is structurally one sentence, one clause, one phrase and one word (also one morpheme).

The above examples show that a sentence is not necessarily longer than a clause, a clause not necessarily longer than a phrase, and a phrase not necessarily longer than a word (in general, we shall not go beyond the level of the word in our analyses). We shall see that sentences may vary in length and complexity from one clause to indefinitely many clauses, clauses from one phrase to indefinitely many phrases, and phrases from one word to indefinitely many words.

In Chapter 2 we shall look at each of these grammatical units in more detail.

1.2.2 LABELLED BRACKETING

The system of bracketing which we have used so far is not very satisfactory. It is difficult to see, for example, which brackets go together to mark off a constituent. The notation introduced above could be improved by adding an appropriate grammatical label to each pair of square brackets. The label indicates what type of constituent (or grammatical category) is contained within the brackets. This convention is called **labelled bracketing**. To illustrate the new system, let us consider again the structure of the sentence *The snake killed the rat and swallowed it* ((1) above).

We shall use square brackets with the label S (short for 'sentence') to mark off the boundaries of the whole sentence, as follows:

(11) $[_{S}$The snake killed the rat and swallowed it$]$

The **category label** is inserted in the bottom corner of the left-hand bracket. This sentence, as we have seen, consists of two clauses: the clause *The snake killed the rat* and the clause (*it*) *swallowed it*. The two clauses are joined together by the coordinator *and*. The clauses can be bracketed and labelled as follows:

(12) $\left[_{S_1}\left[_{S_2}\text{The snake killed the rat}\right]\text{ and }\left[_{S_3}\text{(it)swallowed it}\right]\right]$

The two clauses are labelled S_2 and S_3 here, and the whole sentence is labelled S_1. S_2 and S_3 are clauses inside S_1 (the numbers 1,2,3 etc. are added here and elsewhere just for convenience: they enable us to refer unambiguously to the different Ss). We use the label S for sentences as well as clauses, since clauses can be defined as Ss inside an S or inside a phrase. The clauses in (12) can be further analysed into phrases as follows:

(13) $\left[_{S_1}\left[_{S_2}\left[_{NP}\text{The snake}\right]\left[_{VP}\text{killed }\left[_{NP}\text{the rat}\right]\right]\right]\right.$

$\text{and }\left.\left[_{S_3}\left[_{NP}\text{ (it)}\right]\left[_{VP}\text{swallowed }\left[_{NP}\text{it}\right]\right]\right]\right]$

The label NP stands for noun phrase, and the label VP for verb phrase. *The snake* and *the rat* are NPs, because their most important element is a noun (N); *it*, which replaces an NP, is also an NP (cf. 1.2.4 and 2.4.2.2). The VPs in (13) consist of a verb (V) followed by an NP. The verbs are *killed* and *swallowed.* The NPs *the rat* in *killed the rat* and *it* in *swallowed it* are parts of the VPs, and act as **Complements** of the verbs *killed* and *swallowed* respectively.

The words that make up the above phrases can also be bracketed and labelled as follows:

(14) $\left[_{S_1}\left[_{S_2}\left[_{NP}\left[_{Det}\text{The}\right]\left[_{N}\text{snake}\right]\right]\left[_{VP}\left[_{V}\text{killed}\right]\right.\right.\right.$

$\left.\left.\left[_{NP}\left[_{Det}\text{the}\right]\left[_{N}\text{rat}\right]\right]\right]\right]$

[and]

$\left.\left[_{S_3}\left[_{NP}\text{(it)}\right]\left[_{VP}\left[_{V}\text{swallowed}\right]\left[_{NP}\left[_{N}\text{it}\right]\right]\right]\right]\right]$

The label Det stands for **determiner**, the label N for noun, and the label V for verb. Noun and verb are major **word classes**, and Det is a collective term for various items preceding the noun, e.g.: *the, a, that, this, some, any.* Now compare (14) with (2) in section 1.2.1 above. The only difference between the two is that pairs of brackets are labelled here.

Our syntactic analysis of the sentence does not usually go below the level of the word or even the phrase, but occasionally it will be useful to mark off the morpheme structure of a given word, for example the structure of the past tense forms of verbs, or of the plurals and genitives of nouns. This, too, can be done by means of labelled bracketing, as, for example, in the case of *killed*:

(16) $\left[_{V}\left[_{B}\text{kill}\right]\left[_{Suff}\text{ed}\right]\right]$

Here the label B is used for the **base** (of the verb), and the label Suff for **suffix** (see section 1.1).

Throughout this book we shall frequently use this kind of labelled bracketing to represent sentence structure.

1.2.3 TREE DIAGRAMS AND PHRASE STRUCTURE RULES

Labelled bracketing is one of the most common ways of representing the constituent structure of sentences. However, there are many other methods of marking diagrammatically what elements in a sentence go together and what elements do not. One other very common representation is the **tree diagram**.

The tree diagram is a notational device which is entirely equivalent to labelled bracketing: although it looks different, it provides the same information about the syntactic structure of a sentence.

Consider, for example, the following (simplified) tree diagram of the sentence:

(1) The snake killed the rat and (it) swallowed it.

(16)

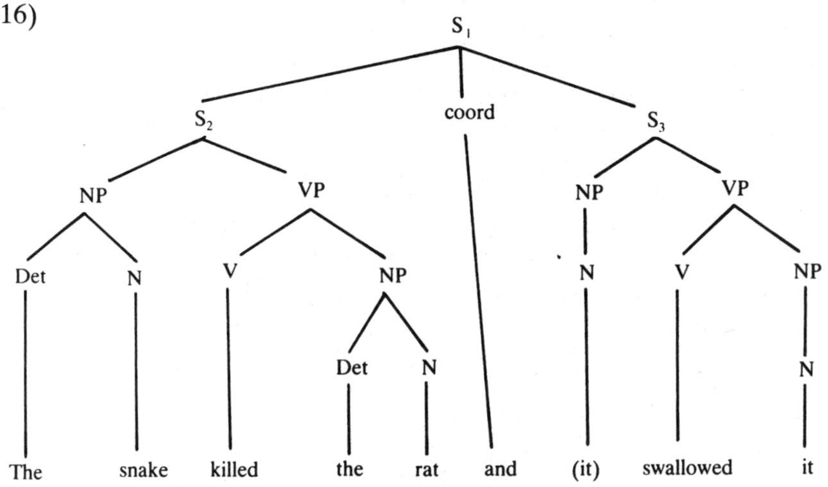

The tree diagram provides the analysis of sentence (1) down to word level (determiner, noun, verb, etc.); in principle, it would also be possible to stop at phrase level (NP, VP, etc.), or to go beyond word level and indicate the morphological structure of each of the words. You can make your grammatical analysis as detailed as you like, or as is necessary for a specific purpose. The syntactic information contained in diagram (16) is essentially the same as that provided by the labelled bracketing in (14) in section 1.2.2. It is largely a matter of taste or practical convenience whether one chooses the notation of (14) in section 1.2.2 or that of (16) above.

To read tree diagram (16) we require some additional terminology. For example, we say that S_1 (the whole sentence) is **expanded** as S_2 and S_3 (two clauses), which are coordinated by *and*. S_1 is said to contain as its **immediate constituents** S_2, S_3 and the coordinator *and*. S_2 is expanded as NP–

VP, and so is S_3. The VP in each case is expanded as V–NP. The constituents mentioned so far are considered to be the main constituents of the sentence. Further down the tree, NP may again be expanded as either Det–N (*the–snake*) or as N (*it*).

There is a convention which is generally used to sum up the system of expanding one unit into other units. It is a set of instructions called **phrase structure rules** (PS rules).

Let us provisionally formulate the following four PS rules:

(17a) S ⟶ S–coord–S

(17b) S ⟶ NP–VP

(17c) VP ⟶ V–NP

(17d) NP ⟶ $\begin{Bmatrix} \text{Det–N} \\ \text{N} \end{Bmatrix}$

The arrows mean: 'expand' or 'rewrite' X as Y (where X represents any element on the left of the arrow, and Y any element on the right). The curly brackets in rule (17d) indicate that NP may be expanded or rewritten as *either* Det–N *or* N.

The category labels in tree diagram (16), such as S_1, S_2, S_3, NP, VP, V, etc., are all attached to the **nodes** of that tree, and the lines connecting these nodes are called **branches**. The node labels in the tree diagram correspond to the labels in the labelled bracketing in 1.2.2. The node labelled S_1 in (16) **dominates** the nodes labelled S_2, coord, and S_3. The node labelled S_2 dominates the nodes labelled NP and VP, but also all the other nodes further down that half of the tree. The same applies to S_3. NP, VP, etc. are said to be dominated by S_2 or S_3. We also see that S_2 and S_3 both contain two NPs. One NP is **immediately dominated** by S_2/S_3, the other by the VP-node. The NP immediately dominated by the VP-node is also dominated by S_2/S_3, but it is not immediately dominated by S_2/S_3. It is important to distinguish between **dominance** and **immediate dominance**. In the latter case there must be no further nodes intervening between the nodes considered.

The **lexical items** (i.e. the words) *the, snake, killed,* etc., are attached to the so-called **terminal** nodes of the tree diagram, i.e. the bottom nodes. The other nodes in the tree diagram are **non-terminal**.

Tree diagram (16) shows, among other things, that *the* (Det) and *snake* (N) combine to form one constituent (an NP), that *killed* (V) and *the rat* (NP) constitute a VP, that the NP *the snake* and the VP *killed the rat* are a sentence/clause (S_2) inside another sentence (S_1), etc. In the same way the right half of the tree diagram also specifies the internal structure of clause S_3.

Subordination of a clause, as in:

(18) I know $\left[_{S}\text{that the snake killed the rat}\right]$

may be represented as follows:

(19)

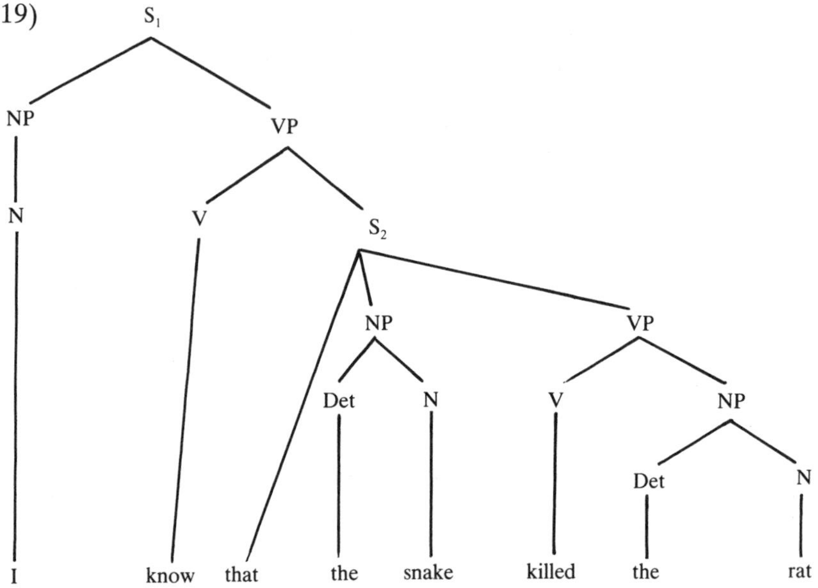

Tree diagram (19) is provisional. We shall look in greater detail at how we should treat the sequence *that– the snake killed the rat* later (see section 2.3).

The provisional set of PS rules in (17) cannot fully describe structures like (19). For example, rule (17a) is optional: it need not apply (after all, not all sentences contain coordinate clauses). We start the rewriting operations for (19) at rule (17b). Also, instead of rewriting VP as V–NP, as stipulated by rule (17c), we must rewrite the VP in (19) as V–S. Consequently, our PS rule (17c) must allow for this possibility: we must adapt it in the following way (the curly brackets again indicate a choice: 'either ... or'):

(17c) $VP \longrightarrow V-\left\{\begin{matrix}NP\\S\end{matrix}\right\}$

The S, which now also occurs on the right-hand side of the arrow, may in its turn be expanded as NP–VP, as indicated in rule (17b), and this VP may now become either V–NP or V–S, and so on. It is possible to have an S embedded inside another S. This kind of embedding (or subordination) may, in principle, be repeated indefinitely many times: there may be indefinitely many Ss embedded inside other Ss. For example:

(20) I know that you think that she hopes that you will say to her that you love her.

Draw a tree diagram representing the syntactic structure of (20).

In diagram (19) S_2 is a subordinate clause, which functions inside S_1: S_2 is dominated by S_1, and immediately dominated by VP.

Ss (clauses) may also appear inside NPs as in:

(21) $[_{NP}$ The snake $[_{S}$ which killed the rat$]]$ belongs to our neighbours.

What we have here is not subordination inside the VP (as in (18) and (20)) but subordination inside an NP. This may be represented as follows:

(22)

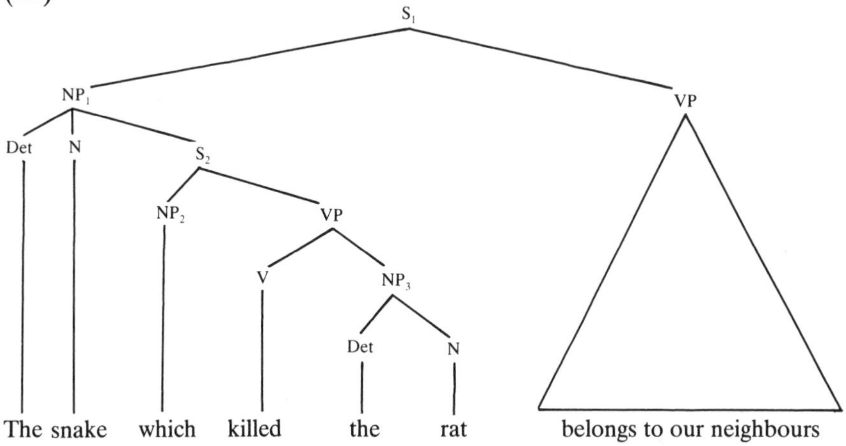

This simplified tree diagram shows that S_2 is immediately dominated by NP_1: S_2 is an immediate constituent of the NP.

The **triangle** under VP in (22) is a device commonly used to indicate that we are not concerned with the internal structure of that constituent. We shall often use the triangle when the internal structure of a constituent is not relevant to the point under discussion.

To describe sentences like (22) we must again adapt the PS rules in (17) above. We reformulate rule (17d) as follows:

(17d) $NP \longrightarrow \left\{ \begin{matrix} \text{Det–N–(S)} \\ \text{N} \end{matrix} \right\}$

The round brackets around S mean that S is optional: we may choose to rewrite NP as Det–N–S or as Det–N. Alternatively, as indicated by the curly brackets, we may also rewrite NP as just N.

1.2.4 SENTENCE AND DISCOURSE

We have said that in syntax the sentence is regarded as the largest or highest unit on the hierarchical scale of constituents; it is the largest unit of syntactic description. But, of course, sentences do not normally occur in isolation. They usually form part of a larger **text** (or **discourse**) which is also organised in a particular way. The sentences of a text follow each other in some 'logical' order, and reflect a certain sequence of thoughts or events. There are often elements in a sentence which mark its relationship with the **context**. Texts are structured, and are more than just a random collection of sentences. Consider, for example, the text 1.2.4, consisting of only four sentences:

> *Text 1.2.4*
> Soon after breakfast Mary Ann brought in The Times. Mr. Carey shared it with two neighbours. He had it from ten till one, when the gardener took it over to Mr. Ellis at the Limes, with whom it remained till seven. Then it was taken to Miss Brooks at the Manor House, who, since she got it late, had the advantage of keeping it.
>
> Adapted from W. Somerset Maugham, *Of Human Bondage.*

The internal structure of this text is shown by a number of factors. For example:

(a) The order in which the four sentences occur is not accidental; it reflects the order in which the events described in the text occur.
(b) The words *it, he* and *she* relate to constituents in previous sentences. Check which elements these words are related to in the text above.
(c) There is a link between 'two neighbours' in the second sentence and 'Mr. Ellis' and 'Miss Brooks' in the two following sentences.
(d) The use of *then* at the beginning of the fourth sentence also indicates that there is a certain temporal sequence of events.

Like sentences, texts have an internal structure. However, the structural organisation of texts is different from that of sentences. The rules conditioning the organisation of texts are the rules of **text grammar** or **discourse grammar**, whereas the rules which determine the structure of sentences make up **sentence grammar** or **syntax**. The rules of text grammar often require an appeal to notions which are not syntactic (see points (a)–(d) above).

In this book we shall only be concerned with the description of sentences. The analysis of longer stretches of discourse will generally be left out of consideration. Although we shall be offering numerous illustrative texts, we shall usually only pay attention to the structure of the individual sentences in the text. Occasionally, we shall go beyond the level of the sentence, if this is necessary for the clarification of some point.

The emphasis of this book is on formal structural properties of sentences rather than on their pronunciation, their meaning or their use in communication: it is a book on English syntax, not on phonology, semantics, or pragmatics.

Throughout this book the terms 'grammar' or 'syntax', 'grammatical' and 'syntactic' will be used interchangeably. The term 'grammar' is also sometimes used in a very general sense to include syntax, phonology, semantics, etc.

1.2.5 EXERCISES

I Draw at least four different tree diagrams, using the set of PS rules below:

(1) S ⟶ NP–VP

(2) VP ⟶ V– $\left(\begin{Bmatrix} \text{NP} \\ \text{S} \end{Bmatrix}\right)$

(3) NP ⟶ Det–N

Insert lexical items at the terminal nodes of the trees. We suggest that you choose from the following:

(a) *the, a, this, that* for the category Det.
(b) *policeman, professor, girl, student* for the category N;
(c) *kissed, warned admired* for the category V if followed by NP;
thought, knew, said for the category V if followed by (*that*)–S;
yawned, snored, laughed for the category V if not followed by NP or S.

II Convert each tree diagram that you have drawn into a labelled bracketing representation.

1.3 CONSTITUENCY TESTS

We have seen that texts consist of sentences and that each sentence/clause may be broken down into the constituents NP and VP. The VP consists of a V, which may be followed by one or more constituents.

The immediate constituents of the sentence/clause (NP–VP) and those of the VP are considered to be the main constituents of syntactic analysis. They may be involved in a number of processes which change the appearance of a basic sentence pattern. These processes always affect complete constituents, and thus enable the student of language to discover what the constituents of sentences are. To illustrate some of these processes, let us consider the text in 1.3.1.

1.3.1 VARIATIONS ON BASIC SENTENCE PATTERNS

Read text 1.3.1:

> *Text 1.3.1*
> Most of the silk we see in Britain comes from silkworms, but wild silk moths in countries like India and Japan also produce it. They all spin cocoons and, although their silk is not as fine as silkworms', several species are cultivated.
>
> The two most important wild silks are tasar and muga. Tasar is produced in a humid and dense belt of tropical forest in India. Once the cocoons have been spun, the largest are used for future breeding. When the moths emerge, the females are tethered by thread tied round the base of their wings to prevent them flying away.
>
> Muga silk is produced exclusively in Assam by the assamiensis caterpillar. The silk varies in colour and texture, depending on their diet. Those fed on the young leaves of the majankori tree produce pale silk — almost creamy white — while those fed on older leaves produce silk of a golden colour.
>
> Adapted from *Observer* (Colour supplement), 14 March 1982.

In the sections below we shall illustrate the most important sentence processes which have applied or may apply to the sentences in this text. We shall deal briefly with operations called *clefting* (1.3.2), *pseudo-clefting* (1.3.3), *passivisation* (1.3.4), *pronominalisation* (1.3.5) and *fronting* (1.3.6). For a more detailed account, see Chapter 4.

1.3.2 CLEFTING

The first sentence of text 1.3.1 contains two coordinate clauses. The first clause is:

(1) Most of the silk we see in Britain comes from silkworms.

The constituent *from silkworms* in (1) may be given more emphasis by placing it at the beginning of the sentence and 'surrounding' it by the words *it was/was . . . that*, as follows:

(2) It is *from silkworms* that most of the silk we see in Britain comes.

(1) and (2) have a different outward appearance (or **form**), but their content (or **meaning**) is more or less the same. The only difference in meaning between them is that in (2) the element *from silkworms* is very emphatically contrasted with something else in the context (*wild silk moths*, in the second coordinate clause): this contrast is more clearly marked in (2) than in (1).

The operations of fronting a constituent like *from silkworms* and surrounding it by *it was/was... that* are part of a process known as **clefting.** If we represent the string *from silkworms* by X, we could summarise the process as follows:

CLAUSE →	It is X that CLAUSE
[with X]	[without X]

So:

(a) Most of the silk we see in Britain comes *from silkworms.*
(b) It is *from silkworms* that most of the silk we see in Britain comes.

Consider also: *Jane gave this book to Bill on Saturday.* Again we show how one can extract a constituent and put it in a more prominent position by applying the process of clefting:

(a) X = *on Saturday*

It was *on Saturday* that Jane gave this book to Bill.

(b) X = *to Bill*

It was *to Bill* that Jane gave this book on Saturday.

(c) X = *this book*

It was *this book* that Jane gave to Bill on Saturday.

(d) X = *Jane*
It was *Jane* that gave this book to Bill on Saturday.

Sentences resulting from the clefting process are called **cleft sentences.**

It is not possible to produce a cleft sentence by putting just anything in the position for X. For example:

(3) *It was *Jane gave* that this book to Bill on Saturday.

Clefting cannot affect the string *Jane gave,* because this is not a constituent in the sentence. (An asterisk in front of a sentence means that the sentence is ungrammatical in English. This convention will be used throughout the book).

Clefting is a useful way of discovering which words in a sentence form constituents and which do not: *Jane* is a constituent, but *Jane gave,* for example, is not.

1.3.3 PSEUDO-CLEFTING

A process closely related to clefting is that of **pseudo-clefting**. This involves the use of *what* to form sentences like:

(4) What Jane did was give this book to Bill on Saturday.

(5) What Jane gave to Bill was this book.

(6) This book is what Jane gave to Bill on Saturday.

These three sentences can all be related to the sentence *Jane gave this book to Bill on Saturday.* Pseudo-clefting affects whole constituents, e.g. *gave this book to Bill on Saturday* and *this book.*

1.3.4 PASSIVISATION

Most of our example sentences above express an activity performed by a person, and affecting some other person, animal or thing which undergoes the activity. The person who performs the activity is the **Agent**, and whoever or whatever undergoes it is called the Patient. Agent and Patient are **roles**.

In the (a)-sentences in (7) and (8) we first mention the Agent, then the Patient. In the (b)-sentences it is the other way round. The change from (a) to (b) is **passivisation**. The examples are taken from text 1.3.1.

(7a) Wild silk moths in countries like India and Japan also produce it.

(7b) It is also produced by wild silk moths in countries like India and Japan.

(8a) People cultivate several species.

(8b) Several species are cultivated.

Like clefting, passivisation is a way of rearranging the information in a sentence: if for some reason the Patient is to be made more prominent, we may use a passive sentence. In passives the Agent role is no longer obligatorily expressed (cf. (8b) above).

In active sentences, normally, the Agent precedes and the Patient follows. In passive sentences the Patient precedes and the Agent, if any, follows.

Passivisation also affects complete constituents. Sentence (7b), for example, shows that *wild silk moths in countries like India and Japan* and *it* are both constituents.

1.3.5 PRONOMINALISATION

Consider the second sentence of text 1.3.1, which begins with *they* and which also contains the word *their.* What do *they* and *their* relate to? To answer this question, we must look at the preceding sentence. The two words *they* and *their* have the same reference as *wild silk moths in countries like India and Japan*: *they* and *their* are co-referential with the NP. Since they can be substituted for an NP, they are called **pronouns**, or more generally **pro-forms**. Substitution by pronouns is called **pronominalisation**. Like clefting and passivisation, pronominalisation can affect constituents only.

1.3.6 FRONTING

The fourth sentence of text 1.3.1 is as follows:

(9) Tasar is produced in a humid and dense belt of tropical forest in India.

This sentence contains the string *in a humid and dense belt of tropical forest in India*, which may be moved to the beginning of the sentence, as follows:

(10) In a humid and dense belt of tropical forest in India, tasar is produced.

We call this process **fronting** (or **preposing**). Only certain sentence elements can be fronted, and these elements must be constituents.

1.3.7 EXERCISES

I Consider the sentence: *Two young Dutch journalists insulted the new Prime Minister of Britain on television last night.*
Clefting and *pseudo-clefting*: produce cleft and pseudo-cleft sentences from this example.
Passivisation: give the Patient element more prominence by making the sentence passive.
Pronominalisation: replace the NPs in the sentence by pronouns, wherever you can.
Fronting: place as many constituents as possible in front position without clefting.

II Try to construct passive sentences corresponding to the following active sentences (passivisation is not always possible):

(1) The government spends thousands of pounds on road safety every year.
(2) The doctor put my aunt on a strict diet.
(3) His uncle died from fatty degeneration of the heart.
(4) The girl with the red hair has won the prize.
(5) The man disappeared last week.
(6) John opened the cellar door.
(7) Anne stirred the mixture continuously.
(8) Someone has killed the dragon.
(9) The squatters have occupied two buildings.
(10) The lady standing in the corner has just bought that famous Rubens painting.

III Comment on the difference between the following two sentences, and explain why (a) fits better in text 1.3.1 than (b):

(a) When the moths emerge, the females are tethered by thread tied round the base of their wings to prevent them flying away.

(b) When the moths emerge, it is the females that are tethered by thread round the base of the females' wings to prevent the females flying away.

IV Comment on the difference between the following pairs of sentences:

(1a) Muga silk is produced exclusively in Assam by the assamiensis caterpillar.
(1b) Exclusively in Assam, the assamiensis caterpillar produces muga silk.

(2a) The silk varies in colour and texture, depending on their diet.
(2b) It is in colour and texture that the silk varies, depending on the caterpillars' diet.

(3a) Those fed on the young leaves of the majankori tree produce pale silk — almost creamy white — while those fed on older leaves produce silk of a golden colour.
(3b) Pale silk — almost creamy white — is produced by those fed on the young leaves of the majankori tree, while silk of a golden colour is produced by those fed on older leaves.

V Indicate which of the italicised strings in the sentences below can be replaced by a pronoun. Observe how the form of the pronoun varies with its position in the sentence.

(1) *Joan* is slimming.
(2) *The poor thing* must have been pretty desperate.
(3) *Her husband* is a real aristocrat.
(4) The doctor called *the young girl* a fool.
(5) I shall speak *to the headmistress.*
(6) His *wife is* Greek.
(7) I like that picture of *your father.*
(8) *The boys* killed *the rats with a long stick.*
(9) *The new-born baby* was adopted by an elderly *couple.*
(10) *David* was widely acclaimed for *his avant-garde paintings.*

VI The following passage is the (slightly adapted) first paragraph of an essay by the American author James Baldwin. Point out factors and devices which serve to express connections between the sentences in this text.

> On the 29th of July, in 1943, my father died. On the same day, a few hours later, his last child was born. Over a month before this, while all our energies were concentrated in waiting for these events, there had been, in Detroit, one of the bloodiest race riots of the century. Two days before my father's funeral, while he lay in state in the undertaker's chapel, a race riot broke out in Harlem. On the morning of the 3rd of August, we drove my father to the graveyard through a wilderness of smashed plate glass.
>
> James Baldwin, *Notes of a Native Son.*

2
CONSTITUENTS

2.1 INTRODUCTION

Let us return to one of our example sentences in Chapter 1:

(1) The snake killed the rat and (it) swallowed it.

We have argued that *sentences* have **structure**, and are not just strings of words which occur in a random order. The words do not just follow each other like the beads on a string or the carriages of a train, all of which are of the same size and structure, connected with each other in one straight line and in exactly the same way. The words of a sentence are strictly organised internally: there is an underlying pattern. For example, *the* goes with *snake* rather than with *killed*, and *it* is more closely associated with *swallowed* than with *and*, *killed* or *snake*. The structure of sentences can be discovered by certain constituency tests.

Similarly, we have argued, it would be naive to think of *texts* as being simply made up of lexical items strung together one after the other. The items in a text are somehow organised: texts also have a certain structure. Texts contain one or more paragraphs, often set off by indentation. Paragraphs in turn consist of sentences, which are usually set off by a capital letter at the beginning and a full stop, an exclamation mark or a question mark at the end. Thus, texts are hierarchically organised into paragraphs, and paragraphs into sentences. There are minimal texts which contain only one paragraph, which in turn consists of only one sentence. Consider, for example, the following notices:

(2) Visitors must not feed the animals.

(3) Shoplifters will be prosecuted.

Announcements such as these are one-paragraph, one-sentence texts. Most texts, however, contain more than one paragraph, and each paragraph more than one sentence.

In this and the following chapters we shall be almost exclusively concerned with the constituent structure of English sentences, not that of texts. As we have seen in Chapter 1, sentences can be analysed into clauses, clauses into phrases, phrases into words, and words into morphemes. Sentences are hierarchically organised into different **constituents**.

2.1.1 EXERCISE

The following exercise illustrates once again what we mean by hierarchical organisation (or structure). In each string below the words have been scrambled. Try to construct one or more sentences from these random strings:

(1) Harvard–George–at–allegedly–cheated.
(2) Peter–dog–are–his–and–great–friends.
(3) Arthur–Paul–squash racket–yesterday–lent–his.
(4) appointed–been–George–manager–has.
(5) joke–affair–whole–John–treated–as–stupid–the–a
(6) the–The–a–rose–boy–girl–bought–red–young–pretty.
(7) not–him–her–She–adventures–London–tell–about–in–did.
(8) makes–dust–All–you–that–thirsty.
(9) She–away–went–days–three–for.
(10) described–25–30–She–old–as–between–and–gunman–years–being–the.
(11) He–her–his–new–books–day–records–and–a–for–lent.
(12) ill–little–boy–been–may–Her–have–yesterday.
(13) should–careful–children–been–have–The–more.
(14) boy–story–girl–The–interesting–French–English–told–the–an.
(15) her–She–long–days–these–wears–hair.

2.1.2 WORD ORDER

Strictly mathematically, each of the strings in 2.1.1 should allow for a great number of combinations. Consider, for example, the string:

(4) Harvard–George–at–allegedly–cheated.

If sentences were random combinations of words, we should at least be able to form the following 'sentences':

(5) Harvard George at allegedly cheated.

(6) Harvard George at cheated allegedly.

(7) Harvard George cheated at allegedly.

(8) Harvard George cheated allegedly at.

(9) Harvard allegedly George cheated at.

(10) Harvard allegedly George at cheated.

... Etc.

Such a random procedure with five words should yield 120 different combinations. However, only some of these strings will be correct English sentences. The sentences which the grammar of English does not allow are said to be **ungrammatical**.

The following sentences are all grammatical, but they may be ordered on a more-or-less descending scale of **acceptability:**

(11) George allegedly cheated at Harvard.

(12) At Harvard George allegedly cheated.

(13) Allegedly George cheated at Harvard.

(14) ?Allegedly at Harvard George cheated.

(15) ?George at Harvard allegedly cheated.

(16) ?George at Harvard cheated allegedly.

Sentences (11)–(13) are all fairly normal, (11) being the most usual string. The sentences (14)–(16) have a very unusual word order, and require a special intonation to sound acceptable. We say that sentences (14)–(16) are **marked stylistically**: they will only occur rarely and in exceptional circumstances, if at all. The other sentences are less marked, and (11) may be said to be the **unmarked** version. In order to be able to say why (14), for example, is less usual than (11), (12) or (13), it is necessary to be able to compare them. These sentences do not differ with respect to the number or kinds of words. What distinguishes them is the order of the words. **Word order** in English is fixed to a large extent, and if a given word order is disrupted the sentence may become less acceptable or even ungrammatical.

In order to specify the word order of English sentences, we might, of course, devise a rule saying: 'if you have the words *Harvard*, *George*, *at*, *cheated*, and *allegedly*, then you can produce grammatical English sentences by arranging the words as follows:

(17) George allegedly cheated at Harvard.

(18) At Harvard George allegedly cheated.

(19) Allegedly George cheated at Harvard.

... Etc.'

Such a rule would yield a list of possible word orders, given these five words. But such an approach would mean that we must formulate a separate rule for each of the following strings:

(20) Jane–supposedly–Yale–cheated–at.

(21) Bill–allegedly–UCL–cheated–at.

... Etc.

If we proceeded in this way, we would end up with a grammar consisting of an enormous set of different rules, each of which would work for only one given sentence. This is obviously very uneconomical, and we must therefore look for more general rules of sentence formation. Syntax should provide a **generalised** account of sentence structure.

2.1.3 CONSTITUENTS

We know now that some words in a sentence are linked more closely together than others. They form grammatical units within the sentence, and any variation in the order of words must respect the fact that there are such units. These grammatical units (sentence, clause, phrase, word and morpheme) are the constituents of a sentence. We have also briefly noted in Chapter 1 that there are various processes which help us to identify such constituents. In sentences (11)–(16) above, for example, *at* and *Harvard* can be seen to be tightly connected: they form a constituent. They are in fact only rarely separated, and the resulting sentence is then not very good.

(22) ?Harvard George allegedly cheated at.

Here follows a list of some of the tests which can be used to identify strings like *at Harvard* as constituents:

(a) The string *at Harvard* can be replaced by one word (*there*):

George allegedly cheated { at Harvard / there }

(b) One can ask a question of the following form:

Where did George allegedly cheat?

and the answer will be *at Harvard. Where* corresponds to (or 'questions') *at Harvard.*

(c) *At* and *Harvard* can be moved around together, as the sentences (11)–(16) illustrate.

(d) *At Harvard* can be the focus element X in a cleft sentence:

It was *at Harvard* that George allegedly cheated.

These tests are used to determine the constituent-hood of *at Harvard.* Their applicability may be summed up as follows:

	At + Harvard	
(a)	Substitution by one word	: yes
(b)	Questioned by one word	: yes
(c)	Move together	: yes
(d)	Can be the focus element X in a cleft sentence	: yes

It is the purpose of this chapter to break down sentences into their components: their constituent structure will be analysed. We shall be looking at the constituents in hierarchical order, starting with the largest unit of our analysis, the sentence, going down to the level of the clause, the next unit down on the scale, and then down to the phrase and to the word. The structure of words will only be discussed where relevant.

Throughout this book the constituent structure of sentences, clauses, phrases, etc. will be indicated by means of labelled bracketing (see 1.2.2) or by means of tree diagrams (see 1.2.3).

2.2 SENTENCES

2.2.1 SIMPLE DECLARATIVE AND INTERROGATIVE SENTENCES

Consider the piece of conversation in text 2.2.1:

> *Text 2.2.1*
> Coroner: The collision occurred at the junction of High Street and Church Road. How far away were you?
> Witness: I was 54 yards, 2 feet, 6 inches away from that spot.
> Coroner: You are very precise. Did you measure the distance?
> Witness: Yes, I measured it carefully.
> Coroner: Why did you measure it?
> Witness: I knew that some idiot would ask me.
> Adapted from Christian Brann, *Pass the Port.*

This conversation clearly involves an exchange of information: the coroner asks questions, and the witness tries to answer them. Sentences can generally be used to give information, and they can be used to ask for information. Identify the questions in the above text.

Questions like *Did you measure the distance?* ask for the answer *Yes* or *No.* They are said to be *Yes–No* questions. If you ask a *Yes–No* question, you want to know whether something did or did not happen. However, if you know that something happened, you might want to hear about the circumstances of the event (e.g. the time, place, reason of the event), or you might want to know more about the participants (the people involved). When the coroner in the text above asks *Why did you measure it?,* he knows that the witness measured the distance, because the witness has just said so. But the coroner does not know the reason for this (*why*); consequently he asks the witness to supply the missing information. Questions which ask for a particular piece of information, rather than for simply *Yes* or *No,* are called *wh*-questions. We call them *wh*-questions because they are often introduced by a word (or phrase) beginning with *wh*-. For example:

(1) *Where* did John hide the money?

(2) *What* did she say?

(3) *When* did he come back?

(4) *Which girl* did Bill like best?

(5) *Who(m)* did you meet there?

However, the *wh*-word does not always open the question. It may also appear inside the first constituent of the sentence:

(6) *For what reason* did you leave early?

(7) *In what way* did John offend her?

(8) *At what distance* were you from that spot?

These are also *wh*-questions. *In what way* can be replaced by *how*, and *at what distance* by *how far. How* and constituents containing *how* are also regarded as *wh*-elements. For example:

(9) *How* did you get to know him?

(10) *How far away* were you from that spot?

(11) *How old* are you?

(12) *How much money* do you earn?

Sentences used to ask questions are *interrogative* sentences; sentences used to supply information are *declarative* sentences.

2.2.2 COMPOUND AND COMPLEX SENTENCES

Compare texts 2.2.2.A and 2.2.2.B:

Text 2.2.2.A
Mary Ann's stories of the sea touched Philip's imagination. One evening he asked whether he might go home with her. His aunt feared that he might catch something. His uncle said that evil communications corrupted good manners.

Adapted from W. Somerset Maugham, *Of Human Bondage.*

Text 2.2.2.B
Mary Ann's stories of the sea touched Philip's imagination. One evening he asked whether he might go home with her; but his aunt feared that he might catch something, and his uncle said that evil communications corrupted good manners.

Adapted from W. Somerset Maugham, *Of Human Bondage.*

Of the two texts, the B-version approximates the original passage in Somerset Maugham's novel more closely.

How many sentences are there in the A-text? How many do you find in the B-text? Note that the second, third, and fourth sentences of A have been joined together in B to form one long sentence.

The boundaries of the sentences in A are still visible in B: the place where the linking has taken place is indicated by means of special punctuation (a comma or a semi-colon) and by means of coordinators such as *and*, *but* and *or*. A clause which is coordinated with another clause in this way is called a **conjoin.** Thus, the second sentence of B consists of three conjoins which have been joined to form one sentence. The three conjoins are:

(13a) One evening he asked whether he might go home with her.

(13b) (but) his aunt feared that he might catch something.

(13c) (and) his uncle said that evil communications corrupted good manners.

A sentence which consists of a string of coordinated clauses (conjoins) is called a **compound** sentence. Here are some further examples of compound sentences:

(14) George cheated at Harvard and Jane cheated at Yale.

(15) Sue went to London and stayed there for a week.

(16) John studied very hard last year but he failed his test.

(17) Paul will go to the cinema tonight, or he will stay at home to read a book.

In examples (14)–(17) simple sentences have been coordinated to form compound sentences.

A third category is that of **complex** sentences. To define these, let us consider the sentences:

(18) I know that the snake killed the rat.

(19) The snake which killed the rat belongs to our neighbours.

In (18) the string *that the snake killed the rat* is a clause, but it is not coordinated with another clause. Rather, it forms part of another clause; it is embedded in another clause. The other clause (the **main** clause) is: *I know that the snake killed the rat.* The embedded clause is a constituent of the VP of the main clause (see 2.4.3). In (19) the string *which killed the rat* is also a clause. This clause forms part of: *The snake which killed the rat*, which is an NP (see 2.4.2). The clause is embedded in the NP; the embedded clause is a constituent of the phrase in which it occurs. Sentences which contain embedded clauses of this kind are said to be *complex.* We shall return to the syntactic differences between compound and complex sentences below.

There are also mixed types of sentences, which involve both coordination and subordination: there may be subordinate clauses within conjoins and subordinate clauses may also be coordinated. An example of the former is sentence (13) above (repeated here as (20)):

(20) One evening he asked whether he might go home with her; but his aunt feared that he might catch something, and his uncle said that evil communications corrupted good manners.

The following are examples of coordination of subordinate clauses:

(21) I know that the snake killed the rat and (that it) swallowed it.

(22) The snake which killed the rat and (which) swallowed it belongs to our neighbours.

These mixed types of sentences are called **compound-complex** sentences.

There are important differences between coordinate and subordinate clauses. For example:

(a) Coordinate clauses are introduced by coordinators (*and, but, or, for,* etc.) and subordinate clauses by subordinators (*when, before, because, if, since, although, that,* etc.). Compare:

(23a) The snake killed the rat *and* it swallowed it.

(23b) The snake killed the rat, *before* it swallowed it.

(b) The coordinator always appears in a position between two coordinated clauses, whereas the subordinator is part of the subordinate clause. As a result, it is impossible to place the second conjoin together with the coordinator in front of the first conjoin. Compare:

(24a) The snake killed the rat and it swallowed it.

(24b) *And it swallowed it, the snake killed the rat.

On the other hand, subordinate clauses and the subordinators which introduce them can be fronted together:

(25a) The snake killed the rat, before it swallowed it.

(25b) Before it swallowed it, the snake killed the rat.

The subordinator and the clause form one constituent; the coordinator and the second conjoin are two separate constituents, which cannot be moved together. This difference between coordination and subordination of clauses may be represented as follows:

coordination: $\left[S_1 \left[S_2\right] \text{coord} \left[S_3\right]\right]$

subordination: $\left[S_1 \quad \left[S_2 \text{ subord} \quad \right]\right]$

(c) Coordination with *and, but* and *or* allows deletion of the subject of the second conjoin, if it is co-referential to the subject of the first conjoin. Deletion of the subject is generally impossible in subordinate clauses. Compare:

(26a) The snake killed the rat and ~~it~~ swallowed it.

(26b) *The snake killed the rat, before ~~it~~ swallowed it.

2.2.3 EXERCISE

Indicate whether the sentences below are simple, compound, complex, or compound-complex, and explain why:

(1) While I attach a very high value to the parental emotion, I do not draw the inference, which is too commonly drawn, that mothers should do as much as possible themselves for their children.

(2) There is a convention on this subject which was all very well in the days when nothing was known about the care of children except the unscientific odds and ends that old women handed on to younger ones.

(3) A mother is not expected to teach her son arithmetic, however much she may love him; so far as the acquisition of book-learning is concerned, it is recognised that children can acquire it better from those who have it than from a mother who does not have it.

(4) Undoubtedly certain things are better done by the mother, but as the child gets older, there will be an increasing number of things better done by someone else.

(5) A woman who has acquired any kind of professional skill ought, both for her own sake and for that of the community, to be free to continue to exercise this skill in spite of motherhood.

(6) A child over nine months old ought not to form an insuperable barrier to its mother's professional activities.

(7) The mother is, in a great many cases, exceptionally selfish towards her children, for, important as parenthood is as an element in life, it is not satisfying if it is treated as the whole of life, and the unsatisfied parent is likely to be an emotionally grasping parent.

2.3 CLAUSES

We use the term 'clause' to refer to sentences which are constituents of other sentences or of phrases. A constituent sentence (or clause) may be coordinated with one or more other constituent sentences to form a compound sentence, or it may be embedded in another sentence or in a phrase to form a complex sentence (see text 2.2.2.B). In simple sentences the boundaries of sentence and clause coincide: a simple sentence is a one-clause sentence, whereas compound and complex sentences always contain at least two clauses.

Let us return to the compound sentence in text 2.2.2.B. In order to show its structure, we shall now bracket each of the conjoins and label them by means of S (for sentence/clause) in the left-hand corner, as follows:

(1a) $[_S$One evening he asked whether he might go home with her;$]$

but

(1b) $[_S$his aunt feared that he might catch something,$]$

and

(1c) $[_S$his uncle said that evil communications corrupted good manners.$]$

Let us start by looking at the structure of (1b) as a separate, independent sentence. If we passivise this sentence, we get:

(2) That he might catch something was feared by his aunt.

Passivisation is a process which operates on sentences: it rearranges the sentence constituents. Since, in our example, passivisation affects the string *that he might catch something,* we conclude that this string is a sentence constituent. Our conclusion is confirmed by pseudo-clefting and by pronominalisation (use of *it, that, what,* etc.):

(3) What his aunt feared was that he might catch something.

(4) His aunt feared $\left\{\begin{matrix}\text{it}\\ \text{that}\end{matrix}\right\}$.

(5) What did his aunt fear?

Bracketing of this constituent provisionally gives us the following result:

(6) $[_S$His aunt feared $[$that he might catch something$]]$

It is clear that the string *he might catch something* is also an S, but what about the element *that*? Sentence (6) is to be bracketed as follows:

(7) $[_{S1}$His aunt feared $[_X$that $[_{S2}$he might catch something$]]]$

S_2 is a sentence inside sentence S_1: it is a constituent of sentence S_1. However, passivisation, pseudo-clefting and pronominalisation (see (2)–(5) above) affect the constituent labelled X in (7), not just S_2.

The role of *that* in (7) is that of linking S_2 (the embedded sentence) to the sentence inside which it occurs: *that* is the subordinator. The constituent X, comprising the subordinator and S_2, is often labelled $\overline{S}$ (S-bar) or S′ (S-prime). It is a unit containing the subordinator and the subordinate clause (cf. 2.2.2).

(8) $\overline{S} \rightarrow$ *that*–S

The element *that* occupies the so-called **complementiser** slot (**COMP slot**) in front of the sentence S_2. Our bracketing of (1b) may now be adapted as follows:

(9) $[_{S_1}$His aunt feared $[_{\overline{S}}$that $[_{S_2}$he might catch something$]]]$

Let us now try to analyse the third conjoin in (1c) above, repeated here as (10):

(10) His uncle said that evil communications corrupted good manners.

Following the procedure we have used above, we find that (10) has essentially the same structure as (1b). Moreover, in both sentences *that* can be omitted (or **deleted**):

(11a) His aunt feared---he might catch something.

(11b) His uncle said---evil communications corrupted good manners.

However, in the passive variants of these sentences *that* is not deletable (cf. also (2)):

(12a) *---he might catch something was feared by his aunt.

(12b) *---evil communications corrupted good manners was said by his uncle.

Now let us finally also consider the structure of the first conjoin in (1a) above, repeated here as (13):

(13) One evening he asked whether he might go home with her.

If you apply some of the tests described above, you will find that *whether he might go home with her* is a constituent. For example, pseudo-clefting yields:

(14) What he asked one evening was whether he might go home with her.

We can ask a question like (15):

(15) What did he ask one evening?

The answer to this would be: *whether he might go home with her.* The string *whether + he might go home with her* is an embedded *Yes–No* question. When *Yes–No* questions are embedded, the subordinator is *whether* or *if*, not *that.* Sentence (13) above may thus be bracketed as follows:

(16)
$$\Big[_{S1}\text{One evening he asked } \Big[_{\overline{S}} \left\{\begin{array}{l}\text{whether}\\ \text{if}\\ \text{*that}\end{array}\right\} \Big[_{S2}\text{he might go home with her}\Big]\Big]\Big]$$

This bracketing means, among other things, that the **COMP slot** can be filled by *whether*, as in (13), and also by *if*, but not by *that.* Together with the embedded sentence S_2 *whether* or *if* form the constituent $\overline{S}$ (S-bar).

Notice that *whether* and *if* cannot be deleted, unlike *that* in (11a) and (11b).

Remember that in addition to *Yes–No* questions English also has *wh*-questions:

(17) Why did you measure the distance?

(18) What did you see there?

Such *wh*-questions may also be embedded in other sentences, but we need no special subordinator to do that. The *wh*-word itself serves as a linking device. For example:

(19) $[_{S_2}$The coroner asked $[_{\bar{S}}$why $[_{S_2}$the witness had measured the distance$]]]$

(20) $[_{S_1}$The policeman asked me $[_{\bar{S}}$what $[_{S_2}$I had seen there$]]]$

We shall explain later how the *wh*-elements come to occupy the COMP slot in front of S_2 (Chapter 4).

Now also compare (21) and (22) below; (22) is more acceptable in American English than in Standard British English. Is there any difference in meaning between them? And what about their form?

(21) The new law requires that seat-belts should be worn by all passengers.

(22) The new law requires for seat-belts to be worn by all passengers.

(21) and (22) have the same meaning, and also basically the same structure. To see this, we may passivise them:

(23) That seat-belts should be worn by all passengers is required by the new law.

(24) For seat-belts to be worn by all passengers is required by the new law.

We may apply pseudo-clefting to both:

(25) What the new law requires is that seat-belts should be worn by all passengers.

(26) What the new law requires is for seat-belts to be worn by all passengers.

What conclusion can we draw with respect to the constituents of these sentences? It seems that (21) requires the following (partial) bracketing:

(27) $[_{S_1}$The new law requires $[_{\bar{S}}$that $[_{S_2}$seat-belts should be worn by ...$]]]$

The string *for seat belts to be worn by all passengers* in (22), as we have seen, structurally resembles the $\bar{S}$ *that seat-belts should be worn by all passengers.* We shall assume, by analogy with (27), that *for* also occupies the COMP slot, and that *seat-belts to be worn by all passengers* is an embedded sentence/clause. The analysis, then, of (22) is as follows:

(28) $[_{S_1}$The new law requires $[_{\bar{S}}$for $[_{S_2}$seat-belts to be worn by ...]]]

Elements which occupy the COMP slot (*that, whether, if, for*, etc.) are often referred to as **complementisers**.

There are, of course, differences between the embedded Ss in (21) and (22). We shall only point out a few here, and return to them later (Chapter 5).

First of all, note that (21) allows a great deal of variation in front of *be worn.* We could replace *should* by *must* or *shall*, and *should be worn* by *are worn.* In fact, *should, must* or *shall* may also be absent. The various possibilities are expressed by (29):

(29) $$\text{The new law requires that seat-belts} \left\{ \begin{matrix} \left(\left\{ \begin{matrix} \text{should} \\ \text{must} \\ \text{shall} \end{matrix} \right\} \right) \text{ be} \\ \text{are} \end{matrix} \right\} \text{ worn ...}$$

In (22), however, no such variation is allowed: in front of *be worn* we only find *to*, and *to* is obligatory. The sequence *to be worn* is called a ***to*-infinitive** of the verb *wear.*

If we replace *seat-belts* by a pronoun, we find another contrast.

(30) The new law requires that *they* should be worn ...

(31) The new law requires for *them* to be worn ...

In (30) we need *they*, in (31) *them.*

The embedded sentence in (21) is **finite**, since the verb phrase is finite (cf. 2.4.3.3); the embedded sentence in (22) is **non-finite**, since its verb phrase is non-finite.

Non-finite clauses may also contain a **bare infinitive** (which is an infinitive without *to*), or they may contain an ***–ing* participle** or an ***–ed* participle**. Consider, for example:

(32) We saw *Mary leave.*

(33) We saw *Mary leaving.*

(34) I do not mind *Mary's leaving.*

(35) We found *all the seats occupied.*

The italicised string in (32) is a non-finite bare infinitive clause, that in (33) is a non-finite *–ing* participle clause, and that in (35) is a non-finite *–ed* participle clause. *Mary's leaving* in (34) is sometimes called a **gerund** clause.

Apart from finite and non-finite clauses of various types, English also has **verbless** clauses. Verbless clauses are clauses in which the verb (usually a form of *to be*) and sometimes other elements have been deleted. Consider, for example:

(36) John believes *the prisoner innocent.*

In this sentence the italicised sequence is a verbless clause, which we assume is a reduced version of the *to*-infinitive clause in (37):

(37) John believes *the prisoner to be innocent.*

The following sentences contain further examples of verbless clauses (italicised):

(38) He considered *the girl a good student.*

(39) *Whenever in trouble,* Bill rang his girl-friend.

(40) He married her *when a student at Harvard.*

See also sections 3.4.11.2 and 3.4.11.3.

Non-finite clauses and verbless clauses are always embedded/subordinate.

2.3.1 EXERCISES

I Bracket all embedded sentences in the following examples. Indicate the boundaries of S_1, $\bar{S}$ and S_2 by labelled bracketing.

(1) John believes that Sue is a spy.
(2) I wonder whether he still remembers that day in April.
(3) That John should have done such a thing is rather worrying.
(4) It is likely that he will propose to her soon.
(5) It would be nice if you could join us for a meal.
(6) I doubt whether he will ever finish the book.
(7) I do not know when the shops close in this town.
(8) I hope they will all come to see me when I am in hospital.
(9) John thinks that George and Mary would make a nice pair.
(10) He asked me why I had written that letter.

II Identify the non-finite clauses in the sentences below. Try to rewrite them as finite clauses:

(1) John believes Bill to be a competent leader.
(2) I am impatient for him to come home.
(3) It was arranged for the children to be adopted.
(4) We are all hoping for Bill to win.

III Identify the verbless clauses in the sentences below. Try to rewrite them as finite or as non-finite clauses:

(1) If available, the books will be sent to you within two weeks.
(2) He drove home after the party, dead drunk.

(3) A *tour de force* by any reckoning, Quirk's grammar carries on the great work of Jespersen but with more economy and greater precision.

See also Chapter 5.

2.4 PHRASES

2.4.1 INTRODUCTION

Read the following text and decide what types of sentences it contains (simple, compound, complex, or compound-complex):

> *Text 2.4.1*
> The tramp read the diary. He laughed. He turned a page, he read it and he laughed again. He leaned towards the German girl and said a few words to her.
>
> The Egyptian was clowning; the noise in the room continued. Soon the young German girl was offering chocolate for the second time. Her voice was very soft.
>
> The tramp was unfolding his magazine slowly. He stopped suddenly, he looked at the chocolate. But she had given him no chocolate. He unfolded his magazine. Then he destroyed it.
>
> V.S. Naipaul, *In a Free State.*

Try to isolate as many phrases as you can in each sentence above. You will see that these constituents fall into various grammatical categories (or constituent types). It is the purpose of this section to look more closely at the different categories of phrases.

2.4.2 NOUN PHRASES

If we go through the text in search of phrasal constituents, we find one very common type, which is represented by constituents such as *the tramp, the diary, he, a page, it, the German girl, a few words, her, the Egyptian, the noise, the young German girl, chocolate,* etc.

It is often possible to replace one item by another. Consider, for example, the following substitution frames:

(1a)	The tramp		the diary
(1b)	The young German girl	read	his magazine
(1c)	The Egyptian		a page
(2a)	The girl		chocolate
(2b)	The very young girl	offered	no chocolate
(2c)	The girl from Berlin		hot chocolate

Constituents which can appear in the same environments (or contexts) are said to have the same **distribution**.

If we look at the examples of constituents listed above, we see that the type of constituent we are here dealing with has as its most important element a word of the **class of nouns** (N): *tramp, diary, page, chocolate, ...* This N may be preceded by such words as *the, a, no,* etc. and also by words such as *German, young, ...* It is, however, quite clear that these additional items are less important than the N. In our text above we found, for example, the constituents *no chocolate* and *the chocolate,* but we also found just *chocolate.*

If a constituent has as its central (non-omissible) element an N, then such a constituent will be labelled NP. The noun is the **Head** of the NP:

(3) $$\begin{bmatrix} {}_{\text{NP}}\text{the } \textit{chocolate} \\ \text{Head} \end{bmatrix}$$

2.4.2.1 Elements before the Head

In text 2.4.1 many NPs begin with words such as *the* or *a.* It is obvious that these words are not the central elements of the NPs. In fact, if you were to jot down a quick sketch of the story told in this fragment, you would probably do so without using *the* or *a.* For example: *Tramp read diary ... He turned page,* etc. And most of the information in the text would be preserved. Conversely, leaving out the Head Ns leads to no text at all: **The read the ... turned a ...,* etc.

Words such as *a* and *the* are useful devices for making more precise what the NP means; they help to **specify** what person or thing is indicated by (or referred to by) the NP. The person or thing referred to by an NP is its **referent.**

Compare, for example, (4a) and (4b) below:

(4a) The tramp read the diary.

(4b) A tramp read a diary.

In (4a) *the tramp* suggests that we already know who, or what tramp, is involved. The referent of *tramp* must already have been introduced in the text before. In (4b), on the other hand, the referent of *tramp* is introduced for the first time. The same applies to *diary.* Since the definite and the indefinite article (*the* and *a*) both serve to **specify** the reference of the NP, they are said to be **Specifiers** of the NP.

In text 2.4.1 there are numerous other instances of NPs with articles functioning as Specifiers. Identify them.

Apart from articles we also find elements like *his* and *her* in front of the Head N, e.g.: *his magazine, her voice. His* and *her* again help to establish the referent: they identify the magazine or voice by indicating the possessor:

his and *her* (possessive pronouns) stand for *the tramp's* and for *the young German girl's* respectively. The forms with *–'s* are genitives. Possessive pronouns and genitives thus also function as Specifiers narrowing down the reference of the NPs in which they occur. Other possessive pronouns are: *my, your, its, our, their,* e.g.: *The baby hates* **its** *pram*; *I like* **my** *new dress*, etc. The demonstrative pronouns *this, that, these* and *those*, and items like *some, any, what, which, whose, each, every, all, half, both, much, many,* and the numerals (*one, two,* ...) may also have a specifier function.

Consider the following examples and identify the NPs (by bracketing) and their Heads (by underlining):

(5) Which reporter will interview all the players?

(6) Two boys found these diamonds.

(7) Both the girls enjoy classical music.

(8) Half the audience started giggling when the three girls began to sing.

If numerals occur in the structure of an NP, they typically follow words like *the, my, our, these,* but precede the Head noun. For example: *the three girls. Half, both, all* and *double* typically precede *the, my, our, these,* etc. For example: *half the bottle, both the girls, all my friends.* Items like those mentioned which precede the NP Head, belong to the grammatical category of **determiner**. Depending on their position relative to each other, determiners may be **predeterminers** (*half, both, all, double*), **central determiners** (*the, a, this, that, my, his,* etc.) or **postdeterminers** (numerals, etc.). In general, we shall use the collective label 'determiner' to refer to all the items just mentioned. Determiners function as Specifiers in the NP. The Head of an NP may also be preceded by adjective phrases (cf. 2.4.5), which **modify** the Head N, as in: *young boys, expensive diamonds, classical music* and *the three gorgeous girls.* Since *young, expensive,* etc. normally precede the Head, they are said to **premodify** it. Premodifiers follow determiners.

An important difference between Specifiers and Premodifiers is that they are realised by totally different categories of words: the function of Specifier is realised by the fairly limited collection of items which we call determiners, whereas the function of Premodifier is usually realised by adjective phrases or other **open class** elements (see the final paragraph of 2.4.2.2).

2.4.2.2 Pronouns

Return to text 2.4.1 once more. It seems that in this text the NPs *the tramp, his magazine, the German girl* are key-phrases. The author repeats them quite often. However, he does not always actually use the NP *the tramp* when he wants to refer to that particular person. Sometimes he uses the substitute form *he*:

(9) *The tramp* read the diary. *He* laughed. *He* turned a page.

He is a word used instead of an NP, it is a **pro-form.** Since it replaces an NP, it is also called a *pronoun.* Can you find other such pronouns in our text?

Words like *he, she, it* and *they* (personal pronouns) are used whenever repetition of the full NP is unnecessary. Constituents which can be replaced by personal pronouns must be NPs. Personal pronouns differ from each other in terms of their relationship to the speaker: *I* refers to the speaker (or writer); *you* refers to the person or persons spoken to (= the addressee(s)); *we* refers to the speaker and some other person or persons; and *he, she, it, they* refer to the person(s) or thing(s) spoken about. This contrast is usually referred to as one of **person**: *I* and *we* are first person, *you* is second person, and *he, she, it, they* are third person.

Moreover, *I* indicates one person only, while *we* indicates more than one. *He* refers to one person, but *they* to more more than one. This contrast between 'one' and 'more than one' is a contrast of **number**; the opposition is one between **singular** and **plural**. (See also 2.5.2.) *You* may be either singular or plural. For example:

(10) You, John, must stand over there.

(11) You will all hear from me soon.

The contrast between *he, she* and *it* is one of **gender**. *He* is said to have **masculine** gender, *she* **feminine** gender and *it* **neuter** gender.

Another contrast found with personal pronouns, in addition to those of (a) number, (b) person and (c) gender, is that between the forms *he* and *him*, and between the forms *she* and *her*, etc. This is a contrast of **case**. Take the following pair of sentences:

(12) Philip liked Mary Anne.

(13) Mary Ann was liked by Philip.

Replace the NPs *Philip* and *Mary Ann* by suitable pronouns. You will see that in (12) you have to choose *he* to replace *Philip*, in (13) you have to choose *him*; in (12) *Mary Ann* has to be replaced by *her* and in (13) by *she.* The choice of the form is not random. The result of bracketing the constituents in (12) and in (13) is as follows:

(14) $[_{S}\,[_{NP}\text{Philip}]\,[_{VP}\text{liked}\,[_{NP}\text{Mary Ann}]]]$

(15) $[_{S}\,[_{NP}\text{Mary Ann}]\,[_{VP}\text{was liked by Philip}]]]$

We use *he* and *she* for the NP which precedes the VP; it is this NP which, together with the VP, makes up the whole sentence. In a tree diagram representation the NP would be immediately dominated by S. Since this NP is the Subject, *he* and *she* are called the Subject forms of the pronouns. We chose *her* and *him* to replace NPs which occur inside a VP: such forms are called Object forms. We shall look more closely at Subjects and Objects in Chapter 3.

We have seen that personal pronouns replace complete constituents, in the same way that clefting, passivisation, etc. affect whole constituents. Pronouns are useful devices for avoiding repetition of the whole NP. Consider, for example:

(16) *John* met *Mary* at the entrance of the station. *He* bought *her* an ice-cream.

As the arrows indicate, *John* and *he* are linked, and so are *Mary* and *her*. *John* and *he* are **co-referential**, and so are *Mary* and *her*. Consider now:

(17) *John* was unable to control *him*.

(18) *Mary* killed *her*.

In (17) *John* and *him* are not co-referential; *him* must be taken to refer to someone else, as in:

(19) *Bill* was very drunk. *John* was unable to control *him*.

In (18) *Mary* and *her* are not related; *her* refers to another female. For example:

(20) *Susan* was threatening to kill the children with a carving-knife.
In the panic which followed *Mary* killed *her*

Him in (19) and *her* in (20) are co-referential to an element outside the sentence: they are **bound** outside the sentence. Because they are not linked to something inside the sentence we can say they are **free** inside the sentence. *Him* and *her* cannot be used in (19) and (20) to express a referential link inside the sentence. In order to say that John lacked self-control, for example, i.e. that 'John cannot control John', we use a special pronoun with *–self* (a reflexive pronoun):

(21) *John* was unable to control *himself*.

If we want to convey that Mary committed suicide, we cannot use *her* (as in (20)), but we must use *herself*: *Mary killed herself*.

Himself and *herself* are pronouns which must be **bound** inside their sentences. Other reflexive pronouns are: *myself, yourself, himself, itself, our-*

selves, yourselves and *themselves.* We return to the notion of 'binding' in Chapters 4 and 5.

Apart from the possessive pronouns *my, your, our,* etc., which belong to the category of determiners (2.4.2.1), English also has the possessive pronouns *mine, yours, his, hers, its, ours, yours* and *theirs.* These can be used to replace a complete NP and can thus occur on their own. For example:

(22) This is your bicycle. *Mine* is over there.

(23) They all admired her new dress. Nobody liked *yours* or *mine.*

(24) These presents are *theirs,* not *ours.*

There is also the category of demonstrative pronouns: *this, that, these* and *those. This* and *that* are singular, *these* and *those* plural. We have seen (2.4.2.1) that, like possessives and articles, they may occur as determiners, functioning as Specifiers of the NP in which they occur. However, the four demonstrative pronouns may also occur independently as NPs. For example:

(25) *This* is my mother and *that* is my father.

(26) *Those* were the days.

Can you think of any personal, reflexive, possessive or demonstrative pronouns apart from the ones that we have mentioned? The correct answer to this question must be negative, for pronouns are said to form **closed sets**, since it is possible and fairly easy to make an exhaustive list of all the pronouns in English. Adjectives, nouns, verbs and adverbs, on the other hand, constitute **open classes** (cf. 2.4.2.1). In these cases it is impossible to list all the items belonging to a class, since such a class can be indefinitely extended by adding newly formed adjectives, nouns, verbs or adverbs.

2.4.2.3 One-word Phrases

Return once more to text 2.4.1. Notice, for example, that the NP *the chocolate* alternates with the noun *chocolate.* Does the latter also count as an NP? To answer this question, we must apply a few constituency tests: clefting identifies the bare N *chocolate* as a constituent:

(27) The young German girl was offering *chocolate.*

(28) It was *chocolate* that the young German girl was offering.

Similarly, passivisation is possible: it shifts *chocolate* to sentence-initial position:

(29) *Chocolate* was being offered by the young German girl.

Fronting produces:

(30) *Chocolate* the young German girl was offering (not tea).

Moreover, one can easily expand the constituent:

(31) The young German girl was offering { *the chocolate* / *hot chocolate* / *very hot chocolate with sugar* }

Chocolate and *the chocolate*, etc. act in precisely the same way with respect to clefting, passivisation and fronting. Hence, it would be very uneconomical to treat them as different grammatical categories. They have the same distribution and they undergo the same processes. Consequently, we shall say that they are both NPs.

2.4.2.4 Elements after the Head

In text 2.4.1 all NPs happen to end with the Head N. This is by no means always the case. Bracket the NPs in the following sentences and underline the Head Ns:

(32) The diary which the tramp was reading was amusing.

(33) The idea that he might like some chocolate did not occur to the German girl.

(34) The question whether the tramp had any money did not arise.

Bracketing of the NP in (32) gives us:

(35) $[_{NP}$The diary $[_{\overline{S}}$which the tramp was reading$]]$

The Head N *diary* is followed by the string *which the tramp was reading.* We have seen (1.2.3) that such a string is an embedded sentence. This sentence/clause is fully integrated within the NP. The clause (labelled $\overline{S}$) follows the Head noun in an NP, and has the function of **Postmodifier**.

Which in the above examples is a relative pronoun; relative pronouns introduce **relative** clauses (see 4.2.6). The other clauses above (with *that* and *whether*) are not relative clauses, but **appositive** clauses, which give an indication of the 'content' of *the idea* or *the question.* They are also said to function as Postmodifiers. There are, however, important differences between relative clauses and appositive clauses, to which we shall return later (4.2.7).

Consider also the italicised NP in (36):

(36) *Two boys with red hair* entered the room.

The string *with red hair* is a prepositional phrase (PP), which postmodifies the Head of the NP (cf. 2.4.4). See also Chapters 3 and 7.

2.4.2.5 Summing up the NP

We have seen that noun phrases in English usually have the structure in (37):

(37)

Category	**Predet** *Half, both, all double*	**Centr.Det** **Art** **Poss pron** **Dem pron**	**Postdet** **Num**	**AdjP/...**	**N**	**S/PP/ ...**
Function	**Specifier**			**Premod**	**Head**	**Postmod**
		the			tramp	
	half	a			page	
		his			magazine	
	both	these		lovely	children	
			two		boys	with red hair
		that		German	girl	
	all	the	ten	French	soldiers	who survivec the crash
					they	
			five	Dutch	students	of English
		no			milk	in bottles
					John	
					he	
		the tramp's			magazine	
		the			news	that he was i

Together with the central determiner (which may be *zero*), the Head (*tramp, page, magazine,* etc.) constitutes the kernel of the NP. In the course of this chapter we shall comment in more detail on all the categories which occur inside the NP.

2.4.2.6 Exercise

Indicate the structure of the following NPs:

(1) two nice English girls without jobs
(2) the girls in the corner
(3) the best Dutch classical music of the seventeenth century
(4) my two greatest friends in this university
(5) the question whether he enjoyed the play

2.4.3 VERB PHRASES

2.4.3.1 Introduction

Consider the following sentence from our text 2.4.1 again:

(38) The tramp read the diary.

Passivisation, fronting and clefting help to establish the following (partial) bracketing:

(39) $\left[_{S}\left[_{NP}\text{The tramp}\right]\text{ read }\left[_{NP}\text{the diary}\right]\right]$

The tramp and *the diary* are NPs. But what about *read*? The word *read* belongs to the class of verbs (*walk, talk, sleep, help,* etc.). We shall look at the properties of verbs in 2.5.3. Is *read* a constituent? Again we need some tests to answer this question. Clefting and fronting yield ungrammatical sentences:

(40) *It is *read* that the tramp the diary.

(41) **Read* the tramp the diary.

In fact, pseudo-clefting shows that *read* and *the diary* constitute one unit:

(42) What the tramp did was *read the diary.*

Moreover, we can replace the string *read the diary* by a special pro-form with *do.* For example:

(43) The tramp read the diary, and the Egyptian *did (so)* too.

(44) The tramp read the diary. *Did* he?

We shall call the string *read the diary* the verb phrase (VP). The verb (V) *read* is the Head of the VP. In our example, the Head (*read*) is followed by an NP. The structure of the VP may thus be represented as follows:

(45) The tramp $\left[_{VP}\text{read }\left[_{NP}\text{the diary}\right]\right]$

Here *the diary* is an NP within a VP. In a sense, the NP completes the VP and is therefore called a **Complement** of the verb *read.*

2.4.3.2 Verb Complements

Consider the following sentences:

(46) The tramp laughed.

(47) The story was interesting.

(48) The tramp read the diary.

(49) He told the girl an interesting story.

(50) He called her a clever girl.

(51) The tramp leaned towards the German girl.

(52) The tramp put the chocolate on the table.

Identify the VPs in these sentences by bracketing.

We find that *laugh* in (46) takes no Complement: the VP consists of the verb only. In (47) the verb requires *interesting* (an adjective phrase) as its Complement. In (48) the verb takes as its Complement the NP *the diary.* In (49) the verb is followed by two Complements, the NPs *the girl* and *an interesting story.* In (50) the verb *call* takes as its Complements the NP *her* and the NP *a clever girl.* In (51) the verb requires a PP (*towards the German girl*). And in (52) the verb *put* is seen to take as its Complements the NP *the chocolate* and the PP *on the table.*

Verb Complements are elements which obligatorily follow the verb in the VP (see 3.1). The verb (*laugh, be, read,* etc.) is the Head of the VP, and the Complements (NP, AdjP, PP, etc.) may have functions like *Direct Object, Indirect Object, Predicative Complement,* etc. We shall return to these functions in Chapter 3.

Consider also the following sentences:

(53) He told the girl that she was clever.

(54) He told an interesting story to the girl.

In (53) we find that the verb phrase contains a *that*-clause as one of the Complements of the verb. The VP here is: *told the girl that she was clever.* Pseudo-clefting and substitution by *do* (*so*) indicate that the *that*-clause is part of the VP:

(55) What he did was *tell the girl that she was clever.*

(56) He told the girl that she was clever and I *did (so)* too.

The structure of (53) is (57):

(57) $\left[_{S}\text{He}\left[_{VP}\text{told}\left[_{NP}\text{the girl}\right]\left[_{\bar{S}}\text{that she was clever}\right]\right]\right]$

Sentence (54) above is an alternative version of (49). The sequence *told*–NP–NP can be rearranged as: *told*–NP–PP (with *to*), without a change in meaning. The two alternatives ((49) and (54) above) may be bracketed as follows:

(58) $\left[\text{He}\left[_{VP}\text{told}\left[_{NP}\text{the girl}\right]\left[_{NP}\text{an interesting story}\right]\right]\right]$

(59) $\left[\text{He}\left[_{VP}\text{told}\left[_{NP}\text{an interesting story}\right]\left[_{PP}\text{to the girl}\right]\right]\right]$

Note that *tell* in (49) above and *call* in (50) both take two NPs as Complements. Compare the two sentences, here repeated as (60) and (61):

(60) He told the girl an interesting story.

(61) He called her a clever girl.

We shall see later that (60) and (61) have quite different patterns of behaviour, and that the two NPs have quite different grammatical functions (see 3.4.3 and 3.4.6).

The examples given above illustrate the most important sentence types of English, in terms of the complementation that the Head of the VP requires. In 3.1 ff. we shall provide a more exhaustive survey of English sentence patterns. For the moment, it is important to note that in the pattern underlying (47) above the adjective phrase (AdjP) may be replaced by an NP or a PP (as in: *The story was a great success* and *The room was in a mess*). Similarly, the V in the pattern underlying (48) may take an $\overline{\text{S}}$ instead of an NP (as in: *He knew that the snake had killed the rat*), etc.

We shall say that a verb **subcategorises** for a certain type of Complement. In other words, a verb occurs inside a certain frame, and is obligatorily followed by certain classes of categories. Such frames are called **subcategorisation frames**. (62a)–(62g) are simplified examples of such frames:

	Subcategorisation frames for verbs	**Verb types**
(62a)	[——]	Intransitive
(62b)	$[\text{——} \left\{ \begin{matrix} \text{AdjP} \\ \text{NP} \\ \text{PP} \end{matrix} \right\}]$	Copula
(62c)	$[\text{——} \left\{ \begin{matrix} \text{NP} \\ \overline{\text{S}} \end{matrix} \right\}]$	Monotransitive
(62d)	$[\text{——} \left\{ \begin{matrix} \text{NP–NP} \\ \text{NP–PP} \end{matrix} \right\}]$	Ditransitive
(62e)	$[\text{—— NP–} \left\{ \begin{matrix} \text{AdjP} \\ \text{NP} \end{matrix} \right\}]$	Complex transitive
(62f)	[—— PP]	Intransitive
(62g)	[—— NP–PP]	Transitive

This list of subcategorisation frames is still provisional, and so are some of the labels given to the different categories of verb ('verb types'). Each frame means that in the position indicated by the dash —— one may insert any verb which takes as its Complement(s) the constituent(s) specified there. As usual, the curly brackets { } indicate a choice: copulas, for example, may take an AdjP, an NP, or a PP, and monotransitive verbs may take an NP or an $\overline{\text{S}}$, etc. The square brackets in (62a–g) mark off the boundaries of the VP. It is only the obligatory elements within the VP that are Complements. The Subject NP, which falls outside the VP, is not a Complement to the verb. See also 3.1.

So far we have only referred to (obligatory) Complements, i.e. those elements whose presence is syntactically required. But we shall see that it is also possible for indefinitely many **optional** constituents to occur in a sentence. For example:

(63) He unfolded his magazine.

(64) He unfolded his magazine (*for the girl*) (*quite unexpectedly*) ...

What is the VP in the above sentences? In (64) we find additional elements (italicised and between brackets) which are optional. We shall say that these elements belong to the VP, but that they are not Complements; they are not needed to complete the VP; they merely add further information: they realise the grammatical function of **Adjunct** (see 3.4.8). The structure of (64) may be represented as follows:

(65) He $\left[_{VP}\right.$unfolded [his magazine] [(for the girl)] [(quite unexpectedly)] ...]

A verb does not subcategorise for Adjuncts. The brackets around *for the girl* and *quite unexpectedly* indicate that these constituents are optional. The dotted line at the end of the sentence is meant to suggest that the number of optional constituents can, in principle, be extended indefinitely. In Chapter 4 we shall see that (optional) Adjuncts may be moved to other positions in the sentence.

2.4.3.3 Elements before the Head

Text 2.4.1 above has past time reference. We might add to the text time-specifying phrases (Adjuncts) such as *last year, in those days, at the time,* etc. Obviously, we cannot add *tomorrow, later on, today, next week,* etc. To change the time reference of text 2.4.1 to the present, we would have to alter all the verb forms, as follows:

(66) The tramp *reads* the diary. He *laughs.* He *turns* a page, he *reads* it and he *laughs* again. Etc.

If we change the time reference of the text from past to present, we find that every time it is the form of the first element in the VP which is affected. For example: *laughed* becomes *laughs,* and *was unfolding* becomes *is unfolding.* The form of the verb is altered from **past tense** to **present tense**.

For each VP in the text a tense choice has been made: either past or present. If a VP is marked for tense, it is said to be **finite**. (*Non-finite* VPs are those which exhibit no contrast between past and present tense.)

We can represent the relationship between the verb and its tense marking by the following notation:

(67) $\left[_{VP}\right.$Tense–V ...]

where ... stands for Complements and Adjuncts in the VP, including zero.

Of course ultimately the tense is attached to the right of (the base of) the V as a suffix: *I work/I workED.*

If we were to rewrite the text so as to change its time reference to the future, we would get sentences like the following:

(68) The tramp *will* read the diary. He *will* turn the page ...

Apart from *will*, one might also use *may*, *must*, *could*, etc. in the same position. In all these cases what we do is add a word in front of the V. These pre-verbal elements are the so-called **modal auxiliaries**, or **modals** (e.g. *shall*, *will*, *may*, *can*, *should*, *would*, *might*, *could*, *must*). They must be added in front of the V, after the tense element (cf. (67)). A closer look at the modals suggests that to some extent they are paired: *will–would*; *may–might*; *can–could*; *shall–should*. This pairing is based on tense contrasts: *will* is present and *would* past, etc. Compare:

(69a) The tramp says that he *will* read the diary.

(69b) The tramp said that he *would* read the diary.

There are three more types of pre-verbal element: *perfect*, *progressive* and *passive*. Consider, for example:

(70) She *had* giv*en* him no chocolate.

Bracket the VP. What type of V is *give*? Bracket and label the Complements. The verb *give* is preceded by *had*, and the form *give* is altered to the past participle *given*. *Given* combines with *have* to form the **perfect aspect**. In our example the **auxiliary** *have* itself is in the past tense *had*. We distinguish between the *present perfect* and the *past perfect*.

Consider also:

(71) He *was* unfold*ing* his magazine.

Here the verb *unfold* is preceded by *was* (the past tense of the **auxiliary** *be*) and the present participle suffix *–ing* is added to it. *Be* + *ing* expresses **progressive aspect**. Again you see that the past tense is attached to the auxiliary. Can you find any other examples of progressive VPs in text 2.4.1?

The third pre-verbal element is that of the **passive voice**. Passive is expressed by the auxiliary *be* and the past participle suffix *–ed*, which is attached to V. For example:

(72) The tramp *was* arrest*ed* by the police.

The examples above show that finite VPs contain an obligatory element, tense. The remaining elements which we have mentioned (modal, perfect, progressive and passive) are all optional: they may, but need not occur in the VP. Tense, the modal auxiliaries and the auxiliaries *have* and *be* function as **Specifiers** of the VP. For convenience, the term 'auxiliary element' will occasionally be used with reference to both tense and auxiliaries.

The following diagram sums up the elements which may occur *before* the Head of the VP:

(73)

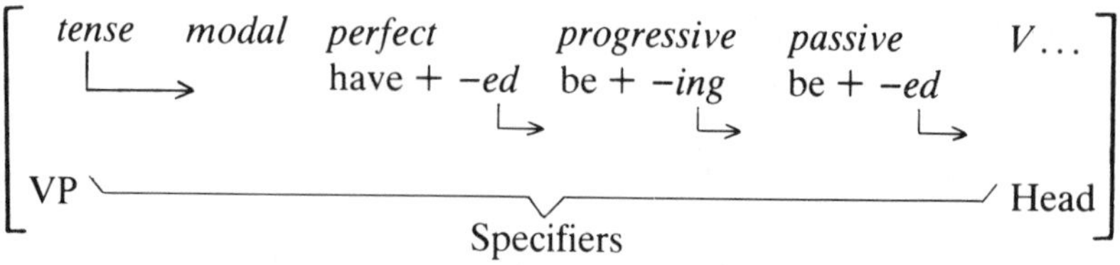

If one or more optional elements are realised, they must ocur in the order given by the diagram. The arrows pointing to the right indicate that the suffixes associated with these elements are moved to the end of the next verb on the right. For example, the VP of:

(74) She may have been working in the garden

has the following structure:

(75)

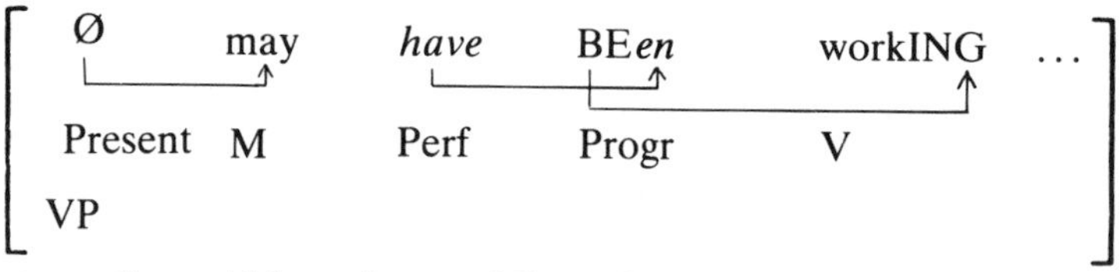

The structure of *would have been sold* is as follows:

(76)

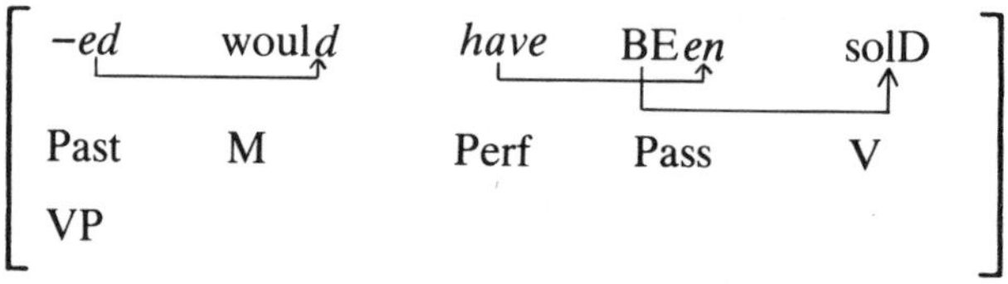

2.4.3.4 The First Auxiliary in the VP

Consider again the following sentences from text 2.4.1 (slightly adapted):

(77) The Egyptian was clowning.

(78) The young girl was offering chocolate for the second time.

(79) She had given him chocolate.

These declarative sentences (cf. 2.2.1) can be turned into *Yes–No* questions, as follows:

(80) Was the Egyptian clowning?

(81) Was the young girl offering chocolate for the second time?

(82) Had she given him chocolate?

As the examples show, *Yes–No* questions are formed by reversing the order of the first constituent in the sentence (*The Egyptian, The young girl*, etc.) and the first element of the VP (*was, had*, etc.). The whole first constituent is involved in this **inversion**, not just part of the constituent; the auxiliary *was* or *had* is moved across the entire constituent to sentence-initial position. Compare, for example:

(83a) $[_{NP}$The new Prime Minister of Belgium$]$ *is* making a statement in the United Nations tomorrow.

(83b) *Is* $[_{NP}$the new Prime Minister of Belgium$]$ making a statement in the United Nations tomorrow?

Not:

(83c) *[The new Prime Minister] *is* [of Belgium] making a statement in the United Nations tomorrow?

Now let us form *Yes–No* questions from (84) and (85) below:

(84) The tramp admires the girl.

(85) He laughed.

Here we always get the additional element *does* or *did* in the corresponding questions. For example:

(86) Does the tramp admire the girl? (Not: *Admires the tramp the girl?)

(87) Did he laugh?

What is the difference between examples (77)–(79) and examples (84) and (85)? Why is there simple inversion in one case, and inversion plus ***do*-insertion** in the other? The answer is that English *Yes–No* questions always need an auxiliary in initial position, and if there is no auxiliary available in the underlying structure (as in (84) and (85)), then the 'dummy' element *do* must be inserted. *Do* is then also called an auxiliary.

It is always *the first auxiliary* in the VP that is involved in the inversion with the Subject NP.

What we have said about the role of the first auxiliary and the use of *do* also applies to the **negation** of English sentences. Negation is normally achieved by inserting *not* after the first element of the VP.

Now negate both sentences (77)–(79) and sentences (84) and (85) above. You will find that (77)–(79) allow simple *not*-insertion (without *do*), whereas (84) and (85) again require *do*-insertion when they are negated. The negative sentences corresponding to (77) and to (84), for example, are the following:

(88) The Egyptian was not/wasn't clowning.

(89) The tramp does not/doesn't admire the girl. (Not: *The tramp admires not the girl).

Why is there *do*-insertion in (89), but not in (88)? The answer is again that negative sentences always need an auxiliary in front of *not.* And if there is no auxiliary available, the auxiliary *do* must be inserted.

The first auxiliary in the VP (a modal, or *have* or *be*) is not only involved in operations like question formation and negation, but also, for example, in **tag formation**. The 'tag question' corresponding to (77) is (90) and that corresponding to (84) is (91) below. Compare:

(90) The Egyptian was clowning, wasn't he?

(91) The tramp admires the girl, doesn't he? (Not: *The tramp admires the girl, admiresn't he?).

The auxiliary in the tag in (90) corresponds with the progressive auxiliary *was* and is negated. In (91) *do*-insertion is again required in the absence of an auxiliary.

Question formation, negation and tag formation are three ways to illustrate the special status of the first auxiliary in the VP: as we have seen, this first element may be a modal (*will, must, should,* etc.), the perfect auxiliary *have,* the progressive auxiliary *be,* or the passive auxiliary *be.* We shall return to the operation of *do*-insertion in section 4.2.3.

However, it is not only the auxiliaries *have* and *be* that are involved in inversion, negation and tag formation, but also the lexical verbs *have* and *be.* For example:

(92a) Her voice was soft.

(92b) Was her voice soft?

(92c) Her voice wasn't soft.

(92d) Her voice was soft, wasn't it?

These lexical verbs behave like auxiliaries here. This is a case of structural indeterminacy or 'reanalysis' (see Chapter 6).

2.4.3.5 Summing up the VP

We have seen that VPs in English usually have the structure shown in (93):

(93)

Category	Tns, M/Perf/ Prog/Pass	V	AdjP/NP/S/ PP/ ...	NP/S/PP/ AdvP/ ...
Function	**Specifier**	**H**	**Verb Complement**	**A**
		laughed		again
		was	interesting	
	must have been	reading	the diary	with great interest
	may have	told	the girl an interesting story	yesterday
	would have	called	her a clever girl	if she had known the answer

This diagram is provisional. We shall return to details of the structure of the VP below. Here it is important to repeat that the only obligatory elements in the VP are: the Head V, its Complements, if any, and the Specifier tense (Tns). The remaining elements are optional. The grammatical functions in VP will be dealt with in Chapter 3. Compare diagram (93) with diagram (37), which sums up the structure of the NP (2.4.2.5).

2.4.3.6 Exercises

I Analyse the VPs of the following sentences, paying particular attention to the elements preceding the Head V. Draw diagrams similar to (75) and (76) above.

(1) Inspector Mills will question the prisoner first.
(2) I am looking forward to hearing from you soon.
(3) The policeman could have arrested the tramp.
(4) Susan has been writing letters all afternoon.
(5) McDonald was booked for hitting his opponent in the stomach.
(6) All these documents have been examined by Dr. Klutzbaum.

II Classify all the lexical verbs in the above sentences ((1)–(6)) in terms of their complementation.

III Wherever possible, change each of the above sentences into:

(a) *Yes–No* questions
(b) Negative statements
(c) Tag questions

Comment on any cases where the three operations yield curious results. Can you think of any other operational tests to show the special status of the first auxiliary?

2.4.4 PREPOSITIONAL PHRASES

Phrases consisting of a preposition (*in, about, under, to, with,* etc.) followed by an NP or an S are called *prepositional phrases* (PPs). We shall assume that the preposition (P) is the Head of the PP, and that what follows the Head is its Complement (**Prepositional Complement**, or Prepc). For example (the P is italicised):

(94) *in* the corner

(95) *to* the tramp

(96) *with* red hair

(97) *about* this topic

The preposition may be preceded by an element which specifies it. For example:

(98) *right* on the spot

(99) *slap* in the middle

(100) *straight* through the wall

(101) *three inches* above the door

The **Specifiers** in the PPs are italicised. The Specifiers in (98)–(100) are adverb phrases, and that in (101) is an NP.

Occasionally the P of a PP is followed by another PP, e.g. *since after the war* and *from behind the green door.* The Prepc is also deletable at times, e.g. *John is inside (the room).*

Notice that PPs may occur within VPs, NPs, etc. Consider, in particular, the following sentences from our text, and decide whether the PPs occur inside a VP or an NP:

(102) He leaned towards the German girl.

(103) The noise in the room continued.

In:

(104) I $[_{VP}$met her at the entrance of the cinema$]$

the PP *at the entrance of the cinema* occurs inside a VP, and the PP *of the cinema* inside the NP *the entrance of the cinema,* which is the Prepc of *at.* The structure of this PP is as follows:

(105) $[_{PP}$at $[_{NP}$the entrance $[_{PP}$of $[_{NP}$the cinema$]]]]$

The normal order of elements in the PP is: P–NP. However, English also has a number of **postpositions**, which typically follow their Complements, as in: *three weeks ago* and *all joking aside*; *ago* and *aside* are like prepositions in that they serve as the Head of a PP.

2.4.4.1 Summing up the PP

The structure of the PP may be summed up as in (106):

(106)

Category	**AdvP/NP**	**P**	**NP/S/PP**
Function	**Specifier**	**H**	**Complement**
		with	red hair
	right	on	the spot
	two minutes	before	her arrival
		about	this topic
		regarding	whether he might come

Compare this diagram with diagrams (37) and (93) in 2.4.2.5 and 2.4.3.5 above.

2.4.4.2 Exercise

Bracket the following sentences, paying particular attention to the structure of the PPs:

(1) She will be wearing a white dress with a dropped waistline.
(2) I will see you at the east gate of the park.
(3) He put the money in an old shoe-box three years ago.
(4) She was born in Trinidad or in Jamaica.
(5) Those two paintings by Salvador Dali are for sale.
(6) Watch out for a tall man with a moustache.

2.4.5 ADJECTIVE PHRASES

Our text 2.4.1 contains phrases such as:

(107) very soft

(108) German

(109) young

These are adjective phrases (AdjPs). The Head of an AdjP is an adjective (*soft, German, young*), just as the head of an NP is an N or the Head of a VP a V, etc. The AdjPs (108) and (109) consist of a Head adjective (Adj) only, whereas in (107) the Head Adj is preceded by an adverb phrase (*very*) which specifies it.

The Head Adj may also be followed by a PP or an S which serves as a **Complement** of the Head Adj. For example (the Complements are italicised):

(110) worried *about the future*

(111) afraid *that she might die*

(112) fond *of the sea*

Decide whether the italicised AdjPs occur inside a VP or inside an NP in the sentence below (the NP itself may be inside a VP or a PP):

(113) Her voice was *very soft.*

(114) He leaned towards the *German* girl.

Bracketing of (113) should yield the following constituent structure:

(115) $[_S [_{NP}$Her voice$] [_{VP}$was $[_{AdjP}$very soft$]]]$

The AdjP *very soft* functions as a Verb Complement in the VP. Bracketing of (114) gives:

(116) $[_S [_{NP}$He$] [_{VP}$leaned $[_{PP}$towards $[_{NP}$the $[_{AdjP}$German$]$ girl$]]]]$

The AdjP *German* functions as a Premodifier in the NP *the German girl.*

NPs may contain more than one AdjP functioning as Premodifier. For example:

(117) the young German girl

(118) the little old lady

(119) that nice young French student

Words like *only*, as in *an only child*, and *utter*, as in *an utter fool*, are also AdjPs. However, they are limited in their distribution: unlike the vast majority of AdjPs, they cannot occur after the Copula *be* in a sentence: **the child is only* or **the fool is utter.* These AdjPs, it appears, can only be used **attributively**, not **predicatively**. Other ADJPs, such as *awake* or *alone*, can only be used predicatively, not attributively, e.g.: **the awake child*, **the alone boy.*

2.4.5.1 Summing up the AdjP

The structure of the AdjP may be summed up as in (120):

(120)

Category	**AdvP**	**Adj**	**PP/S**
Function	**Spec**	**H**	**Complement**
		young	
	extremely	handsome	
	very	worried	about the future
		afraid	that she might die
	rather	fond	of the sea

Compare this diagram with diagrams (37), (93) and (106) above.

2.4.5.2 Exercises

I AdjPs usually describe some sort of quality that is attached to a person or thing, e.g. *She is nice* attaches 'niceness' to 'she'. Identify the AdjPs in the following sentences. What is the NP each AdjP is related with?

(1) His decision was very unwise.
(2) The young girl was left in absolute misery.
(3) She looks very attractive.
(4) This important decision was reached after painful negotiations.
(5) The old Vicar considered their behaviour sinful.
(6) The idea seems to me to be rather provocative.
(7) They painted the door dark red.
(8) She married the Duke young.

II Complete the sentences below by adding a Complement PP with the appropriate preposition. Bracket the AdjP and then the VP.

(1) She was not aware . . .
(2) She is angry . . .
(3) She was very envious . . .
(4) You are guilty . . .
(5) Children are often afraid . . .

2.4.6 ADVERB PHRASES

Text 2.4.1 also contains phrases such as:

(121) again

(122) soon

(123) very

(124) slowly

(125) then

These are adverb phrases (AdvPs). The Head of an AdvP is an adverb (Adv), just as the Head of an NP is an N or the Head of a VP a V, etc. The AdvPs in (121)–(125) consist of a Head Adv only; our text contains no instances of AdvPs containing elements which specify the Head. Examples of such AdvPs are the following:

(126) very soon

(127) extremely slowly

AdvPs may occur in a VP or in an AdjP. Decide whether the italicised AdvPs below occur inside a VP or an AdjP (the AdjP itself may be inside an NP or a VP):

(128) He left *very recently.*

(129) She copied the documents *quite accurately.*

(130) An *unexpectedly* large crowd took part in the demonstration.

(131) He is *typically* British.

(132) He arrived *rather unexpectedly.*

(133) The film was *marvellously* funny.

(134) She has a *really* sweet personality.

Observe that AdvPs take no Complements.

2.4.6.1 Summing up the AdvP

The structure of the AdvP may be summed up as in (135):

(135)

Category	**Adv**	**Adv**
Function	**Spec**	**H**
	very	recently
		typically
		then
	extremely	slowly

Compare this diagram with diagrams (37), (93),(106) and (120) above.

2.4.6.2 Exercises

I Add AdvPs to the italicised AdjPs in the sentences below:

(1) She became *angry.*
(2) His attitude is *intolerable.*
(3) George is *tired.*
(4) She is *afraid that she might die.*

II Add AdvPs denoting 'manner' to the following sentences:

(1) The old man sat down ...
(2) She spoke to him ...
(3) The Vicar considered the matter ...
(4) The professor explained the problem ...

2.5 WORDS

2.5.1 INTRODUCTION

Every speaker of English will intuitively recognise what the words in an English sentence are. Faced with the string:

(1) SoonafterbreakfastMaryAnnbroughtinTheTimes

he will no doubt be able to identify the individual words in this sentence quite easily, and he will know that the appropriate word boundaries are as in (2) below, rather than as in (3):

(2) Soon after breakfast Mary Ann brought in The Times.

(3) *Soo naf terbre akfast Mary Ann broug htin TheT imes.

If you know a language well enough, you can do this sort of demarcation of word boundaries quite automatically, by intuition. It is your **linguistic competence** which allows you to do this. Of course, such competence is maximal only for your mother tongue, and it is less than perfect for other languages which you do not speak fluently. And you have no such competence for the languages which you do not speak. If you do not know a language, you will find it impossible to identify the word boundaries in even the simplest sentences. The following string is an example of a very simple Welsh sentence followed by its translation in English:

(4) Bethymayemrysyneiwneud? : What is Emrys doing?

If you do not know Welsh, you will not be able to decide that the word boundaries are as follows:

(5) Beth y may Emrys yn ei wneud?

Words are grammatical units which a speaker of a language can intuitively recognise. After all, very little grammatical education is needed to be able to play Scrabble, and this game essentially relies on the recognition of words. The same applies to other word games.

2.5.1.1 Word Classes: the Distribution of Words

In order to form sentences, words must appear in a particular structural relationship and in a particular order. The distribution of each class of words is different. Distributional properties of words are known intuitively by a native speaker.

Consider, for example, the extract below, which is taken from W. Somerset Maugham's *Of Human Bondage.* We have left out ten words from the text. Try to complete the text by inserting an appropriate word:

(6) Philip had led the .... (1) life of an only child, and .... (2) loneliness at the vicarage was no .... (3) than it had been when his .... (4) lived. He made friends .... (5) Mary Ann. She was a chubby little .... (6) of thirty-five, the daughter of .... (7) fisherman, and had come to the .... (8) at eighteen; it was her first .... (9) and she had no intention of .... (10) it.

You will probably find that at some of the points in the text you could insert quite a number of appropriate words, while at other points you are far more restricted in your choice. At 1, for example, you might have thought of words like *solitary, lonely, unhappy, isolated, secluded, sheltered, protected, miserable, uneventful, self-centred, boring, dull, happy, uninteresting, stable, tedious, romantic, full, empty,* etc. But at point 2 you can only choose between *Philip's* and *his,* and perhaps *the.*

We now give the list of the actual words, as they occurred in the original text: *solitary, greater; his, a; mother, person, vicarage, place; leaving; with.* Can you identify which word went where in the text above? See also text 2.5.8.

Words can be classified depending on the type of environments in which they can appear. At 1 in the text none of the words suitable for 2 would have been appropriate; and vice versa. The environment in which a word occurs (the **context**) serves as an important criterion for setting up classes of words. Words which can appear in the same context will be said to have the same distribution: they belong to the same **word class**. In this section it is our purpose to look more closely at word classes.

2.5.2 NOUNS

In section 2.4.2 we have identified NPs as constituents whose Head is a noun (the Head Ns are italicised):

(7) The *tramp* was reading his *diary.*

(8) The German *girl* was pouring hot *chocolate.*

Thus a word is a noun (N) if it can fill the blank in frames like:

(9) $[_{NP}$The ....$]$ was reading $[_{NP}$his ....$]$

(10) $[_{NP}$The German ....$]$ was pouring $[_{NP}$hot ....$]$

As we have seen, Ns may be preceded by determiners, but also by AdjPs to form NPs.

Nouns may vary in form. Compare:

(11a) The *tramp* is reading his *diary.*

(11b) The *tramps* are reading their *diaries.*

The sentences show a contrast between singular and plural nouns: *tramp* and *diary* refer to only one person or thing; *tramps* and *diaries* refer to more than one person or thing. This contrast between singular and plural is one of **number** (see also 2.4.2.2 above).

Consider now the following:

(12) {The boy / Philip} was ill.

(13) {The maid / Mary Ann} brought the newspaper.

Philip and *Mary Ann* take the same position as the sequence article +

noun. In fact, we shall consider them to be a special category of nouns: **proper nouns**. They do not normally take an article (* *The Jane was ill*) and usually occur in the singular only (**Janes*). However, some proper nouns always occur in the plural and take a definite article: *The Hebrides, The United States, The Times.*

2.5.3 VERBS

In 2.4.3 we have introduced VPs. Bracket the VP in the sentences below and underline the Head V in each clause:

(14) Mary Ann had come to the vicarage when she was eighteen.

(15) Philip asked her whether he might come with her.

(16) Her parents lived in a little house near the harbour.

The head Vs in (14)–(16) are *come* (twice), *ask* and *live.* These are called **main verbs** or **lexical verbs**. The item *had* in *had come* in (14) is an **auxiliary** (of the Perfect), and *might,* in *might come* in (15) is a **modal** (auxiliary). For the main differences between lexical verbs and auxiliaries, see 2.4.3 above.

Lexical verbs are verbs which function as the Head of a VP, and which as such can be the only verb in a sentence. Lexical verbs can be preceded by one or more auxiliaries.

Auxiliaries cannot normally occur on their own, although in some cases the lexical verb functioning as the Head may have to be recovered from the context: we say then that the lexical verb (and other material accompanying it in the context) is deleted. Examples are:

(17) A: Who has broken the window? B: John has (broken the window).

(18) A: Can you speak Danish? B: No, I can't (speak Danish).

The italicised elements in the following VPs are all auxiliaries, the verb *arrest* in each example being the lexical verb:

(19a) ... *will* arrest ...

(19b) ... *has* arrested ...

(19c) ... *will have* arrested ...

(19d) ... *would have been* arrested ...

2.5.4 ADJECTIVES

In section 2.4.5 we have described AdjPs as constituents whose Head is an adjective. Consider, for example, the following AdjPs (the Head Adjs are italicised):

(20) *solitary*

(21) very *nice*

(22) rather *hot*

Adjectives in English do not change in form to show number (unlike French adjectives, for example):

(23a) an *old* tramp

(23b) two *old* tramp*s*

Some adjectives may have different forms depending on the degree of the quality they express:

(24) Mary Ann is *nice*, Philip is *nicer*, but the Vicar is *nicest.*

The form *nice* is said to be the **base**; *nicer* is the **comparative degree** (usually followed by a phrase or a clause beginning with *than*), and *nicest* is the **superlative degree**. Base, comparative and superlative are the three **degrees of comparison**.

Longer adjectives cannot be 'graded' by adding *–er*/*–est* to the base. Instead we must put *more* and *most* before the adjective to form the comparative and the superlative.

(25a) She is *ambitious.*

(25b) She is *more ambitious* than her sister.

(25c) She is the ˈ*most ambitious* student in the first year.

There are also irregular degrees of comparison such as: *good–better–best*; *bad–worse–worst*; and *little–less–least.*

2.5.5 ADVERBS

Adverbs function as the Head of AdvPs (the Head Advs are italicised in the examples below):

(26) *marvellously*

(27) very *slowly*

Adverbs are often formed by adding the suffix *–ly* to the corresponding adjectives, e.g.: *marvellous–marvellously*; *beautiful–beautifully.* However, not all adverbs are formed with *–ly.* For example, *soon, well, then, there, fast, now* have no regular corresponding adjective forms. *Early, fast, hard, kindly,* and *late* are both adverbs and adjectives.

Like adjectives, adverbs may be put in the comparative and the superlative degrees. A few short adverbs like *soon, early* and *late* take *–er* and *–est,* but the majority of adverbs require *more* and *most,* and some are irregular. For example: *early–earlier–earliest*; *beautifully–more beautifully–*

most beautifully; *slowly–more slowly–most slowly*; *well–better–best*; and *badly–worse–worst.*

2.5.6 PREPOSITIONS

Prepositions function as the Head of a PP (cf. 2.4.4). Prepositions may consist of only one word (e.g.: *on, at, in, inside*), or of more than one word (e.g.: *in relation to, with respect to, because of, in favour of, in aid of*). These multi-word prepositions are 'frozen' units, which have become single lexical items. Their internal make-up is irrelevant for our purposes: as a whole they function as one preposition (see also multi-word conjunctions below (2.5.7)).

Prepositions may be separated from their Complements in cases like (28) and (29) (the PP is italicised):

(28) *That book* I have been looking *for* for weeks.

(29) *What* is this *in aid of*?

See also 4.2.4.3.

English also has some *postpositions* like *ago,* as in: *three days ago* (cf. 2.4.4).

2.5.7 CONJUNCTIONS

Conjunctions serve to link sentences/clauses, or phrases. They may consist of only one word (*and, but, or, that, if,* etc.) or more than one word (*so that, in order that, as soon as* etc.).

Conjunctions may also be subdivided into **coordinators** (*and, but, or, for,* etc.) and **subordinators** (*that, if, although, so that, as soon as,* etc.) (cf. 2.2.2). The coordinators in the following examples are italicised:

(30) John got up *and* walked out.

(31) Not Paul, *but* Bill failed his finals.

(35) We had to hurry, *for* we were late.

The examples below contain subordinators (italicised):

(33) *When* he is ill, he does not go to church.

(34) He didn't go, *because* he felt ill.

(35) They came back early, *in order that* they could see the film on TV.

Since subordinating conjunctions occur in the COMP slot they are often referred to as **complementisers**.

2.5.8 EXERCISES

I Bracket the sentences, clauses and phrases in the following text:

> *Text 2.5.8*
> Philip had led the solitary life of an only child, and his loneliness at the vicarage was no greater than it had been when his mother lived. He made friends with Mary Ann. She was a chubby little person of thirty-five, the daughter of a fisherman, and had come to the vicarage at eighteen; it was her first place and she had no intention of leaving it; but she held a possible marriage as a rod over the timid heads of her master and mistress. Her father and mother lived in a little house off Harbour Street, and she went to see them on her evenings out. One evening Philip asked whether he might go home with her.
> Adapted from W. Somerset Maugham, *Of Human Bondage*.

II Are the sentences in the above text simple, compound, complex or compound-complex?

III List all the NPs, VPs, AdjPs, AdvPs and PPs in the text.

IV Try to classify all the words in the text into different classes: make lists of all nouns, all verbs, all adjectives, all adverbs, etc.

V Find the pronouns in the text and try to establish what NP they replace.

VI Consider the following sentences:

(1) *The young* are often selfish. They have never really learnt to share.
(2) *The French* are renowned for their good taste.
(3) John is always trying to achieve *the impossible.*
(4) Only *the absurd* is worth writing about.

Would you call the italicised strings NPs or AdjPs? Give evidence to justify your answer.
What (syntactic) differences are there between the italicised strings in (1) and (2) and those in (3) and (4) above?

VII Consider the following sentences:

(1) You <u>might</u> have <u>come</u> home a bit earlier.
(2) All the applicants <u>should</u> have <u>been</u> examined.
(3) When <u>asked</u> about his favourite author, he always <u>mentions</u> J.D. Salinger.
(4) They <u>wanted</u> me <u>to come</u> at once, but I refused.
(5) I remember <u>seeing</u> him <u>doing</u> that trick blindfolded.
(6) She <u>had</u> a curious feeling of <u>having</u> been there before.

Determine whether the underlined verbs are auxiliaries or lexical verbs. For each auxiliary, state whether it is a modal or not, and for each lexical verb, indicate whether it is a finite or non-finite form.

3
FUNCTIONS

3.1 INTRODUCTION: THE VERB AND ITS COMPLEMENTS

Let us return once more to text 2.4.1, repeated here as text 3.1.

> *Text 3.1* (= 2.4.1)
> The tramp read the diary. He laughed. He turned a page, he read it and he laughed again. He leaned towards the German girl and said a few words to her.
>
> The Egyptian was clowning; the noise in the room continued. Soon the young German girl was offering chocolate for the second time. Her voice was very soft.
>
> The tramp was unfolding his magazine slowly. He stopped suddenly, he looked at the chocolate. But she had given him no chocolate. He unfolded his magazine. Then he destroyed it.
>
> V.S. Naipaul, *In a Free State.*

Identify NPs, VPs and PPs in the text by bracketing and labelling. If you look carefully at the structure of each clause, you will find there is always a combination of one NP and one VP per clause. To illustrate this point, let us analyse all the clauses of the first paragraph of text 3.1:

(1) $[_S [_{NP} \text{The tramp}] [_{VP} \text{read} [_{NP} \text{the diary}]]]$

(2) $[_S [_{NP} \text{He}] [_{VP} \text{laughed}]]$

(3) $[_S [_{NP} \text{He}] [_{VP} \text{turned} [_{NP} \text{a page}]]]$

(4) $[_S [_{NP} \text{he}] [_{VP} \text{read} [_{NP} \text{it}]]]$

(5) $[_S [_{NP} \text{he}] [_{VP} \text{laughed} [_{AdvP} \text{again}]]]$

(6) $[_S [_{NP} \text{He}] [_{VP} \text{leaned} [_{PP} \text{towards the German girl}]]]$

(7) $[_S [_{NP} \text{(he)}] [_{VP} \text{said} [_{NP} \text{a few words}] [_{PP} \text{to her}]]]$

The first NP in (7) is ellipted, as the parentheses indicate, but it is clear from the context that the NP must be *he.*

Each clause contains a VP preceded by an NP, as is reflected by one of the phrase structure rules of English:

(8) $S \longrightarrow NP\text{–}VP$

The effect of this rewrite rule may also be represented by the following tree diagram (see also 1.2.3):

(9)

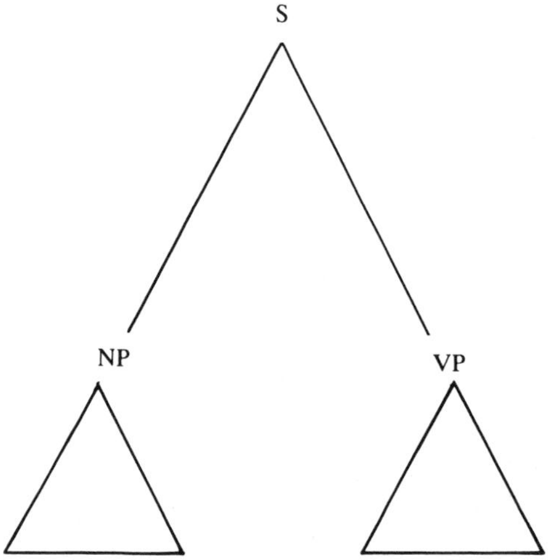

The NP immediately dominated by S is the **Subject** NP (3.3.1), and the VP is the **Predicate** of S (3.3.2). On the use of the 'triangles' in (9), see 1.2.3.

Bracket the remaining clauses of text 3.1 and identify the Subject NP and the Predicate of each clause. There are four Ss (i.e. clauses) in the second paragraph, and six in the third.

As we have seen (Chapter 2), lexical verbs can be classified according to the type of complementation they take (that is, in terms of the subcategorisation frames in which they can occur). We repeat here the classification of verbs given in 2.4.3.2, with one example sentence for each verb type.

	Verb types	Frames	Examples
(a)	Intransitive, e.g. *laugh*	$[_{VP} \text{—}]$	He laughed
(b)	Copula, e.g. *seem*	$[_{VP} \text{—} \left\{\begin{matrix} AdjP \\ NP \\ PP \end{matrix}\right\}]$	He seemed $[_{AdjP}$ very cheerful$]$
(c)	Monotransitive, e.g. *kill*	$[_{VP} \text{—} \left\{\begin{matrix} NP \\ \overline{S} \end{matrix}\right\}]$	He killed $[_{NP}$ the mouse$]$

(d) Ditransitive, e.g. *give*	$\left[_{VP}\text{—} \begin{Bmatrix} NP–NP \\ NP–PP \end{Bmatrix}\right]$	He gave [$_{NP}$the girl] [$_{NP}$a book]
(e) Complex transitive, e.g. *call*	$\left[_{VP}\text{—}\ NP– \begin{Bmatrix} AdjP \\ NP \end{Bmatrix}\right]$	He called [$_{NP}$him] [$_{NP}$a fool]
(f) Intransitive + PP, e.g. *lean*	[$_{VP}$— PP]	He leaned [$_{PP}$towards the girl]
(g) Transitive + PP e.g. *put*	[$_{VP}$— NP–PP]	He put [$_{NP}$his head] [$_{PP}$on her shoulder]

In the following sections we shall look at the behaviour of Complements in more detail, refining and completing the above schema as we go along. Moreover, we shall also deal with Adjuncts in VPs, which are not included in this survey of basic patterns, since Adjuncts are not obligatory constituents.

It is important to point out that the verb itself may contain more than one word, e.g.:

(10) He *went out.*

(11) He *gave up* alcohol.

Go out is a multi-word verb which takes no Complement, whereas *give up* is a multi-word verb which needs an NP Complement.

(12) *go out*: [$_{VP}$——]

(13) *give up*: [$_{VP}$——NP]

Go out is intransitive, and *give up* is monotransitive. Both are **phrasal verbs** (cf. Chapter 6).

It is clear that subcategorisation frames are not based on syntactic information only; the **meaning** of the lexical verb (the Head of the VP) also plays an important part in the setting up of such frames. As a rule, verbs express **activities** of some kind (but the term 'activity' is to be interpreted here in a fairly wide sense, to include such events, happenings, states of affairs and situations as are expressed by verbs like *die, dream, fall, hate, possess, resemble*). Activities usually involve one or more **participants**. The activity 'kill', for example, expressed by the verb *kill*, involves two participants: the Agent and the Patient. In order to refer to the activity of 'killing', we must therefore also refer to these two essential participants. In the sentence *John killed the tramp*, the Agent is expressed by *John*, the Patient by *the tramp*. The constituents *John* and *the tramp* are respectively the Subject of S and the Complement of V. Thus, a subcategorisation frame can be seen as a grammatical specification of a verb, which also reflects the *semantic content* (that is, the meaning) of the verb.

3.2 GRAMMATICAL FUNCTIONS

Compare the following sentences:

(1) The girl showed the diary to the tramp.

(2) The tramp showed the diary to the girl.

These two sentences contain identical words, and their constituent structure is also exactly the same. Both sentences are to be bracketed as follows:

(3) $[_S [_{NP} \quad] [_{VP} \quad [_{NP} \quad] \quad [_{PP} \quad]]]$

Match the constituents in (1) and in (2) to the bracketing in (3). The tree diagrams (4) and (5) represent (1) and (2) respectively:

(4)

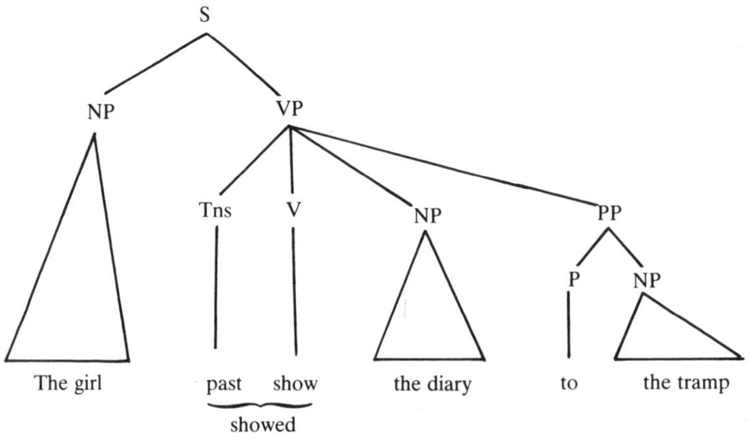

(5)

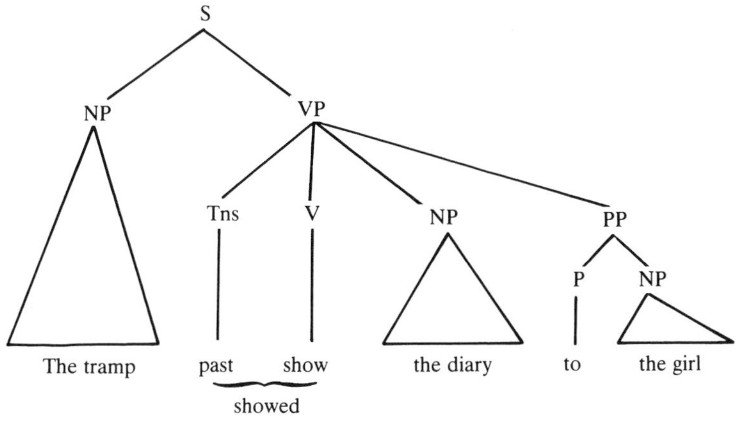

The trees as such are identical, but the lexical items *the tramp* and *the girl*, two NPs, occur at different structural positions in the tree. In (4), the NP *the girl* is immediately dominated by S (it is the Subject (Su)), whereas in (5) it is the NP *the tramp* which is immediately dominated by S (and is thus the Su). As you can see, Subject NPs are *outside* the VP.

In (4) *the tramp* occurs inside the VP: it is immediately dominated by PP, and it is also dominated by VP. In (5), *the girl* is in the same structural position: it is immediately dominated by PP, and it is also dominated by VP. On the distinction between immediate dominance and dominance, see 1.2.3.

The difference in the position of the NPs clearly has an effect on the behaviour of such NPs in the sentence. For example, only the two NPs inside the VP (e.g. *the diary* and *the tramp*) may switch places. Compare:

(1) The girl showed the diary to the tramp.

(6) The girl showed the tramp the diary.

(7) *The diary showed the girl to the tramp.

We shall say here that the change from (1) to (6) above also involves the deletion of the preposition *to.* The NP outside the VP (*the girl*) is not affected by the operation which changes (1) into (6). This operation is called **Dative Movement**.

On the other hand, if we passivise sentence (1) we find that it is the NP outside the VP that is affected, as well as one of the two NPs inside the VP. The Subject NP is shifted rightwards and the preposition *by* is added to it. The other NP is moved leftwards out of the VP. Compare:

(1) *The girl* showed *the diary* to *the tramp.*

(8) *The diary* was shown to the tramp *by the girl.*

(9) *The tramp* was shown the diary *by the girl.*

Again we assume that in the change from (1) to (9) the preposition *to* is deleted. We conclude that, depending on their structural position, the NPs and PPs in (1) and (2) have different syntactic properties.

Constituents are said to have different **grammatical functions** (GFs). In (1), for example, *the girl* is Subject (Su); *the diary* is Direct Object (Od), *to the tramp* is Indirect Object (Oi). We shall say that in (1) the Subject is **realised by** an NP, the Od is realised by an NP, and the Oi by a PP. For (1), we may provisionally abbreviate this information as follows: NP/Su, NP/Od, and PP/Oi. Conversely, we might want to say, for example, that the NP *the girl* in (1) **realises** the GF of Su: NP/Su, or NP **functions** as Su.

The slash convention introduced here provides a quick way of indicating the GFs and their realisations in a given sentence.

In the sections which follow we shall look at all the important GFs in English. We begin with the functions in S (3.3), and then proceed to the functions in VP (3.4).

3.2.1 EXERCISES

I Replace the NPs in (1) and (2) above by pronouns. Which of them have subjective forms, and which have objective forms?

II Provide counter-examples to the following claim:

In standard English subjective forms of pronouns occur as Subject and objective forms as Object.

3.3 GRAMMATICAL FUNCTIONS IN S

3.3.1 SUBJECT

The Subject of a sentence has been defined as the NP which combines with the VP to form an S. In other words, the Su is the NP which is immediately dominated by S in a tree diagram representation. Consider:

(1) The tramp was laughing.

In (1) the Subject NP is *the tramp.* Here are two alternative representations:

(2) $[_S [_{NP}$ The tramp$] [_{VP}$ was laughing$]]$

(3)

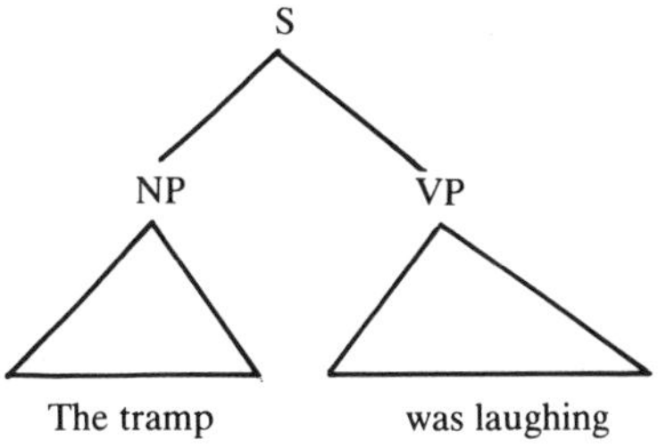

Identify the Subject in (4) and in (5) below, using both labelled bracketing, as in (2), and a tree diagram representation, as in (3):

(4) The Egyptian was clowning.

(5) The German girl was offering us some chocolate.

Let us consider some of the syntactic characteristics of Subject NPs such as *the tramp, the Egyptian* and *the German girl* in (1), (4) and (5) above. We have already noted (2.4.3.4) that NPs functioning as Su invert with the first auxiliary element (*was* in our examples) in the formation of questions. For example:

(6) Was the tramp laughing?

The switch of the Subject NP and the first auxiliary element is called Subject–Auxiliary Inversion (SAI). The mechanics of this process will be dealt with in section 4.2.1.

Another characteristic of Subject NPs in finite clauses is that they normally **agree** in number with the first element in the VP. If, for example, we put the NP *the tramp* in the plural, we get sentence (7) instead of (1):

(7) The tramps *were* laughing.

The change from singular to plural here does not only affect the Subject NP but also the VP: *was* also has to be replaced by a plural form. **Agreement** is overtly marked in finite clauses on the first auxiliary element, or, if there is no auxiliary element, on the lexical verb itself. Note that other elements in the VP may also be affected by this. Compare, for example:

(8a) The tramp never enjoys himself.

(8b) The tramps never enjoy themselves.

A third way of recognising Subject NPs is that pronouns replacing them will normally have the subjective form (*he, she, they,* etc.), not the objective form (*him, her, them,* etc.). For example:

(9a) He was laughing.

(9b) *Him was laughing.

The three characteristics of Subject NPs mentiond here (SAI, agreement and substitution by pronouns) can be used to identify the Subject of a finite clause. Using these three tests, identify the Subject NPs in (10)–(14) below:

(10) The patient has been examined by Dr MacDonald.

(11) The tramp was shaving himself.

(12) The exam is at the end of next term.

(13) That painting Sue does not like.

(14) After breakfast the boys wandered out into the playground.

Discuss any problems that you are faced with in applying all three tests to the above sentences.

3.3.2 PREDICATE

We have seen that the Subject NP and the VP together make up a sentence:

S⟶NP–VP

The VP 'predicates something' of the Subject; its function is 'predicative'. Since the function of VP is that of predicating, we shall call it the **Predicate** (Pred) of the sentence. We shall see below that constituents inside the VP may also have some kind of predicative function.

3.3.3 SENTENCE ADJUNCTS

Apart from Su and Pred, the sentence may also contain elements which are peripheral in the structure of the sentence: they fall outside the major constituents NP and VP. These peripheral sentence elements are of two types:

(a) items which serve to specify the speaker's attitude towards the rest of the sentence; examples are: *unfortunately, certainly, in my view, in fact.* For example:

(15) *Unfortunately,* the match was cancelled because of bad weather.

(b) items which serve to connect sentences in a text; examples are: *moreover, however, nevertheless, yet.* For example:

(16) John had planned to swim across the Channel last year. *However,* when the time came he did not have the courage.

The items under (a) and (b) are collectively referred to as **Sentence Adjuncts** (Sas). We shall return to them in section 3.4.9.

3.4 GRAMMATICAL FUNCTIONS IN VP

Having looked at the two major grammatical functions in the sentence: Subject (Su) and Predicate (Pred), we shall now consider the functions realised by constituents within the VP. In section 3.5 we shall discuss the grammatical functions in NPs, AdjPs, AdvPs and PPs.

The VP, as we have seen, may contain elements of various types which either precede or follow the Head of the VP (a lexical verb). We have distinguished between Complements in the VP and Adjuncts in the VP. Complements are obligatory constituents, which are needed to complete the VP. They are 'selected' by the lexical verb (cf. 3.1 above). In addition to Complements of V, the VP may also contain optional Adjuncts, generally denoting place, time, manner, condition and the like.

The functions in the VP that will be dealt with are: Predicative Complement (3.4.1), Direct Object (3.4.2), Indirect Object (3.4.3), Adverbial Complement with intransitive verbs (3.4.4), Adverbial Complement with transitive verbs (3.4.5), and a complex grammatical function which is a combination of Predicative Complement and Adverbial Complement (3.4.6).

3.4.1 PREDICATIVE COMPLEMENTS

The function of a *Predicative Complement* (Pc) is that of ascribing some property to the Subject of the sentence. This function is normally realised by NPs, AdjPs or PPs, and the verbs that select such a Complement belong to the class of copulas (*be, look, seem*, etc.). Examples:

(1) Jane seemed *a good student.*

(2) John looked *foolish* in that tracksuit.

(3) She is *an actress.*

(4) Bill was *in a filthy mood.*

The Head of the VP in (1) is the copula *seem.* It is followed by an NP. In (2) the VP-Head is followed by an AdjP, in (3) by an NP again, and in (4) by a PP. It is these obligatory constituents following the V which have the GF of Pc (Predicative Complement). They have been italicised.

We have noted that the VP as a whole also has a predicative function: it predicates something of an NP. Characteristically, elements in a predicative relation (NP/Su and VP, for example) will show agreeement:

(5a) John *is* working in France at the moment.

(5b) John and Jane *are* working in France at the moment.

Similarly in (6) the Predicative Complement (to the Subject) agrees in number with the Subject NP:

(6a) She is *an actress.*

(6b) They are *actresses.*

In many languages (French, for example) AdjPs also show agreement with the elements they have a predicative relation with. Copulas characteristically serve to 'link' the Subject NP and the property expressed by the Pc. 'Being a good student', for example, is seen as a property of the person referred to as Jane in (1) above, while in (2) 'foolishness' is ascribed to John.

3.4.1.1 Exercise

What is the Predicative Complement (Pc) in each of the following sentences?

(1) Mary is in love with her driving instructor.
(2) He is a tall, thin man with a sallow face and a long nose.
(3) The milk has turned sour.
(4) The vending machine is out of order.
(5) Mr Wilson was the richest man in Blackstable.
(6) The room is in a mess.
(7) His hair was very white.
(8) Your uncle has grown old.
(9) That trip is out of the question.
(10) She got angry with him.

3.4.2 DIRECT OBJECT

Bracket the major constituents in (7) below. Draw a tree diagram and identify the Subject.

(7) The tramp was unfolding the magazine for the second time.

As you can see, the VP contains two constituents in addition to the VP-Head and its Specifiers: an NP and a PP:

(8) $[_{VP}$ was unfolding $[_{NP}$ the magazine$]$ $[_{PP}$ for the second time$]]$

Which of these is an Adjunct? That is, which of them can be left out easily?

The NP *the magazine* must be regarded as obligatory in this context. It is a Complement of V: *unfold* subcategorises for (or selects) an NP:

unfold: $[_{VP}$ —— NP$]$

The NP *the magazine* cannot be omitted.

(9) *The tramp was unfolding for the second time.

If we passivise sentence (7), we find that the NP-Complement becomes the Subject of the passive sentence:

(10) *The magazine* was being unfolded by the tramp for the second time.

An NP-Complement of V which becomes the Subject of a passive sentence is said to have the function of Object. More specifically, *the magazine* is the Direct Object (Od) of *unfold.* Verbs such as *unfold* which subcategorise for a constituent functioning as Od are said to be monotransitive.

3.4.2.1 Exercise

Bracket NP/Su and VP in the following examples. Are there any Complements inside VP? Are there any Object NPs?

(1) He spoke a few words to the German girl.
(2) He looked a dull guy.
(3) She had forgotten his name.
(4) He destroyed all the magazines.

3.4.3 INDIRECT OBJECT

Consider the following example:

(11) She had given the tramp no chocolate.

The VP contains two NPs:

(12) $[_{S}\text{She } [_{VP}\text{had given } [_{NP}\text{the tramp}] [_{NP}\text{no chocolate}]]]$

Both NPs are Complements to the lexical verb *give,* which is ditransitive. Both NPs are, in fact, Objects since both can become the Subject of a passive sentence:

(13) *No chocolate* had been given to the tramp.

(14) *The tramp* had been given no chocolate.

But the two NPs (italicised) do not behave in quite identical ways. In (13) we have to add the P *to* to the NP *the tramp,* but in (14) we cannot insert *to* before *no chocolate.* This is related to the fact that there is an alternative version of (11), in which the NP *the tramp* can be replaced by a PP with *to*; the NP *no chocolate* cannot be replaced by a PP with *to.*

(15) She had given no chocolate to the tramp.

(16) *She had given the tramp to no chocolate.

Both NPs in (11) are Objects: *no chocolate* is the Direct Object (Od), and *the tramp* is the Indirect Object (Oi). It is characteristic of the Oi that it can often be replaced by a PP with either *to* or *for.* An example of the latter:

(17) She poured the tramp a drink.

(18) She poured a drink for the tramp.

However, occasionally there is only one possibility of realising the Oi, e.g.

(19) She struck him a blow.

(20) *She struck a blow to him.

Ditransitive verbs like *give*, *offer* and *pour* normally have one of the following subcategorisation frames:

(21) $\left\{ \begin{array}{l} [\text{—— NP–NP}] \\ [\text{—— NP–PP}_{to}] \end{array} \right\}$ OR $\left\{ \begin{array}{l} [\text{—— NP–NP}] \\ [\text{—— NP–PP}_{for}] \end{array} \right\}$

3.4.3.1 Exercises

I Bracket the Indirect Object NPs and PPs in the sentences below:

(1) She showed him her drawings.
(2) This song gives me a headache.
(3) John taught Bill linguistics.
(4) They offered the kidnappers a large sum of money.
(5) He told us an incredible story.
(6) John suggested a rather interesting solution to us.
(7) The princess donated all her money to the Church.
(8) I do not envy you your job.
(9) Arthur demonstrated his new invention to his friend.
(10) That adventure is going to cost them their lives.

II Which of the sentences above have an alternative Indirect Object construction? (I.e. in which cases can the NP/Oi be replaced by a PP/Oi and vice versa?)

3.4.4 ADVERBIAL COMPLEMENTS WITH INTRANSITIVE VERBS

Consider the following sentences:

(22) The newspaper remained with Mr Ellis for three hours.

Bracket the VP. What kinds of constituents does the VP contain?

(23) The newspaper $\left[_{VP}\right.$remained $\left[_{PP}\right.$with Mr Ellis$\left.\right]$ $\left[_{PP}\right.$for three hours$\left.\right]\left.\right]$

There are two PPs in the VP, of which the second seems to be optional and the first obligatory:

(24) The newspaper remained with Mr Ellis.

(25) *The newspaper remained for three hours.

For three hours is an optional VP-Adjunct. *With Mr Ellis* is a Verb Complement. *Remain* in this case requires a PP: $[_{VP}$—— PP].

Remain is an intransitive verb: it does not take an Od. But at the same time *remain* subcategorises for a PP. The subcategorised PP specifies the place where the newspaper remained. Constituents which give us more information concerning the place, manner, time, duration, etc. of an activity are said to have an **adverbial** function, and if such an element (like the PP *with Mr Ellis*) is obligatory, we call it an **Adverbial Complement** (Ac).

Note that *remain* does not just subcategorise for a PP introduced by *with*; other prepositions are also possible:

(26) The newspaper remained at the vicarage.

(27) The sun remained behind the clouds all day.

(28) The paper remained on the shelf.

(29) The books remained in the library.

Alternatively, the Adverbial Complement of *remain* may be realised by an AdvP:

(30) He remained *there.*

(31) The women remained *upstairs.*

The AdvP again is a Complement: it is non-omissible. Furthermore, it specifies the location of the activity: it has an adverbial function.

The following examples illustrate other uses of verbs which take an Ac (the Ac is italicised):

(32) He leaned *against the sideboard.*

(33) He is *in London.*

(34) He is *at his club.*

(35) His birthday is *next Saturday.*

(36) The performance lasted *(for) two hours.*

(37) The enterprise cost *thousands of pounds.*

(38) This parcel weighs *two kilos.*

In these examples *be* is not a copula: the Complements (*in London, at his club*, etc.) do not assign a property to the Subject NP, but rather specify the place of 'being' ((33), (34)), or the time of 'being' in (35). The verbs in the remaining sentences are also intransitive, but they require an Ac to describe the activity or state. An Ac may be realised by various syntactic categories. For example, the verb *last* in (36) takes an Ac realised by either a PP or an NP.

Identify the Ac in each of the following sentences and label the category which realises the function Ac:

(39) John belongs to several social clubs.

(40) She specialises in biochemistry.

(41) Your new car drives very smoothly.

(42) The fire lasted three days.

(43) John lives in Paris.

(44) She stayed at the Hilton.

(45) John condescended to help us.

(46) His father lived to be 90.

It is not always easy to decide with certainty whether a constituent following the lexical verb is obligatory or optional. There are many cases which are less clear-cut than those above: the criterion for deciding on the non-omissibility of a constituent in the VP is whether the remaining part of the sentence is still grammatical or whether the meaning of the lexical verb changes drastically as a result of omitting that particular constituent. Let us see what happens to the sentences above if we leave out the PPs, AdvPs, or Ss that follow the lexical verb (the * indicates ungrammaticality and the ! a drastic change in meaning):

(47) *John belongs.

(48) *She specialises.

(49) *Your new car drives.

(50) *The fire lasted.

(51) !John lives.

(52) !She stayed.

(53) *John condescended.

(54) !His father lived.

NPs such as *several social clubs, biochemistry* and *his attempt* in the examples above cannot become the Subject of corresponding passive sentences. These NPs are not Objects of the lexical verbs, but form part of the PPs which function as Ac here. Hence, there is a difference between the following sentences:

(39) John belongs to several social clubs.

(55) Somebody has slept in my bed.

Sentence (55) can be passivised as follows:

(56) My bed has been slept in.

This suggests that *my bed* in (55) is an Od (cf. Chapter 6). However, since (39) cannot be passivised in the same way, *several social clubs* in (39) is not to be regarded as an Od: *to several social clubs* is a PP functioning as Ac.

3.4.4.1 Exercise

Which of the following sentences contain Adverbial Complements? Bracket the Acs and indicate how they are realised.

(1) He has gone off the rails.
(2) He lives in a council house in Dagenham.
(3) The Lake District is up in the top left-hand corner of England.
(4) This new encyclopedia costs 70 pounds.
(5) Slap in the middle of England stands the City of Oxford.
(6) The child was in tears.
(7) He darted towards the door.

3.4.5 ADVERBIAL COMPLEMENTS WITH TRANSITIVE VERBS

In section 3.4.4 we have seen that verbs like *remain, belong, last* require an Ac to complete the VP. The verbs were also seen to be intransitive: they have no Od. In this section, we shall see that transitive verbs may also select an Ac. Consider, for example:

(57) John put the money in a box.

(58) He worded the letter very carefully.

(59) The children always remind me of their grandfather.

The verbs *put, word* and *remind* are transitive: they take an NP/Od, which can regularly become the Subject of a passive:

(60) The money was put in a box.

(61) The letter was worded very carefully.

(62) I am always reminded of their grandfather.

The VP of sentence (57), for example, has the following structure:

(63) $\left[_{NP}\text{put} \left[_{NP}\text{the money}\right]\left[_{PP}\text{in a box}\right]\right]$

It contains an NP and a PP. The PP *in a box* is a Complement of the V and expresses the location of 'putting'. *Where* did he put the money?: *In a box.* This constituent is thus an Ac. Bracket sentences (58) and (59) above in the same way.

The Ac for *put* can also be realised by an AdvP:

(64) John put the money *there/upstairs.*

The verb *put* has the following subcategorisation frame:

(65) $\left[_{VP} \text{——NP–} \begin{Bmatrix} \text{PP} \\ \text{AdvP} \end{Bmatrix} \right]$

The verb *word* in (58) above is also a transitive verb, which selects both an Od and an Ac. Ac is realised by an AdvP (*very carefully*). While the Ac in (57) expresses location, that in (58) expresses manner. In (58) the AdvP could be replaced by a PP (*in a careful way*). In (59) we find another verb taking an Object NP and a PP as Complement. Though we can see that the PP is obligatory, it would be difficult to say what semantic contribution the PP makes. It is clear, however, that the PP is non-omissible:

(66) *The children always remind me ——.

Note that in sentence (59) *me* is the Direct Object; the NP *their grandfather* is not an Object, but the Prepc of *of* (cf. 2.4.4).

3.4.5.1 Exercise

Which of the following sentences contain Adverbial Complements? Bracket the Acs and indicate how they are realised.

(1) The doctor put her on a diet.
(2) He kept his money in a shoe-box.
(3) The Government has brought the country close to economic ruin.
(4) The police posted 20 men around the house.
(5) A really efficient pit crew can put 40 gallons of fuel in a car and change two wheels in 12 seconds.
(6) She devoted her life to charity.

Note: It is doubtful whether in sentence (5) the PP *in 12 seconds* is an optional Adverbial or an Ac. What do you think?

3.4.6 PREDICATIVE COMPLEMENT + ADVERBIAL COMPLEMENT: A COMPLEX FUNCTION

Now consider the following examples:

(67) The government set the prisoners free.

(68) The Vicar flung the door open.

Bracket the major constituents. Note that the VPs contain an obligatory Complement in addition to the Od. For example:

(69) The government $\left[_{VP}\text{set} \left[_{NP}\text{the prisoners}\right] \left[_{AdjP}\text{free}\right]\right]$

What is the function of the AdjP *free*? Since it is obligatory, it is a Complement within the VP. It narrows down the meaning of *set* (and is thus adverbial), but it also links up with the Direct Object NP: it predicates something of the NP *the prisoners.* The AdjP *free* is thus both adverbial and predicative in function. The same applies to *open* in sentence (68). We shall say that the VPs in (67) and (68) have a complex pattern of functional relations, represented schematically in (70):

(70)

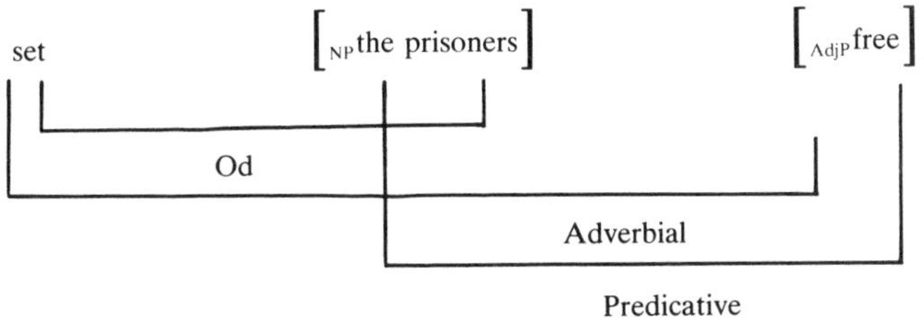

In a sense, *free* is both a Predicative Complement and an Adverbial Complement. This combination of functions could be abbreviated as **Pc+Ac**. Verbs which select a Pc+Ac are called *complex transitive.* This term is a shorthand label for the complex functional schema given in (70). Consider also:

(71) She called her baby George.

(72) She called the proposal absurd.

Bracket the VP and its constituents in (71) and (72). In each case you see that there is an NP which is the Direct Object of the verb (passivisation confirms this). But, in addition, there is a Complement which narrows down the activity of 'calling'; it is a Complement with an additional adverbial function, just as in (67) and (68). Note that the second NP following the verb in (71) is not an Object: unlike the first NP, *George* cannot become the Subject of a passive. Compare:

(73) Her baby was called George.

(74) *George was called her baby.

The functional pattern of the VP in (71) is like that given in (70) above. In this case, however, the predicative function of the NP (*George*) is perhaps stronger than its Adverbial function. Still, there is a clear relation between the NP *George* and both the verb *call* and the NP *her baby.* Again the GF of *George* is that of Pc+Ac, and *call* is here a complex transitive verb.

Complex transitive verbs such as *call, set* and *fling* require two Complements, one of which is the Direct Object, while the other has an adverbial and, perhaps more importantly, a predicative function relating it to the Direct Object.

3.4.6.1 Exercise

Bracket the Pc+Acs in the following sentences and indicate how they are realised.

(1) Who left the door open?
(2) Shall we call it a day?
(3) They elected Mr Owen chairman.
(4) John treated the whole affair as a joke.
(5) She threw the window open.

Note: see sections 3.4.11.2 and 3.4.11.3 for alternative analyses of the sentences above.

3.4.7 VERB PATTERNS AND FUNCTIONS: A SUMMARY

In 3.1 we have presented a provisional summary of the most important different types of VP in English, based on the types of complementation that lexical verbs require.

Looking at the internal structure of VPs in English, we have distinguished the following types of Complement to the verb:

(a) Predicative Complement (Pc): section 3.4.1.
(b) Direct Object (Od): section 3.4.2.
(c) Indirect Object (Oi): section 3.4.3.
(d) Adverbial Complement with intransitive verbs (Ac): section 3.4.4.
(e) Adverbial Complement with transitive verbs (Ac): section 3.4.5.
(f) The complex GF of Pc+Ac: section 3.4.6.

Verbs such as *laugh, snore* and *yawn* have no Complement (cf. *He laughed*). This is not the same as **'zero' complementation**. The term 'zero' complementation is used with reference to cases like *He is reading*, which may be opposed to *He is reading a book*. 'Zero' is only used if there is a corresponding explicit Complement (e.g. NP/Od), and not if there is no corresponding explicit Complement normally, as in the case of *He laughed/snored/yawned*, etc.

Table 3.4.7 sums up the seven most important VP-structures in English. In each VP the lexical verb (V) is the Head, and the Head selects certain Complements. Since the Subject NP falls outside the VP and since it is obligatory for all VPs (cf. S→NP–VP), there is no need for us to state that a VP takes a Subject NP: every S must have a Subject position.

The structure of the VP is represented in terms of subcategorisation frames of V. In table 3.4.7 on page 82 the first column gives the label for the type of verb. This label is merely a shorthand device for summing up the subcategorisation frame given in the second column. For example, a verb which takes a Direct Object as its only Complement, is a monotransitive verb. As the curly brackets in the second column show, the Od may be realised by either an NP or an $\overline{\text{S}}$. Some verbs do not take the $\overline{\text{S}}$-option (*eat*, for example), others normally only take the sentential realisation (*think, wonder*), and others again take either realisation (*believe, reveal*). The third column gives one or two examples of each type. In the last column we have summed up the function labels and the various ways in which GFs can be combined in basic sentences. Su[V], for example, means that this is a sentence containing a Subject and a VP with only a V and no Complement. Su[V–Od] means that the sentence has a Subject and a VP containing an Od as Verb Complement.

Let us at this point also sum up what we have said about grammatical functions. In the first place, we have distinguished between the two major sentence functions of Subject (Su) and Predicate (Pred). The former GF is realised by the NP immediately dominated by S, and the latter is realised by the VP. The Predicate says something about the Subject. Secondly, we have drawn a distinction between Complements and Adjuncts in the VP, the criterion being that of omissibility. Complements are defined as obligatory constituents in the structure of the VP, which are required by the V to complete the VP. Adjuncts of V are optional constituents of the VP.

The different Complements can be characterised syntactically. For example, Direct and Indirect Objects are affected by passivisation and become Subjects of passive sentences; the order NP/Od–PP_{to}/Oi is an alternative to the order NP/Oi–NP/Od; predicative NPs usually show number agreement with the Subject; Adverbial Complements cannot become the Subject of a passive etc. Moreover, there is a general tendency for Predicative Complements to be realised by AdjP, NP or PP, Direct Objects by NP or $S(\overline{S})$, Indirect Objects by NP or PP, Adverbial Complements by PP, AdvP and occasionally NP or $S(\overline{S})$, etc.

In analysing sentences, we shall generally want to include information about the constituents of a sentence and about the GFs of the sentence-constituents; we shall normally use a slash to separate the constituent from the GF, e.g. NP/Su, etc. The analysis of a sentence like *She gave John the money*, for example, is: NP/Su [V–NP/Oi–NP/Od]. The square brackets mark the boundaries of the VP/Pred. The hyphens are added for convenience to separate the V and the Verb Complements. Similarly, the pattern for *George cheated at Harvard* is: NP/Su [V–PP/A], that for *A man that cannot love a horse cannot love a woman* is: NP/Su [V–NP/Od], and that for *She called her baby George* is: NP/Su [V–NP/Od–NP/Pc+Ac].

3.4.7.1 Exercise

Produce English sentences with the following patterns:

(1) NP/Su [V–NP/Pc]
(2) NP/Su [V–NP/Oi–NP/Od]
(3) $\overline{S}$/Su [V–$\overline{S}$/Pc]
(4) AdvP/A–NP/Su [V–NP/Od–PP/A– – – –]
Note: the dashes – – – in the VP mark the original position of the Adjunct AdvP, which has been fronted.
(5) NP/Su [V–PP/Ac]

Table 3.4.7

Verb type	*Subcategorisation frame*	*Examples*	*Functions*
Intransitive	[——]	John snores Mary is slimming	Su [V]
Copula	[—— {AdjP / NP / PP}]	She is {a happy student / in a filthy mood}	Su [V–Pc]
Monotransitive	[—— {NP / S}]	Susan loves Bill Mary says that Susan loves Bill	Su [V–Od]
Ditransitive	[—— {NP–NP / NP–$PP_{to/for}$}]	She gave John the money or: She gave the money to John	Su [V– {Oi–Od / Od–Oi}]
Intransitive + Adverbial Complement	[—— {PP / AdvP}]	She is {in London / upstairs}	Su [V–Ac]
Transitive + Adverbial Complement	[—— NP– {PP / AdvP}]	He put the money in a box	Su [V–Od–Ac]
Complex transitive	[— NP– {AdjP / NP}]	She called him {foolish / a fool}	Su [V–Od–Pc+Ac]

(6) NP/Su [V]
(7) NP/Su [V–NP/Od–PP/Ac]
(8) NP/Su [V–NP/Od–AdjP/Pc+Ac]
(9) NP/Su [V–NP/Oi–NP/Pc]
(10) NP/Su [V–NP/Oi–PP/Pc–$\overline{S}$/A]

3.4.8 ADJUNCTS AND COMPLEMENTS

The table in 3.4.7 gives only the elements which are minimally required in a sentence with a certain type of V. Of course, optional Adjuncts can be added fairly freely. So, starting from a basic structure such as:

(75) The doctor put the girl on a diet

which contains the transitive verb *put* and its two Complements (Od and Ac), we might add to this sentence any number of optional Adverbial Adjuncts (A). Consider, for example:

(76) Last year the doctor reluctantly put the girl on a diet because she was overweight.

Last year is an Adjunct (of time) realised by an NP, *reluctantly* is an Adjunct (of manner) realised by an AdvP, and *because she was overweight* is an Adjunct (of reason) realised by an $\overline{S}$. If these elements are omitted, the sentence does not become ungrammatical. Nor does the lexical verb *put* change its meaning.

3.4.8.1 Exercise

The following examples contain various kinds of optional Adjuncts. Identify these omissible elements by underlining them, and state how they are realised. For each sentence determine what sentence type it is (cf. 3.4.7).

(1) He must have left here on Friday morning.
(2) His room looked quite tidy yesterday.
(3) They always discuss their finances before leaving.
(4) He may soon regret his decision.
(5) They appointed him Vice Chancellor last week.
(6) On Friday she saw her cousin in the department store.
(7) He was born in Jamaica on 1 August 1963.
(8) Yesterday they were still waiting for further news.
(9) I will no longer tolerate your bad behaviour.
(10) *Of Human Bondage* is generally considered to be Somerset Maugham's masterpiece in a long, versatile, and extremely distinguished literary career.

Adjuncts may occur in various positions and some can easily be moved around in the sentence. Try preposing them.

3.4.9 SENTENCE ADJUNCTS AND VP-ADJUNCTS

Consider text 3.4.9:

Text 3.4.9

William walked slowly down the road. He felt that he should dislike the little girl intensely. He decided that he should never meet her again. She was certainly a very unreasonable person. Yet he couldn't dislike her. He hoped that he should see her again. He believed sincerely that a friendship with her would be exciting. Anyway, William had always preferred people who quarrelled with him. He was bored with people who agreed with him. He considered the little girl quite attractive.

Adapted from Richmal Crompton, *William The Detective.*

We shall first look at the simple sentences in the text. Complex sentences will be dealt with in section 3.4.11. Identify the simple sentences in text 3.4.9. Underline all the Adjuncts in those sentences.

There are four simple sentences in the text:

(77) William walked slowly down the road.

(78) She was certainly a very unreasonable person.

(79) Yet he couldn't dislike her.

(80) He considered the little girl quite attractive.

Bracket the VP and Subject NP. Identify the constituents inside VP and label them. Is the verb *walk* in (77) intransitive or transitive? Are there any Verb Complements? We may decide that the verb *walk* requires an obligatory indication of location: *down the road*, which in that case functions as Adverbial Complement (Ac). In this context *slowly* seems less obligatory in the VP. Compare:

(81) William walked down the road.

(82) ?William walked slowly.

We suggest that (77) is a sentence of the Su[V–Ac] type, with an additional Adjunct *slowly*:

(83) $$\left[_{S}\left[_{Su}^{NP}\ \text{William}\right]\left[_{VP}\ \text{walked}\left[_{A}^{AdvP}\ \text{slowly}\right]\left[_{Ac}^{PP}\ \text{down the road}\right]\right]\right]$$

The Adjunct *slowly* is a manner Adjunct. In general, Adverbial Adjuncts are Modifiers of the activity expressed by the verb.

Sentence (78) above contains a copula (*be*) with a Predicative Complement (Pc) realised by an NP:

(84) $\left[_{\substack{\\ S}} \left[_{\substack{NP\\Su}} \text{She}\right] \left[_{\substack{\\ VP}} \text{was} \left[_{\substack{AdvP\\Sa}} \text{certainly}\right] \left[_{\substack{NP\\Pc}} \text{a very unreasonable girl}\right]\right]\right]$

Certainly is also an optional Adjunct (A), but there is an important difference between *certainly* and *slowly* in (77) above. *Certainly* does not refer to the time of an event, or to place or manner, but it indicates the speaker's attitude towards the rest of the sentence: (78) means 'it was certainly true that she was a very unreasonable girl', or: 'what was certain is this: she is an unreasonable girl'. *Certainly* is an Adjunct which relates to the content of the sentence and is therefore said to be a **Sentence Adjunct (Sa)**. The Sa may also be realised by PPs:

(85) *In fact,* she was a very unreasonable girl.

(86) *In my opinion,* she was a very unreasonable girl.

Certainly, in fact and *in my opinion* modify the truth value of the sentence. They do not relate to the content of the VP, but to that of the sentence as a whole.

Yet in sentence (79) above is also an Sa: its function is to connect sentences. In this case, it connects *He couldn't dislike her* with the preceding sentence(s) in text 3.4.9. Other examples are AdvPs such as *however, nevertheless, then* or PPs such as *in addition, in spite of that,* etc.:

(87) *However,* what could he do about it?

(88) *Nevertheless,* we must get on with the job.

We conclude that English has two main types of (optional) Adjuncts: Adverbial Adjuncts (As) and Sentence Adjuncts (Sas). Adverbial Adjuncts appear inside the VP (they may thus also be called VP-Adjuncts), Sas relate to the entire sentence (S-Adjuncts).

There are two syntactic tests which may be used to differentiate between As, on the one hand, and Sas, on the other:

(a) focusing: it is possible to focus on certain As but not on Sas:

(89) He walked down the road *slowly,* not quickly.

(90) *She arrived home before dark, *fortunately,* not unfortunately.

(91) *What could he do about it, *however,* not moreover?

Sometimes, it is also possible to use an A as the focused element in a cleft sentence; Sas can never be focused in this way. Compare:

(92) It is only *recently* that I saw him.

(93) *It is { *certainly* / *in fact* / *however* } that she is a very unreasonable girl.

(b) *wh*-questioning: As can be questioned with wh-items, e.g.:

(94) How did he walk down the road? *Slowly.*

(95) When did you see him? *Recently.*

Sas cannot be questioned in this way:

(96) When was she a very unreasonable girl? **Certainly.*

3.4.9.1 Exercise

Identify the functions (Su, V, O, etc.) in the sentences below, and indicate by what constituents (NP, VP, etc.) they are realised. Remember that the optional elements here may be VP-Adjuncts (A) or S-Adjuncts (Sa).

(1) Britain has changed dramatically in the past two decades.
(2) They set him an almost impossible task.
(3) You're making Mummy very unhappy by disobeying.
(4) George allegedly cheated at Harvard.
(5) Peter and his dog are great friends.
(6) His parents taught him the facts of life.
(7) His wife's death left him a broken man.
(8) Agriculture and fishing have become this country's major industries.
(9) I would not put it past her.
(10) Fred testified reluctantly.
(11) John worded the letter very carefully.
(12) Thomas Hardy is perhaps the greatest writer of rural life and landscape in the language.
(13) Paul lent Arthur his old squash racket.
(14) His death will leave a large gap in the English literary scene.
(15) Alexander Pope was a most enigmatical personality.
(16) John treated the whole affair as a joke.
(17) Always keep this one thing in mind.
(18) Dylan Thomas died in New York at the end of 1953.
(19) Cornflowers make splendid pot plants.
(20) Everyone called John Brown a fool.
(21) Unfortunately, the experiment was no success.
(22) Mary bought herself a new English dictionary.
(23) She wears her hair long these days.
(24) Mrs Robinson is wonderful.
(25) Chomsky sees his theory as superior to that of De Saussure.

3.4.10 PREDICATIVE ADJUNCTS

In text 3.4.9 we have seen the example:

(97) William walked slowly down the road.

Slowly is a VP-Adjunct; it occurs inside VP. Its function is that of expressing the manner of walking. We shall now look at some cases in which a VP-Adjunct also has a non-adverbial function.

Bracket constituents in the following sentences. Try to determine which VP-constituents are Complements and which are optional Adjuncts:

(98) They have painted the house red.
(99) They have appointed John Brown their new manager.
(100) I always eat vegetables raw.
(101) She married young.
(102) The queen named the ship Georgina II.
(103) She returned him his letters unopened.

Let us first look at (98). We assume that the AdjP *red* in (98) is optional, but that the NP *the house* is obligatory. We suggest the following bracketing:

(104) [$_{S}$ [$_{NP}$They] [$_{VP}$have painted [$_{NP}$the house] [$_{AdjP}$red]]]

What is the GF of the NP *the house*? What is the function of *red*? Obviously, *red* says something about the activity of 'painting', but in addition it predicates something of the NP/Od: 'the house is red as a result of the painting': thus *red* is used both adverbially and predicatively. Schematically, we may represent the internal relations inside the VP of (98) as follows:

(105)

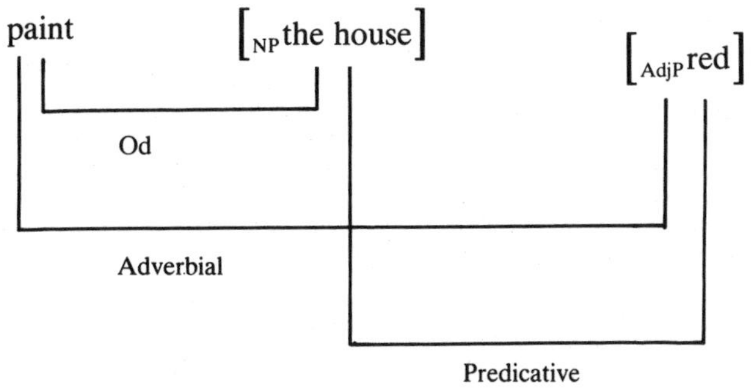

Structures like (105) are very similar to the pattern introduced for complex transitive verbs such as *set ... free* (see 3.4.6):

(106)

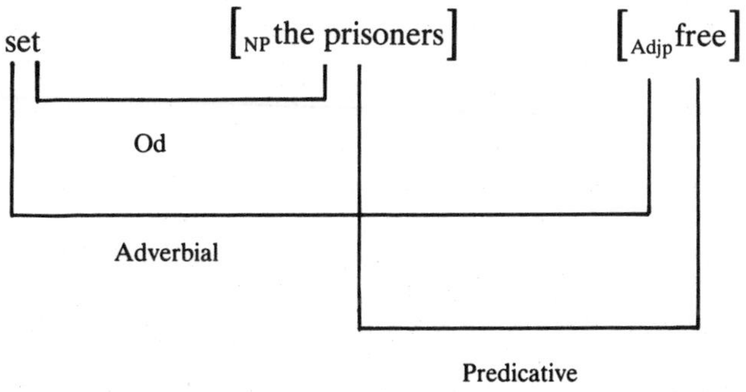

Is there any difference between (105) and (106)? The only difference is that *free* is non-omissible (**The government set the prisoners*), while *red* can be omitted without altering the sense of *paint* too much (*They have painted the house*). As we have seen (3.4.6), the AdjP *free* in (106) has the GF of Pc+Ac. The contrast can also be observed in the following paraphrases:

(107a) They have painted the house, and (more specifically) they painted it red.

(107b) *The government set the prisoners, and (more specifically) they set them free.

Observe also the following contrast:

(108a) If they have painted the house red, they have painted the house.

(108b) *If the government set the prisoners free, they set the prisoners.

This means that the difference between (105) and (106) is minimal and relates entirely to the type of V: *set* requires an AdjP (or a PP), while *paint* does not need the Adjunct. Adjuncts like *red* in *paint the house red*, which are both predicative and adverbial, but which are optional, are called **Predicative Adjuncts**. They are labelled **P+A**. It is clear, however, that P+A (105) and Pc+Ac (106) are otherwise very much alike.

In example (99) above we find a similar pattern. If we bracket the S we get:

(109) [$_S$They [$_{VP}$have appointed [$_{NP}$John Brown][$_{NP}$their new manager]]]

The first NP in the VP is an Od, the second an Adjunct: *They have appointed John Brown* is also a good sentence; however, *their new manager* has a double relation: it specifies the appointing, and it predicates something of the Object: 'John Brown is their new manager':

(110)

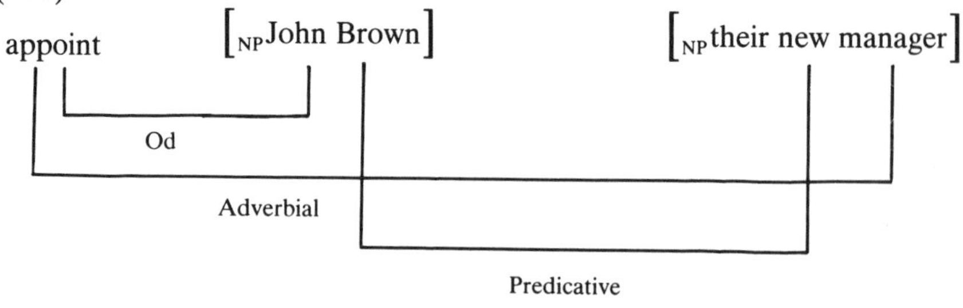

Again the pattern resembles that of complex transitive verbs like *set, fling* and *call* (3.4.6): cf. *They called John Brown a fool.* In example (109), however, the NP *their new manager* is not obligatory and must be labelled P+A, rather than Pc+Ac. Compare:

(111) They called these two men fools.

(112) They have appointed these two men their managers.

The fact that there is number agreement in both cases shows that there is a predicative relation between the two NPs in (111) and (112): *two men–fools*, and *two men–their managers.*

Apply the same analysis to the examples (100) and (103) above. (103) is interesting in that the verb *return* takes an Od and an Oi as well as a P+A:

(113)

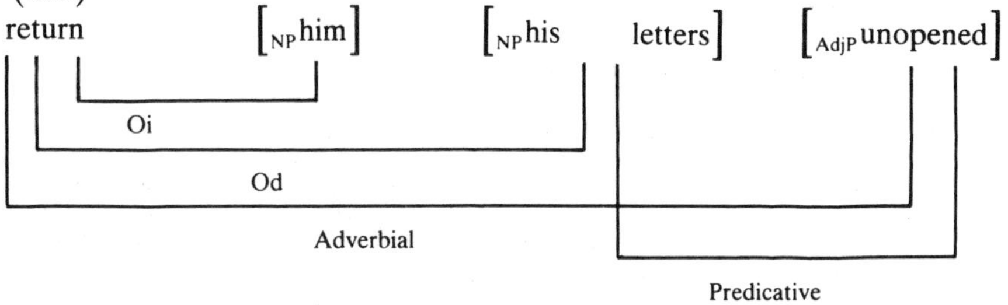

Let us also look at (101): *She married young*. This sentence must be bracketed as follows:

(114) [S She [VP married [AdjP young]]]

The AdjP *young* must be considered to be optional: after all, *She married* is a possible sentence, although perhaps somewhat unusual. You can paraphrase the sentence by 'She was young when she (got) married', or 'She (got) married while still young'. In other words, *young* is an Adverbial Adjunct (A). It specifies the time of the 'marrying'. But *young* also ascribes a property to the Subject: thus *young* is also predicative. Schematically:

(115)

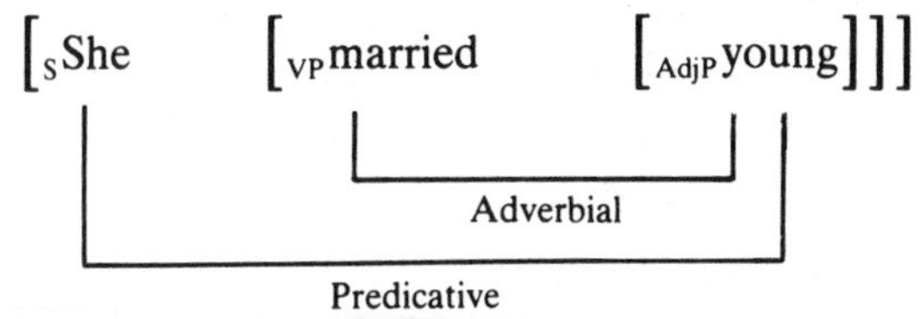

The AdjP *young* predicates something of the Subject NP, and expresses the time of the activity of the verb: it is predicative and adverbial at the same time: a P+A. This pattern is, of course, very close to that found with copulas:

(116) She was young.

where *young* is a Complement and predicates something of the Subject: a

Pc. The crucial difference is that in (101/115) *young* is not obligatory (*marry* does not require the AdjP), while with the copula *be* in (116) the AdjP is needed.

Also consider the following sentences:

(117) He left the house angry with his wife.

(118) Unaware of the danger, he walked into the room.

The analyses of (117) and (118) are as follows:

(119) $[_{S}[_{NP}\text{He}][_{VP}\text{left }[_{NP}\text{the house}][_{AdjP}\text{angry with his wife}]]]$

(120) $[_{S}[_{AdjP}\text{Unaware of the danger}][_{NP}\text{he}][_{VP}\text{walked }[_{PP}\text{into the room}]]]$

The function of the NP *the house* in (119) is that of Od. What is the function of AdjP *angry with his wife*? It does not seem to be a Complement, since it can easily be left out: *He left the house.* It is an Adjunct in VP, indicating both how he left the house, and (more importantly, perhaps) what state of mind 'he' was in when he left the house.

The AdjP has a dual function: it is adverbial, and it is predicative. If you compare (119) and (115) (*She married young*), you will find that the link between the AdjP and the V is stronger in (115) than in (119). In (119) the predicative function of the AdjP seems more important than its adverbial function. This is even clearer with the AdjP *unaware of the danger* in (118/120) above. The predicative function of this phrase is far more obvious than its adverbial function. Its adverbial function is less prominent, for example, than that of *young* in *She married young.* In spite of this difference, we shall also call the AdjPs in (117) and (118) P+As, bearing in mind that in some cases the predicative function may be more dominant than the adverbial function. (This is particularly clear when AdjPs such as *angry with his wife* or *unaware of the danger* occur initially in the sentence.)

3.4.10.1 Exercise

Identify the Predicative Adjuncts (P+As) in the following sentences. How are the P+As realised?

(1) They painted the door green.
(2) She married the Prince of Wales young.
(3) Curious, he opened the letter.
(4) Lord Soames died a Catholic at the age of 85.
(5) My friends from New York have arrived safe and sound.
(6) After 25 years in the United States John returned home a millionaire.
(7) Enthusiastic about his new job, Bill rang his wife.
(8) Green with envy, she hit him in the face.

Note: see also section 3.4.11.3 for an alternative analysis of the sentences above.

3.4.11 COMPLEX SENTENCES: FUNCTIONS OF CLAUSES

3.4.11.1 Finite Clauses

So far we have only looked at simple sentences, and we have identified the various GFs associated with NP, PP, AdjP or AdvP. We must now also consider what functions can be realised by embedded clauses. The following sentences from text 3.4.9 above contain embedded clauses:

(121) He felt that he should dislike the little girl intensely.

(122) He decided that he should never meet her again.

(123) He believed sincerely that a friendship with her would be exciting.

Sentence (121) can be analysed as follows:

(124) $\left[_{S} \left[_{NP}\text{He}\right] \left[_{VP}\text{felt that he should dislike the little girl intensely}\right]\right]$

Look carefully at the structure of the VP: in addition to a V (*felt*), it contains a *that*-clause, which is said to be embedded in the VP. Remember that we have bracketed such *that*-clauses as $\bar{S}$s (S-bars; i.e. complementisers + S):

(125) $\bar{S} \longrightarrow$ COMP–S

(126) $\left[_{\bar{S}} \ \underset{\text{COMP}}{\text{that}} \ \left[_{S}\text{he should dislike the little girl intensely}\right]\right]$

The GF of the *that*-clause is that of Direct Object. Since it is an Od, it should be possible to make it the Subject of a passive sentence. Consider:

(127) *That he should dislike the little girl intensely* was felt by William.

This may not be a very elegant sentence, but it is grammatical. A good way of improving the sentence would be by means of the process called '*it*-extraposition' (see 4.4.1). This would give:

(128) It was felt by William that he should dislike the little girl intensely.

We find then that Subjects and Objects may be realised not only by NPs but also by clauses ($\bar{S}$/Su or $\bar{S}$/Od).

Analyse sentences (122) and (123) above in the same way.

The following tree diagram also represents the structure of (121):

(129)

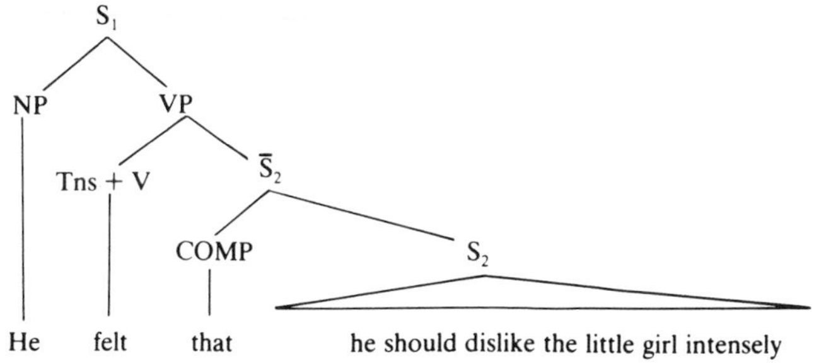

The internal structure of S_2 (the embedded clause) is as follows:

(130) $\left[_{S2}\left[_{NP}\text{he}\right]\left[_{VP}\text{should dislike}\left[_{NP}\text{the little girl}\right]\left[_{AdjP}\text{intensely}\right]\right]\right]$

The details of (130) can be added to tree diagram (129):

(131)

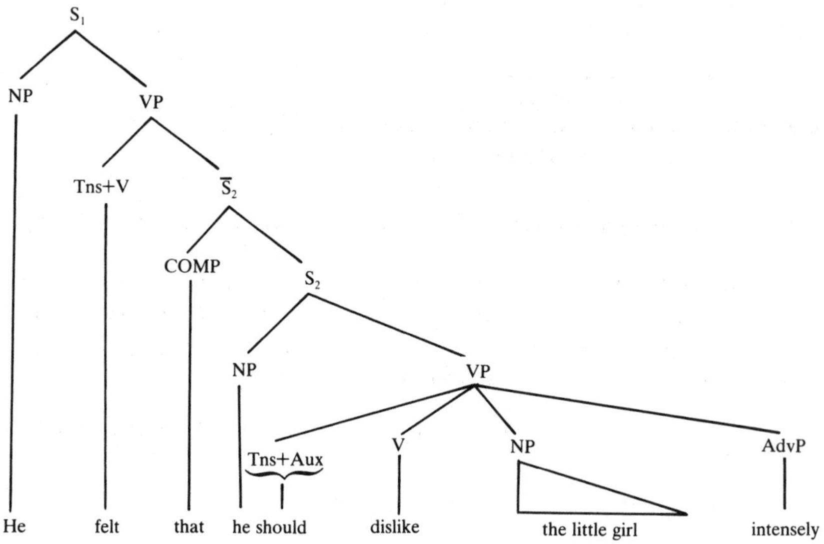

Tree diagram (131) contains, among other things, two Ss (which have been given the subscripts 1 and 2 to distinguish them) and one $\overline{S}$. S_1 is the main clause; the node S_1 dominates all the constituents of the sentence. $\overline{S}_2$ is the embedded S. In this sentence it functions as the Direct Object of the verb *feel.* In other words, $\overline{S}_2$ is an Object clause. $\overline{S}_2$ is COMP–S_2, and the element *that* in COMP serves as a subordinator.

Each S has its own Subject NP and VP. The Head of the VP in S_1 is *feel,* and in S_2 *dislike.* Both verbs are monotransitive, requiring an Od as their Complements.

Draw similar tree diagrams for sentences (122) and (123) above.

Identify embedded clauses in sentences (132)–(139). Bracket the Subject NP and the VP of the main clause. What is the function of each embedded S? Note that the COMP slot may be filled by *that, whether* or *if.*

(132) One evening he asked her whether he might go home with her.

(133) His aunt feared that he might catch something.

(134) His uncle said that evil communications corrupted good manners.

(135) John believes that Sue is a good student.

(136) I wonder if he still remembers that day in April.

(137) That John should have done such a thing is rather worrying.

(138) That he will propose to her soon is unlikely.

(139) I doubt whether he will ever manage to finish the book.

Embedded clauses very often function as Adjuncts (A). For example:

(140) Someone called to William *when he was walking down the road.*

(140) I will meet you at the station *if I can.*

Bracket the NP and VP in the main clause of (140) and (141). In each case the VP contains an embedded $\bar{S}$. For example:

(142) $[_{S}\, [_{NP}$ Someone$]\, [_{VP}$ called to $[_{NP}$ William$]\, [_{\bar{S}}$ when he was walking ...$]]]$

The *when*-clause ($\bar{S}$ *when*) is optional and serves to express the time of the activity of 'calling'. $\bar{S}$ *when* is an A, rather than a Verb Complement. It is also a VP-Adjunct, rather than a Sentence Adjunct, as the focusing and *wh*-question tests show. It is possible to focus on $\bar{S}$ *when*:

(143) It was when he was walking down the road that someone called to William.

And it is possible to ask a *wh*-question about $\bar{S}$ *when*:

(144) *When* did someone call to William?

The analysis in (142) is thus confirmed by these two tests.

Identify VP-Adjuncts realised by embedded clauses in the following sentences:

(145) When Mrs Carey passed the dissenting ministers in the street, she stepped over to the other side of the street.

(146) If there was not time for this she fixed her eyes on the pavement.

The following sentences contain examples of Sentence Adjuncts (Sas) realised by embedded clauses:

(147) John will come back soon, *as far as I know.*

(148) Philip does not like it here, *if I am not mistaken.*

The italicised clauses above function as Sas, not VP-Adjuncts (see 3.4.9). The two tests used above to distinguish between VP-Adjuncts and Sentence Adjuncts ((a) focusing and (b) *wh*-questioning) can again be applied. For example:

(a) focusing: it is *not* possible to focus on Sa:

(149) *It is as far as I know that John will come back soon.

(b) *wh*-questioning: Sas *cannot* be questioned with *wh*-items:

(150) When will John come back? **As far as I know.*

3.4.11.2 Non-finite and Verbless Clauses

Compare the three variants in:

(151) John believes *that the prisoner is innocent.*

(152) John believes *the prisoner to be innocent.*

(153) John believes *the prisoner innocent.*

Example (151) contains a finite Object clause, and (152) a non-finite one. In (151) and (152) *the prisoner* is the NP/Su of the embedded $\overline{S}$, and the AdjP *innocent* in both cases in the Predicative Complement (Pc) in the VP of the embedded clause. The structure of (152) may be represented as follows:

(154) John believes $\left[_{\overline{S}} \left[_{NP} \text{the prisoner}\right] \left[_{VP} \text{to be} \left[_{AdjP} \text{innocent}\right]\right]\right]$

The whole clause ($\overline{S}$) is the Direct Object of *believe*: what does John believe? That the prisoner is innocent.

Sentence (153) is almost identical with (152). They have the same meaning: the string *the prisoner innocent* is a reduced form of *the prisoner to be innocent*; it has the same GF: Od of *believe*:

(155) John believes $\left[\left\{ \begin{array}{l} \text{the prisoner to be innocent} \\ \text{the prisoner innocent} \end{array} \right\} \right]$

Although the string *the prisoner innocent* contains no verb, we shall treat it as a clause, since there is a predicate relationship between the NP *the prisoner* and the AdjP *innocent.* Such a string is called a **verbless clause** or a **small clause** (labelled $S_{\emptyset}$). The string *the prisoner innocent* is regarded as a verbless clause by analogy with the clauses in sentences (151) and (152).

Inside the verbless clause *the prisoner* is the Su and *innocent* the Pc, just as in (151) and (152).

In (156)–(163) we give some further examples of verbless Object clauses (italicised); rephrase each sentence, using a finite *that*-clause and a non-finite infinitive clause.

(156) I want *the dress ready by five o'clock.*

(157) He expects *me in his office at 12.*

(158) He considered *the girl a good student.*

(159) He thinks *the decision very unwise.*

(160) He judged *the man in his fifties.*

(161) He found *the assignment more difficult than he had expected.*

(162) You can count *yourself lucky.*

(163) His attitude made *real communication impossible.*

In 3.4.6 we have discussed complex transitive verbs, such as *set* in:

(164) They $\left[_{\mathrm{VP}}\text{set}\left[_{\mathrm{NP}}\text{the prisoners}\right]\left[_{\mathrm{AdjP}}\text{free}\right]\right]$

According to the analysis proposed there, *set* takes as its Complements (a) an NP functioning as Od, and (b) an AdjP functioning as Pc+Ac:

(165) *set*: [—— NP–AdjP]

An alternative analysis would be to treat the sequence NP–AdjP in (164) as one constituent: a verbless clause (or small clause):

(166) They $\left[_{\mathrm{VP}}\text{set}\left[_{\mathrm{S}_{\emptyset}}\left[_{\mathrm{NP}}\text{the prisoners}\right]\left[_{\mathrm{AdjP}}\text{free}\right]\right]\right]$

set is then said to take as its Complement an $S_{\emptyset}$:

(167) *set*: [—— $S_{\emptyset}$]

Inside $S_{\emptyset}$ the NP *the prisoners* is the Su; the AdjP *free* is a Pc. One reason for adopting such an analysis is the parallelism with sentences containing non-finite *–ing*-clauses such as:

(168) They $\left[_{\mathrm{VP}}\text{set}\left[_{S_{ing}}\left[_{\mathrm{NP}}\text{the prisoners}\right]\left[_{\mathrm{VP}}\text{working on a new task}\right]\right]\right]$

The verbless clauses above are used as Od. Verbless clauses may also be used, for example, as Prepc of *with*:

(169) With $\left[_{\mathrm{S}_{\emptyset}}\text{John in hospital}\right]$ we cannot go out.

Compare (169) with (170) below, where P takes an NP as its Complement:

(170) With $\left[_{\mathrm{NP}}\text{this sort of weather}\right]$ we cannot go out.

Sentence (169) can be analysed as follows:

(171) $\left[_{\mathrm{PP}}\text{With}\left[_{\mathrm{S}_{\emptyset}}\left[_{\mathrm{NP}}\text{John}\right]\left[_{\mathrm{PP}}\text{in hospital}\right]\right]\right]$ we cannot go out.

With may also take a non-finite clause as its Prepc:

(172) With $\left[_{S_{ing}}\text{him being so slow nowadays}\right]$ we'll never get there.

3.4.11.3 Empty Subjects in Non-finite and Verbless Clauses

Compare the following pairs of sentences:

(173a) *When he was waiting for the train,* John noticed that he had lost his ticket.

(173b) *When waiting for the train,* John noticed that he had lost his ticket.

(174a) *Whenever he was in trouble,* Bill rang his girl-friend.

(174b) *Whenever in trouble,* Bill rang his girl-friend.

Sentences (173a) and (174a) contain finite embedded clauses (italicised) functioning as A: the embedded clauses are optional and they express the time of the activities expressed by *notice* and by *ring* in the main clause. The (b)-sentences are clearly reduced versions of the corresponding (a)-sentences. It is by analogy with the finite clauses in (173a) and (174a) that we also regard the italicised strings in (173b) and (174b) as clauses.

The *when*-clause in (173b) is non-finite, and the *whenever*-clause in (174b) is verbless. In both cases, the subordinate clause lacks an overt Subject, but the Subject can usually be inferred from the rest of the sentence or the context. We assume that non-finite and verbless clauses of this type do contain a Subject position, but that this position is 'not lexically realised': the open Subject positions in (173b) and (174b) are interpreted as 'John' and 'Bill' respectively (cf. *he* in (173a) and (174a)). The underlying structures of (173b) and (174b) may thus be represented as follows:

(175) When ( ) waiting for the train, John noticed that he had lost his ticket.

(176) Whenever ( ) in trouble, Bill rang his girl-friend.

We shall say that the Subject of the main clause (*John, Bill*) **controls** the **empty** Subject position of the subordinate clause (see Chapter 5). In sentence (177) below we shall read *you* into ( ):

(177) When ( ) waiting for your train, take care of your luggage.

Non-finite clauses may also be passive:

(178) When he had been arrested by the police, he rang up his lawyer.

(179) When arrested by the police, he rang up his lawyer.

Like *waiting* in (177), *arrested* in (179) is non-finite, but *waiting* is active and *arrested* is passive (cf. the corresponding finite (a)-sentences).

The *waiting*-clause (S*ing*) and the *arrested*-clause (S*ed*) in (177) and (179) are participle clauses with empty Subjects.

Infinitive clauses may also have empty Subjects. For example:

(180) John decided ( ) to study English.

(181) George promised Mary ( ) to leave.

In the verbless clause *whenever in trouble* (174b), the PP *in trouble* functions as Pc, just as in (174a). Compare:

(182a) $\left[_{\bar{S}}\text{whenever}\left[_{S}\left[_{NP/Su}\text{he}\right]\left[_{VP}\text{was}\left[_{PP/Pc}\text{in trouble}\right]\right]\right]\right]$

(182b) $\left[_{\bar{S}}\text{whenever}\left[_{S}\left[_{NP/Su}(\quad)\right]\left[_{PP/Pc}\text{in trouble}\right]\right]\right]$

(183) The books will be sent *if available.*

(184) He married her *when a student at Harvard.*

Analyse the italicised verbless clauses in the same way as *whenever in trouble* (cf. (182a) and (182b)). What element controls the Subject position in *if available* and in *when a student at Harvard*? What is the GF of *available* and of *a student at Harvard*?

In 3.4.10 we have introduced the GF of P+A. For example, in:

(185) They $\left[_{VP}\text{have painted}\left[_{NP/Od}\text{the house}\right]\left[_{AdjP/P+A}\text{ red}\right]\right]$

(186) She $\left[_{VP}\text{married}\left[_{AdjP/P+A}\text{ young}\right]\right]$

An alternative analysis would be, however, to consider such AdjPs as *red* and *young* in (185) and (186) as constituents of verbless clauses without lexical subjects:

(187) They $\left[_{VP}\text{have painted}\left[_{NP/Od}\text{the house}\right]\left[_{S_{\emptyset}/A}\left[_{NP/Su}(\quad)\right]\left[_{AdjP/Pc}\text{red}\right]\right]\right]$

The verbless clause itself has the GF of A (VP-Adjunct). Inside the verbless clause, the Subject position is not lexically realised and it is controlled by the NP/Od *the house* ('the house is red'). The AdjP *red* is a Pc, again inside $S_{\emptyset}$. Similarly, there is an alternative analysis for (186):

(188) $\left[_{NP/Su}\text{She}\right]\left[_{VP}\text{married}\left[_{S_{\emptyset}/A}\left[_{NP/Su}(\quad)\right]\left[_{AdjP/Pc}\text{young}\right]\right]\right]$

In 3.4.6 we have proposed the following analysis:

(189) They $\left[_{VP}\text{set}\left[_{NP/Od}\text{the prisoners}\right]\left[_{AdjP/Pc+Ac}\text{free}\right]\right]$

In view of the preceding discussion of verbless clauses, we might also consider the following analysis:

(190) They $[_{VP}$set $[_{NP/Od}$the prisoners$]$ $[_{S_{\emptyset}/Ac}$ $[_{NP/Su}($ $)]$ $[_{AdjP/Pc}$free$]]]$

Free is here an AdjP which functions as a Pc inside a verbless clause. The verbless clause itself lacks a lexical Subject; ( ) is controlled by NP/Od *the prisoners.* As a whole the verbless clause has the GF of Ac: it is a Complement to the V *set.*

3.5 GRAMMATICAL FUNCTIONS IN PHRASES: A BRIEF SURVEY

In section 2.4 we have looked in some detail at the internal structure of phrases in English. Noun phrases are constituents headed by an N, verb phrases by a V, etc. In this section we shall provide a brief survey of the internal structure of each phrasal type. Diagrams (1)–(5) provide information about (a) the type of constituent found inside the phrase, (b) the order of the constituents, (c) the function of the constituent inside the phrase:

(1) *Noun phrases*:

	the five	French	students	from Paris
Category	Art (Num)	(AdjP)	Noun	(PP)
Function	Specifier	Premod.	Head	Postmod.

(2) *Verb phrases*:

	will	show	the girl	his paintings	after dinner
Category	Pres (M)	Verb	NP	NP	(PP)
Function	Specifier	Head	Complements		Adjunct

(3) *Adjective phrases*:

	very	fond	of her
Category	(Adv)	Adj	PP
Function	Specifier	Head	Complement

(4) *Adverb phrases*:

	quite	unexpectedly
Category	(Adv)	Adverb
Function	Specifier	Head

(5) *Prepositional phrases*:

	right	on	the spot
Category	(Adv)	P	NP
Function	Specifier	Head	Complement

If we look at the structures above more closely, we see that there is a degree of parallelism between all the phrase structures:

(a) each phrase type has a Head;
(b) the Head may be preceded by Specifiers;
(c) the Head may be followed by Complements and by optional constituents (Modifiers in NP and Adjuncts in VP).

It is thus possible to give a more abstract schema of phrase structure which gives us a general representation for all phrasal categories:

$$\text{X-phrase:}\quad \text{Specifier–}\underset{\text{X}}{\text{Head}}\text{–Complement–}\begin{Bmatrix}\text{Mod}\\ \text{A}\end{Bmatrix}$$

where X stands for N, V, etc.

However, this abstract schema has to be adjusted for the individual phrase types. In NPs, for example, Modifiers (AdjPs) may also precede the Head. VPs, AdjPs and PPs have Complements, but not NPs and AdvPs. Furthermore, the Specifier is realised in quite distinct ways depending on the category: in NPs, for example, Spec is realised by Det, whereas in VPs Spec is realised by tense, modal, etc. (cf. also Chapter 7).

3.5.1 EXERCISES

I Discuss in greater detail the general differences between phrase-types, and define the difference between phrases and clauses.

II By what type of category is the GF of Su realised in the following examples?

(1) Workers angry about pay is just the situation that the company wanted to avoid.
(2) Under the bed is a cosy spot.
(3) Singing comprehensibly in English is almost as hard for foreigners as writing idiomatically.
(4) From London to Paris is a long way.
(5) Unwanted is a terrible way to feel.

III Identify non-finite and verbless clauses in the sentences below. What is their GF? What is their internal structure?

(1) The body of Sir Trevor, a plastic bag held by an elastic band over his head, was found on Tuesday morning by his chauffeur.
(2) It all started, as a lot of things do, on a couch in a hotel room, one sunny afternoon with the curtains drawn, the door locked and most of my clothes hanging on the peg behind the door.
(3) The daughter of a boxer, Mae West first set foot on a stage when William McKinsley was sitting in the White House.
(4) Huckleberry Finn was a young wayfarer who knew how to stretch the truth when in the right company.
(5) The collapse of cubism left Bomberg stunned.

4

PROCESSES

4.1 INTRODUCTION

In Chapter 3 we have given a survey of the basic sentence patterns in English, looking at straightforward sentences in which the basic patterns described by the phrase structure rules are left virtually undisturbed. Sentence (1) below, for example, is such a 'basic sentence':

(1) Jane gave this book to Bill on Saturday.

Starting from a set of PS rules (2a), and after insertion of the appropriate lexical material (chosen from the set in (2b)), we arrive at the underlying structure or deep structure (2c):

(2a)
$$S \longrightarrow NP\text{–}VP$$
$$NP \longrightarrow \begin{Bmatrix} Det\text{–}N \\ N \end{Bmatrix}$$
$$VP \longrightarrow Tns\text{–}V\text{–}NP\text{–}PP\text{–}PP$$
$$Tns \longrightarrow Past$$
$$PP \longrightarrow P\text{–}NP$$

(2b) N : Saturday, Bill, Jane, book
Det: this
V : give
P : on, to

(2c)
$$\left[_{S} \left[_{NP}\text{Jane} \left[_{VP} \left[_{Tns}\text{Past}\right] \left[_{V}\text{give}\right] \left[_{NP}\text{this book}\right] \left[_{PP}\text{to} \left[_{NP}\text{Bill}\right]\right] \left[_{PP}\text{on} \left[_{NP}\text{Saturday}\right]\right]\right]\right]\right]$$

All we need to do now is to ensure that the past tense marker ends up on the right of the verb *give*, producing *gave*. The step from the underlying structure (2c) to (1) is the operation of a morphological rule which ensures proper attachment of affixes.

It is possible, however, to vary the basic patterns of sentences by performing additional operations on the underlying or deep structure. Starting from (2c) once again we may arrive at quite different patterns:

(a) by forming a *Yes–No* question:

Did Jane give this book to Bill on Saturday?

(b) by forming a *wh*-question:

What did Jane give to Bill on Saturday?

To whom did Jane give this book on Saturday?

(c) by fronting the Adjunct PP:

On Saturday Jane gave this book to Bill.

(d) by passivising the sentence:

This book was given to Bill (by Jane) on Saturday.

Bill was given this book (by Jane) on Saturday.

(e) by clefting:

It was Jane who gave this book to Bill on Saturday.

It was to Bill that Jane gave this book on Saturday.

It was on Saturday that Jane gave this book to Bill.

(f) by pseudo-clefting:

What Jane did was give this book to Bill on Saturday.

Example (1) as well as the examples listed under (a)–(f) above are all related to the string (2c). Underlying structures are defined as structures resulting from lexical insertion (2b) in the structures described by the PS rules (2a). Surface structures result from applying one or more operations to the underlying structures. In cases like example (1) only one morphological operation has been performed (attachment of the affix), but often more drastic changes will occur (cf. (a)–(f) above).

Schematically our description is organised as follows:

(a) underlying structure

$\Downarrow$ PROCESSES

(b) surface structure

Let us return once more to example (1). Instead of inserting Ns and Det (as in (2b)) into the NP slots generated by the PS rules (2a), we may also choose to insert pro-forms:

(3a) $[_{S} [_{NP} \textit{She}] [_{VP} [_{Tns} \text{Past}] [_{V} \text{give}] [_{NP} \textit{it}] [_{PP} \text{to } [_{NP} \textit{him}]] [_{PP} \text{on Saturday}]]]$

(3a) is again an underlying structure. After attaching the past tense affix to V, we arrive at the surface structure (3b):

(3b) She gave it to him on Saturday.

Inserting pronominal elements rather than full lexical NPs is referred to as **pronominalisation**.

4.2 LEFTWARD MOVEMENT: wh-MOVEMENT AND RELATED TRANSFORMATIONS

4.2.1 QUESTIONS: DIFFERENT TYPES

In Chapter 2 we have noted that English has various types of questions. We have distinguished between:

(a) *Yes-No* questions, e.g.:

Did you measure the distance?

(b) *Wh*-questions, e.g.:

Why did you measure it?

and between:

(c) Direct questions, e.g.:

May I go home with you?

(d) Indirect questions, e.g.:

One evening he asked whether he might go home with her.

All these interrogative sentences are related to basic declarative structures, e.g. *You measured the distance, I may go home with you,* etc. In the following sections we shall consider three main operations which relate questions to basic sentence patterns. The three operations are: *Subject–Auxiliary Inversion,* do-*insertion* and wh-*movement.*

4.2.2 SUBJECT–AUXILIARY INVERSION

In the following text you will find three instances of direct *Yes-No* questions. Identify them.

Text 4.2.2

One morning the elder girl hung back in my room. She had something to say. She said: 'Shall I show you my rude drawings?' I was interested. She showed me the drawings: a child's view of unclothed dolls. I was greatly moved. She said: 'Do you like my rude drawings?' 'I like your drawings, Yvonne.' 'I will show you some more tomorrow. Would you like to keep these?' 'I'd rather you kept them, Yvonne.' 'No, you can have these. I can always do some for myself.'

V.S. Naipaul, *The Mimic Men.*

The direct *Yes-No* questions in the text are:

(1) Shall I show you my rude drawings?

(2) Do you like my rude drawings?

(3) Would you like to keep these?

What distinguishes them from the basic patterns to which they are related is the order of the first two elements in the sentence: the auxiliary and the Subject NP. Compare (1) and (3) with (4) and (5) below:

(4) I shall show you my rude drawings.

(5) You would like to keep these.

The operation which changes the order of elements in a sentence (for example, to get from (4) to (1) or from (5) to (3)) is called a **transformation**. The change from (4) to (1) may be represented as follows:

declarative: $\left[_{S}\left[_{NP}\text{I}\right]\left[_{VP}\left[\begin{matrix}\text{shall}\\ \text{+Present}\end{matrix}\right]\left[\text{show you my rude drawings}\right]\right]\right.$

interrogative: $\left[_{S}\left[\begin{matrix}\text{Shall}\\ \text{+Present}\end{matrix}\right]\left[_{NP}\text{I}\right]\left[_{VP}\text{show you my rude drawnings}\right]\right]$

In order to form *Yes-No* questions like (1) and (3) we move the first auxiliary to the left and place it in front of the Subject. The moved auxiliary may be a modal auxiliary (*shall, will, must, can*, etc.), perfect *have*, progressive *be*, or passive *be*; all these auxiliaries are marked for either present or past tense.

The following is a more abstract formulation of the rule involved in *Yes-No* question formation. The movement transformation works on basic patterns as follows:

underlying structure: $\left[\text{S}\left[\text{NP}\right]\left[\text{VP}\left[\begin{matrix}\text{aux (n't)}\\ \text{+Tense}\end{matrix}\right]\ \text{V}\ldots\right]\right]$

surface structure: $\left[\text{S}\left[\begin{matrix}\text{aux (n't)}\\ \text{+Tense}\end{matrix}\right]\left[\text{NP}\right]\left[\text{VP}\ \ \text{V}\ldots\right]\right]$

The abbreviation 'aux' is used for 'auxiliary' (see 2.4.3.3).

Produce *Yes-No* questions from the following declarative sentences by applying the above transformation:

(6) George can speak German and French.

(7) The postman has been attacked by our neighbour's dog.

(8) Mary has been sunbathing all afternoon.

(9) Bill was washing his hair when the phone rang.

(10) John hadn't seen his friend so angry before.

(11) Jane hasn't left home yet.

(12) Jane has *not* left home yet.

As you can see, the transformation affects only the tensed auxiliary. If a contracted negator *–n't* is attached to the tensed auxiliary, it must be moved along to the left (see (10) and (11) above). The morpheme *–n't* is not an independent word; it must attach to the auxiliary. The uncontracted form *not*, on the other hand, is independent and does not move along with the auxiliary (see (12) above).

The operation described above is generally referred to as *Subject–Aux Inversion*, or *SAI* for short.

4.2.3 *DO*-INSERTION

Consider now example (2) again:

(2) Do you like my rude drawings?

We may assume that this corresponds to the basic pattern in (13):

(13) You like my rude drawings.

In (13) the VP contains no auxiliary element apart from the obligatory tense element: there is no modal auxiliary, or *have* or *be*. The underlying structure of (2) is as follows (cf. (13)):

(14) $\left[_{S}\left[_{NP}\text{You}\right]\left[_{VP}\left[\text{Tense}\right]\ \text{like my rude drawings}\right]\right]$

In such cases there is not only Subject–Aux Inversion, but also *do*-insertion. In other words, the transition from (13) to (2) involves two changes, instead of one:

(a) SAI: the tense element is moved out of the VP and placed in front of NP/Su;
(b) *do* is inserted.

We have seen that SAI affects the first auxiliary and the present or past tense element associated with it. If there is no auxiliary in the sentence, SAI affects only tense, which, as we have seen (2.4.3.3), is also an auxiliary element. But it is clear that in such cases we cannot stop after SAI, or else we would end up with an isolated tense affix in front of the Subject NP:

(15) $[_S [\text{Tense}] [_{NP}\text{you}] [_{VP}\text{like my rude drawings}]]$

Tense can never occur on its own; it must always be attached to a verb or an auxiliary. One way of 'saving' this isolated (or *stranded*) tense-marker is to insert a prop-word, which has the function of *carrying* tense: this support-word is the auxiliary *do* (step (b) above: *do*-insertion). *Do*-insertion attaches *do* to the stranded tense element.

(16) $[_S [\begin{smallmatrix}\text{DO}\\ +\text{Tense}\end{smallmatrix}] [_{NP}\text{you}] [_{VP}\text{like my rude drawings}]]$

SAI (followed by *do*-insertion if necessary) can also occur in cases like the following:

(17) No sooner *had he* entered the house than the police arrived.

(18) Never *did I* suffer more than on that unfortunate day!

(19) On no account *will he* do such a thing again.

SAI and *do*-insertion are **triggered** by the presence of negative VP-Adjuncts such as *no sooner*, *never* and *on no account*.

4.2.3.1 Exercise

In text 4.2.3.1 you will find instances of direct *Yes-No* questions. Identify them and discuss their formation.

Text 4.2.3.1

It was a bitterly cold morning and I was thankful for the Volvo's efficient heating system. I had slipped Mozart's clarinet concerto into the stereo and was looking forward to a pleasant drive when I saw the hitchhiker. His placard read: Cambridge — Volvo preferred. It intrigued me and breaking the habit of a lifetime, I stopped. He slipped into the passenger seat, placing his bag carefully at his feet.

'Thank you very much sir, for stopping.'

'I was intrigued by your sign; flattered I suppose,' I replied.

'Oh, I admire Volvos very much. I'm reading engineering and I know what goes into them.'

'What exactly is it that you admire?'

'It's the little things. Do you know what happens when one of your tail lights fails?'

'Yes, a light flashes on the dashboard to tell me.'

'That's true, but did you know you can replace the bulb from inside the boot?'

I confessed that I didn't and made the point that such news was hardly likely to start a rush on 6-cylinder Volvos.

'Ah, but it should.'

I told him he was preaching to the converted and turned off the stereo, as it was evident my passenger wanted to talk.

'Tell me, do you ever drive really fast? I hope you don't mind my asking?' He grinned like a boy.

'Well, since you're reading engineering and not law, I confess that there have been times when I have gone over 70 mph. On the Continent, of course, and in the presence of a trained nurse.'

Adapted from Volvo advertisement, *Punch*, 21 November 1979.

4.2.4 *WH*-MOVEMENT

So far we have looked at *Yes-No* questions and the two operations involved in forming them (SAI and *do*-insertion). Let us now consider the formation of *wh*-questions.

In text 4.2.4 you will find several instances of such *wh*-questions.

> *Text 4.2.4*
> I was brought up in Cornwall. On one sad night during the war a sentry of the Home Guard shot what he took to be an interloper. At the subsequent enquiry his commanding officer said:
> 'Did you challenge him?'
> 'Yes, sir.'
> 'What did you say?'
> 'Who goes there?'
> 'What did he say?'
> 'Friend, sir.'
> 'What did you do?'
> 'I shot him, sir.'
> 'Then why did you shoot him?'
> 'If it had been a real friend, he'd have said "Don't be silly", and I'd have let him pass.'
> Adapted from Christian Brann, *Pass the Port.*

Two *wh*-questions from the text are:

(20) What did you say?

(21) Who goes there?

In what follows we shall argue that the structure underlying (20) is roughly:

(22) $\left[_{S}\left[_{NP}\text{You}\right]\left[_{VP}\text{Past say}\left[_{NP}\text{what}\right]\right]\right]$

and that leftward movement of *what*, as well as SAI and *do*-insertion are required to give us (20). The underlying structure of (21) is as follows:

(23) $\left[_{S}\left[_{NP}\text{Who}\right]\left[_{VP}\text{Present go}\left[_{AdvP}\text{there}\right]\right]\right]$

We shall say that *wh*-movement also applies here, but since *who* already appears at the beginning of the sentence, the rule is said to apply **vacuously**. As we shall see, *do*-insertion is not required in this case.

Form *wh*-questions from the following sentences, replacing the italicised item by a *wh*-phrase. For example:

John put his money *in the top drawer of his desk.*

becomes:

Where did John put his money?

(24) The wedding is to take place *on 13 April.*

(25) Susan will be wearing *her blue dress* tonight.

(26) *A man with red hair* was waiting for Jane.

(27) I heard *the telephone, not the door-bell.*

(28) These are *Charles's* shoes.

(29) John hit Bill *because he hated him.*

(30) George got here *by train.*

(31) The terrorists assassinated *the ambassador.*

4.2.4.1 Subcategorisation Frames and *Wh*-movement

We must first justify our choice of (22) and (23) as the structures underlying (20) and (21) above. Our argument is largely based on the subcategorisation of lexical verbs (cf. 3.4.7). Subcategorisation frames can be seen as providing the slots into which to insert the verb. *Assassinate,* for example, ((31) above) has the following frame:

(32) *assassinate*
+V, [—— NP]

This means that *assassinate* is a verb which is subcategorised as taking an NP.

(33) $[_{S}[_{NP}$The terrorists$][_{VP}$assassinated $[_{NP}$the ambassador$]]]$

Notice that a frame *must* be fully realised. Otherwise the sentence will be ungrammatical:

(34) *$[_{S}[_{NP}$The terrorists$][_{VP}$assassinated $[_{NP}$——$]]]$

In basic sentences in English the NP/Od typically follows the verb. Consequently, (35) below is ungrammatical:

(35) *$[_{S}[_{NP}$The terrorists$][_{VP}[_{NP}$the ambassador$]$ assassinated$]]$

If you form a *Yes-No* question from *The terrorists assassinated the ambassador,* you will find that the sentence is grammatical only if the NP/Od follows the verb, as stipulated by the subcategorisation frame for *assassinate.* For example:

(36) $[_{S}$Did $[_{NP}$the terrorists$][_{VP}$assassinate $[_{NP}$the ambassador$]]]$

Not: **Did the terrorists the ambassador assassinate?*

Now consider the following *wh*-question:

(37) *Who(m)* did the terrorists assassinate?

If you try to fit this into the subcategorisation frame (32) above, you will get the impression that the NP/Od after the lexical verb is not realised:

(38) Who(m) did the terrorists assassinate $[_{NP}$——$]$

But what happens if we insert a constituent in the apparently empty position? We get:

(39) *Who(m) did $\left[_{NP}\text{the terrorists}\right]\left[_{VP}\text{assassinate}\right.$

$\left.\left[_{NP}\text{the ambassador}\right]\right]$

Of course, (39) is not grammatical.

We must conclude that the Object position in (38) is somehow already occupied. And indeed we can easily provide a filler; the sentence-initial *wh*-phrase *who(m)* can fill the position:

(40) $\left[_{S}\left[_{NP}\text{The terrorists}\right]\left[_{VP}\text{assassinated}\left[_{\substack{NP\\+WH}}\ \text{who(m)}\right]\right]\right]$

Under *who(m)* you now see the symbol [+WH]. This is said to be a *feature* of the *wh*-phrase: *who(m)* is a *wh*-NP (here an interrogative pronoun).

Compare now again (41) and (42) below (slightly simplified):

(41) $\left[_{NP}\text{The terrorists}\right]\left[_{VP}\text{assassinated}\left[_{\substack{NP\\+WH}}\ \text{who(m)}\right]\right]$

(42) $\left[_{\substack{NP\\+WH}}\ \text{Who(m)}\right]\text{ did }\left[_{NP}\text{the terrorists}\right]\left[_{VP}\text{assassinate}\right]$

It would be very uneconomical to devise two separate frames for *assassinate*: one for (41) and one for (42), as follows:

(43) $\left[_{VP}\text{——}\substack{NP\\+WH}\right]]$

(44) $\left[_{VP}\text{——}\right]$

Frame (43) suggests that *assassinate* requires an obligatory NP/Od, whereas (44) implies that the same verb requires no Complement. Obviously, (41) and (42) are related structures. How can we express the relationship between (41) and (42)? How can we make a **generalisation** about the two patterns?

Let us assume that *assassinate* always has the frame:

(45) $\left[_{VP} \text{——} \underset{\text{+WH}}{\text{NP}}\right]$

We start from (41):

(46) $\left[_{S}\left[_{NP}\text{The terrorists}\right]\left[_{VP}\text{Past assassinate}\left[_{\underset{+WH}{NP}}\text{ who(m)}\right]\right]\right]$

We can move the *wh*-phrase $[\underset{+WH}{NP}]$ from its original position, and place it in front of the sentence. Assume that it is placed in a special **slot** marked as [+WH], which occurs in front of S:

(47) $\left[_{+WH}\right]\left[_{S}\ldots\right]$

The movement of the *wh*-phrase to the +WH slot (i.e. wh-*movement*) may be represented schematically as follows:

(48) $\left[_{\underset{+WH}{NP}}\text{ Who(m)}\right]\left[_{S}\text{the terrorists Past assassinate ---}\right]$

After the movement a gap is left behind, which is marked here by dashes ---. We can find its original filler in the special sentence-initial slot. After this first operation we get:

(49) Whom the terrorists assassinated ---.

Of course, this is not a well-formed question. To make this a correct question, we need two additional operations (SAI and *do*-insertion):

(50) Whom the terrorists Past assassinate ---?

(51) Whom Past the terrorists assassinate ---? (SAI)

(52) Whom did the terrorists assassinate ? (*do*-insertion)

Having discussed *wh*-question formation with regard to verbs such as *assassinate* (which requires an NP/Od as Complement), let us now turn to a verb like *give*. To derive the sentence *To whom did the princess give the money?*, we start from the following underlying structure:

(53) $\left[_{+WH}\right]\left[_{S}\text{The princess Past give the money}\left[_{\underset{+WH}{PP}}\text{ to whom}\right]\right]$

Application of *wh*-movement, SAI and *do*-insertion to this underlying structure gives us (54):

(54) $\left[_{\underset{+WH}{PP}}\text{ To whom}\right]\left[_{S}\text{did the princess give the money}\left[_{PP}\text{---}\right]\right]$

The moved constituent here is a $[^{PP}_{+WH}]$, which matches a gap marked PP. We shall say that the *wh*-phrase at the *wh*-slot in front of S matches or **binds** the gap.

Summing up, we have seen that wh-questions are formed by (a) moving a constituent containing a *wh*-word into the +WH slot in front of the sentence, and by (b) SAI, with or without *do*-insertion. Operation (a) is the transformation called ***wh*-movement**. It typically leaves a gap --- bound by a *wh*-word. The *wh*-word is called **the binder** or the ***wh*-operator**. The gap marks the original position (i.e. the **extraction site**) of the *wh*-word. SAI is triggered here by the presence of the *wh*-word in front of S.

4.2.4.2 Exercise

The following interrogative sentences all start with a *wh*-phrase. Indicate the gap corresponding to (or bound by) the phrase:

(1) *Where* did you go after the film?
(2) *Who* did you meet there?
(3) *What* did you drink?
(4) *How good a president* was J.F.K.?
(5) *Who* did you say John introduced you to after the play?
(6) *Where* did you say Mary put the dustbin?
(7) *What* did you say Mary wants to buy for John?
(8) *How far away* were you?
(9) *Why* did you measure it?
(10) *Who* do they think is spying on them all the time?

4.2.4.3 Prepositional Phrases in *Wh*-questions

Consider the following '*echo-question*' containing a $[^{PP}_{+WH}]$:

(55) John bought the necklace $\left[_{\substack{PP\\+WH}} \text{ for whom}\right]$?

Wh-movement can operate in two ways: (a) it may affect the whole PP:

(56a) $\left[_{+WH}\text{For who(m)}\right]\left[_{S}\text{did John buy the necklace }\left[_{PP}---\right]\right]$

(b) it may affect only the *wh*-word *whom*, which is an NP:

(56b) $\left[_{+WH}\text{Who(m)}\right]\left[_{S}\text{did John buy the necklace }\left[_{PP}\text{for }\left[_{NP}---\right]\right]\right]$

In both cases the moved constituent matches the type of gap (PP or NP). In (b) it is only the NP following the preposition that is moved. The preposition left behind is said to be **stranded**. In (a) the moved *wh*-word (*who(m)*) trails the preposition along with it. If movement affects more than just a *wh*-constituent, we say that the other elements are **pied-piped**. **Pied-piping** is usually optional with PPs (cf 2.4.4).

In some cases native speakers feel that pied-piping is obligatory. Try, for example, to produce *wh*-questions corresponding to (57)–(59) below:

(57) He offended her in what way?

(68) You got home by what time?

(59) She asked you to pick her up at what station?

Preposition stranding yields particularly awkward sentences when the PPs are Adverbial Adjuncts of time or place, as in (59): ? *What station did she ask you to pick her up at*? Certain prepositions (e.g. *during, notwithstanding*) never allow stranding: * *Which holiday did he meet her during*?

4.2.4.4 *Wh*-movement of Subjects

Normally, as we have seen, *wh*-question formation involves:

(a) *wh*-movement
(b) SAI, with or without *do*-support.

With Subject *wh*-phrases, however, this is not true. Consider, for example:

(60) *Who* left last night?

Since a Subject *wh*-phrase occupies a sentence-initial position, we shall say for the sake of generality that *wh*-movement takes place here as well, but that its effect is not visible. *Wh*-movement is said to apply **vacuously** here.

(61) $[\ _{+WH}][_S [_{NP}\text{who}]_{+WH} [\text{Past leave}]]$

(62) $[_{NP}\text{who}]_{+WH} [_S [_{NP}---] [\text{Past leave}]]$

There is no SAI. Evidence that the NP/Su is indeed affected by *wh*-movement can be found in certain complex sentences. Look for the gap corresponding to the *wh*-phrase in the following examples:

(63) *Who* did you say had left the garage open?

(64) *Which boy* did you say has broken the window?

Who is the Subject of *had left the garage open*, and *which boy* is the Subject of *has broken the window*. We shall return to examples like these below.

4.2.4.5 *Wh*-movement and $\bar{S}$

We have so far developed a schema for *wh*-question formation, which is based on the assumption that in underlying structure such sentences contain an interrogative *wh*-element and are preceded by a slot for *wh*-items. *Wh*-movement extracts the *wh*-phrase from its original position in S, leaves a gap marked by ---, and moves the *wh*-phrase into the slot marked for receiving it:

(65) $[_{+WH}\text{What}]\ [_{S}\text{John will send --- to Mary}]$

The presence of *what* triggers SAI:

(66) What will John send to Mary?

We shall say that the slot marked for *wh*-words at the beginning of the sentence together with the following S again constitute an $\bar{S}$ (*S-bar*); see 2.3. After *wh*-movements the *wh*-phrase will occupy the slot labelled +WH:

(67) $[_{\bar{S}}\ [_{+WH}\text{What}]\ [_{S}\text{will John send --- to Mary}]]$

4.2.4.6 Exercises

I Form two different *wh*-questions from each of the declarative sentences below:

(1) John asked for more pay.
(2) John was arguing fiercely about the decision.
(3) They were talking to the Vice-Chancellor about the new lecturer.
(4) Sylvia has written an angry letter to her ex-husband in Brazil.
(5) The miners are applying for a 10% wage increase.

II In the sentences above indicate the gap left by *wh*-movement by means of dashes, and label the original position.

4.2.5 INDIRECT QUESTIONS

4.2.5.1 Indirect Yes-No Questions

We have seen that questions may be direct or indirect; text 2.2.2.A, for example, contains the following indirect question (italicised):

(68) One evening he asked her *whether he might go home with her.*

Let us look at the structure of (68). First, we note that the phrase *one evening* has been fronted. It is an Adjunct, whose normal position we have assumed is after *He asked her* (or even at the end of the sentence):

(69) He asked her one evening whether he might go home with her.

(70) He asked her whether he might go home with her one evening. (ambiguous)

Bracketing (69) for main clause constituents yields the following:

(71) $[_{S}\underset{Su}{[_{NP}}\text{He}]\ [_{VP}\text{asked}\ \underset{Oi}{[_{NP}}\text{her}]\ \underset{A}{[_{PP}}\text{one evening}]$
$\underset{Od}{[_{\bar{S}}}\ \text{whether he might go home with her}]]]$

The constituent *whether he might go home with her* is an Object clause: it is the Direct Object of *asked.* In 2.3 we have argued that *whether* (like *that* or *if*) occupies the COMP slot in $\bar{S}$:

(72a) He said $\left[_{\bar{S}}\left[_{COMP}\text{that}\right]\left[_{S}\ldots\ \right]\right]$

(72b) He asked her $\left[_{\bar{S}}\left[_{COMP}\text{if}\right]\left[_{S}\ldots\ \right]\right]$

(72c) He asked her $\left[_{\bar{S}}\left[_{COMP}\text{whether}\right]\left[_{S}\ldots\ \right]\right]$

Unlike *that,* the complementisers *whether* and *if* indicate that the subordinate clause is a question. *Whether* and *if* cannot be deleted.

Indirect questions (i.e. subordinate clauses) introduced by *whether* or *if* correspond to direct questions of the *Yes-No* type. Compare:

(73a) He asked her: 'May I go home with you?'

(73b) He asked her $\left\{\begin{array}{l}\text{whether}\\ \text{if}\end{array}\right\}$ he might go home with her.

In 4.2.2 we have seen that direct *Yes-No* questions undergo SAI. Indirect *Yes-No* questions, on the other hand, are not subject to SAI. Consider:

(74) $\ldots\left[\left[_{COMP}\text{whether}\left[_{Su}\text{he}\right]\left[_{Aux}\text{might}\right]\text{go home with her}\right]\right]$

The normal Su–Aux word order is preserved here, and the presence of the complementiser (*whether* or *if*) signals that the subordinate clause is a question.

4.2.5.2 Indirect *Wh*-questions

Text 4.2.3.1, as we have seen, contains the following complex sentence:

(75) Do you know *what happens when one of your tail lights fails*?

The italicised string is an indirect *wh*-question, corresponding to the direct question:

(76) What happens when one of your tail lights fails?

How do we form structures with indirect *wh*-questions? Let us assume that we start from the basic sentence patterns as described in 3.4.7. Assume that we have a sentence such as:

(77) Mary wondered: 'What is John doing?'

The string with quotation marks is an example of direct speech or thought: we report Mary's thoughts or words directly. However, we may also decide to report them indirectly by means of an embedded sentence:

(78) Mary wondered what John was doing.

Underlying this example we shall assume the basic pattern:

(79) Mary wondered $[_{\bar{S}}[_{COMP}]\,[_{S}\text{John}\,[_{VP}\text{was doing}\,[_{NP}\text{what}]]]]$

where the NP *what* is the Direct Object and follows the verb *do*. As you see, the COMP slot is left unfilled here. The *wh*-phrase which we find inside the subordinate clause in (79) is moved out of S into COMP:

(80) Mary wondered $[_{\bar{S}}[_{COMP}\text{what}]\,[_{S}\text{John}\,[_{VP}\text{was doing}\,[_{NP}\text{- - -}]]]]$

Wh-movement leaves behind a gap bound by the moved element in COMP. With direct questions, as we have seen, *wh*-movement is followed by SAI. There is no SAI in embedded *wh*-questions; remember that there was no SAI in embedded *Yes-No* questions either.

Explain what we mean by saying that in examples like (75) *wh*-movement applies 'vacuously' (cf. 4.2.4). Provide the analysis of (75), and indicate the difference between (75) and (78).

We have seen now that *wh*-movement and SAI may be used together to form *wh*-questions, but SAI and *wh*-movement can also occur independently: they are elementary operations which are not necessarily linked. For example, SAI occurs on its own in:

Yes-No questions: *Did you measure it?*

Declarative sentences with fronted negative Adjuncts: *Never had he felt so happy.*

Wh-movement occurs without SAI in:

Indirect questions: *She wondered what he was doing.*

Exclamations: *What fools they have been*!

Note that neither *wh*-movement nor SAI is necessarily linked with question formation: SAI occurs with fronted negative Adjuncts in declaratives and *wh*-movement occurs with exclamations.

4.2.5.3 Long *Wh*-movement

Let us look at the sentence:

(81) Who do they think is spying on them all the time?

This is, of course, a *wh*-question. *Wh*-movement has put the *wh*-word in front position. Where does *who* come from? Obviously, it is not the Subject of the main clause: *they* is the Subject NP of the *think*-clause. Underlying the sentence we assume the basic pattern (82) below:

(82) They think $\left[_{\bar{S}}\left[_{COMP}\right]\left[_{S}\text{who is spying on them all the time}\right]\right]$

The clause *(that) who is spying on them all the time* is subordinate; it is an Object clause of *think*. *Wh*-movement again takes out *who* and moves it first to the COMP of the embedded clause ($\bar{S}$), and then in a second move to a COMP slot in front of the main clause:

(83) $\left[_{COMP}\text{Who}\right]\left[\text{do they think}\left[_{\bar{S}}\left[_{COMP}\right]\right.\right.$

$\left.\left.\left[\text{--- is spying on them all the time}\right]\right]\right]$

As you see, the fronting of *who* also triggers SAI (with *do*-insertion) in the main clause: *they think* becomes *do they think.*

Examples (84)–(87) below are further instances of long *wh*-movement: the dashes locate the vacated position (the gap bound by the *wh*-phrase):

(84) *Who* did John say he met --- on the bus?

(85) *Who* did Mary tell you she had seen --- on the train?

(86) *Who* did Bill say --- was asking for me the other day?

(87) *At what time* do they think the taxi will reach the airport ---?

Long *wh*-movement as in the sentences above need not be restricted to only one clause-leap: the *wh*-element may move over more than one clause:

(88) *Who* did John say that Bill thought that Mary wanted to see ---?

Here are some further examples of long *wh*-movement, in which you are asked to signal the gap by dashes:

(89) Where did you say Bill had found the book?

(90) Can you ask Iris who she thinks will arrive first?

4.2.6 RELATIVE CLAUSES

Read the text below. First identify questions: are there any *Yes-No* questions? And *wh*-questions? Locate the gap corresponding to the *wh*-word. You will find several examples of subordinate clauses introduced by a *wh*-word which are not questions, but relative clauses (see 2.4.2.4).

Text 4.2.6
The day on which Lawlessness reared its ugly head at Blandings Castle was one of singular beauty. The sun shone down from a sky of corn-flower blue, and what one would really like would be to describe in

> leisurely detail the smooth green lawns on which it shone.
>
> But those who read thrillers are an impatient race. They chafe at scenic rhapsodies and want to get on to the rough stuff. They ask: when did the dirty work start? Who were mixed up in it? Was there blood? How much blood was there? And most particularly: where was everybody and what was everybody doing at the time of the crime?
>
> The chronicler who wishes to grip his audience must supply this information at the earliest possible moment.
>
> The wave of crime which was to rock one of Shropshire's stateliest homes to its foundations broke out towards the middle of a fine summer afternoon, and the persons whom it involved were all living there at the time.
>
> Adapted from P.G. Wodehouse, *Lord Emsworth and Others.*

The NPs listed below all contain a postmodifying (or relative) clause and are thus complex: the GF of Postmodifier is realised by a clause:

(91) The day *on which Lawlessness reared its ugly head at Blandings Castle*

(92) The smooth green lawns *on which it shone*

(93) Those *who read thrillers*

(94) The chronicler *who wishes to grip his audience*

(95) The wave of crime *which was to rock one of Shropshire's stateliest homes to its foundations*

(96) The persons *whom it involved*

We have seen (2.4.2.5) that complex NPs have the following structure:

Category	Det	AdjP	N	$\overline{\text{S}}$
Function	Spec	Premod	Head	Postmod
	The The	handsome German	policeman girl	who directed us to the station who gave me this book

The NPs (91)–(96) above all have the same structure as *The German girl who gave me this book.* The Head noun *girl* is postmodified by an $\overline{\text{S}}$: *who gave me this book.* Analyse (91)–(96) according to this pattern.

In each case the Postmodifer is realised by an $\overline{\text{S}}$ consisting of a *wh*-phrase followed by a sentence with a matching gap.

Superficially, the pattern of the postmodifying $\overline{S}$ is similar, but not quite identical, to that of indirect *wh*-questions (see 4.2.5.2). Compare:

(97) I wonder *who(m) John talked to.*

(98) the girl *who(m) John talked to*

On the analogy of *wh*-questions, we assume that (98) has the following underlying structure:

(99) $\left[_{NP}\text{The girl} \left[_{\overline{S}} \left[_{COMP}\ \right] \left[_{S}\text{John talked to whom}\right]\right]\right]$

The element *whom* is moved to the COMP slot in front of S, and *to* is stranded:

(100) $\left[_{NP}\text{The girl} \left[_{\overline{S}} \left[_{COMP}\text{whom}\right] \left[_{S}\text{John talked to ---}\right]\right]\right]$

Whom binds the gap at the site of extraction ---. Note that *wh*-movement is obligatory. The presence of a *wh*-word inside an NP always triggers *wh*-movement: **the girl John talked to whom* is ungrammatical. It is also important to observe that SAI does not operate inside postmodifying clauses.

In *wh*-question formation, as we have seen, there is a choice with respect to the movement of *wh*-PPs: one can either strand the P and extract the NP only, or one can pied-pipe the P. In the example above we have stranded the P; we could also have pied-piped. Compare:

(101) I wonder *to whom John talked.*

(102) the girl *to whom John talked*

Apply *wh*-movement to the italicised *wh*-words in the sentences below. Apply pied-piping whenever necessary (—— indicates COMP):

(103) the house —— John lives in *which*

(104) the book —— Sue is waiting for *which*

(105) the girl —— John is in love with *whom*

In (103)–(105) above pied-piping is optional. Consider now the following NPs:

(106) the woman —— I live in whose house

(107) the man —— I met whose daughter for the first time last year

(108) the cathedral —— the cardinal was murdered on the steps of which

How should *wh*-movement be carried out here? Pied-piping is obligatory in this case, for we cannot just move *whose*, *which*, etc. here. For example:

(109) *the woman *whose* I live in --- house

We must pied-pipe in one of the following two ways:

(110) the woman *in whose house* I live ---

(111) the woman *whose house* I live in ---

What is the difference between (110) and (111)?

Our discussion so far has shown that the same transformation of *wh*-movement can be applied to form both *wh*-questions and postmodifying clauses in NPs. We have seen that as far as pied-piping is concerned, *wh*-movement inside complex NPs mirrors exactly that in *wh*-questions.

As in the case of *wh*-questions, we shall assume that *wh*-movement also operates on Subject *wh*-phrases, although there is no obvious gap in the surface structure: it operates vacuously. On the analogy of *wh*-questions, we shall assume that the underlying structure (112) below becomes (113), as a result of *wh*-movement in the NP:

(112) $\big[_{NP}\text{the man}\ \big[_{\overline{S}}\big[_{COMP}\big]\ \big[_{S}\big[_{NP}\text{who}\big]\ \text{carried the gun}\big]\big]\big]$

(113) $\big[_{NP}\text{the man}\ \big[_{\overline{S}}\big[_{COMP}\text{who}\big]\ \big[_{S}\big[_{NP}\text{---}\big]\ \text{carried the gun}\big]\big]\big]$

We have seen that the postmodifying $\overline{S}$ in a complex NP is linked to the Head N by a *wh*-word. The *wh*-words which relate the subordinate clause and the Head, are relative pronouns. The relative pronoun in front of S is said to bind a gap inside the relative clause.

4.2.6.1 Exercise

The following underlying NP structures are 'ready for *wh*-movement'.

(a) Find the *wh*-phrase, bracket it and label it (both the category and the GF).
(b) Move it and indicate the site of the gap by dashes ---. Use an arrow to mark the *binding* relationship.

(1) The report $\big[_{\overline{S}}\big[_{COMP}\big]\ \big[_{S}\text{John wrote which}\big]\big]$

(2) The rumour $\big[_{\overline{S}}\big[_{COMP}\big]\ \big[_{S}\text{the demonstrators spread which in town}\big]\big]$

(3) The stories $\big[_{\overline{S}}\big[_{COMP}\big]\ \big[_{S}\text{John told me which last night}\big]\big]$

(4) The man $\big[_{\overline{S}}\big[_{COMP}\big]\ \big[_{S}\text{I was watching whom yesterday}\big]\big]$

(5) The girls $\big[_{\overline{S}}\big[_{COMP}\big]\ \big[_{S}\text{Eric fancies whom}\big]\big]$

4.2.6.2 The Meaning of Relative Clauses

Postmodifying (relative) clauses may help to identify the referent of the

Head noun: they may narrow down the reference of the Head. For example, in: *the man who lives next door*, the relative clause *who lives next door* indicates who exactly the speaker is talking about. The clause provides information that is essential for the identification of the referent. Relative clauses of this kind are necessary if it is not clear from the context who the speaker is referring to. They are said to be **restrictive**. Here are some additional examples of restrictive relative clauses (italicised):

(114) What is the name of the film *which is now showing at the ABC*?

(115) The books *which I ordered* have finally arrived.

(116) The man *who saw the accident* was not prepared to testify.

See also examples (91)–(96), (98), (103)–(108), etc.

Relative clauses may also be **non-restrictive**, as in:

(117) The Pope, who was expected to visit Poland again this summer, decided to go to France instead.

Clauses of this kind are said to be non-restrictive because no further identification of the referent (the Pope, in this case) is needed. These modifying clauses provide additional, non-essential information about the Head of the NP. We shall turn to non-restrictive clauses in 4.2.6.6 below.

It is worth noting that the distinction between restrictive and non-restrictive relative clauses also applies to other types of postmodification and premodification.

4.2.6.3 Deletion in Relative Clauses

Consider:

(118) The film which we saw at the ABC last week has been banned from all official programmes.

(119) The man whom you see over there is the owner of the company.

The relative pronoun in these sentences can be deleted. We shall use the symbol Ø to mark the deleted element, and call it the **zero** relative pronoun:

(120) The film Ø we saw at the ABC last week has been banned ...

Deletion of the *wh*-word is impossible:

(a) if it functions as the Subject of the embedded sentence, e.g.:

(121a) The man who is standing over there is the Prime Minister of Pakistan.

(121b) *The man Ø is standing over there is the Prime Minister of Pakistan.

(b) if it is preceded by a preposition, e.g.:

(122a) The man for whom we were all waiting did not come.

(122b) *The man for Ø we were all waiting did not come.

Compare:

(123) The man $\left\{\begin{matrix}\text{whom}\\ \text{Ø}\end{matrix}\right\}$ we were all waiting for --- did not come.

If the preposition is stranded, the moved *wh*-word on its own can be deleted.

Notice the use of the zero relative pronoun in Subject position in structures of the type: *There is a gentleman at the door Ø wishes to see you* (cf. 4.4.3) and of the type: *It is Jane Ø gave the book to Bill* (cf. 4.5.1).

4.2.6.4 *That* in Relative Clauses

One also often finds the complementiser *that* instead of *who(m)* or *which* at the beginning of restrictive relative clauses. Consider, for example:

(124) The young girl that plays the violin so well is Egyptian.

(125) The man that we liked so much turned out to be a real crook.

The GF of Postmodifier is realised by an embedded clause preceded by *that*:

(126) $[_{\bar{S}}\text{that } [_{S}\text{plays the violin so well}]]$

(127) $[_{\bar{S}}\text{that } [_{S}\text{we liked so much}]]$

The sentence (S) together with *that* is an $\bar{S}$. There is a great deal of similarity between these Ss and restrictive relative clauses. For example:

(a) both occur inside an NP,
(b) both are restrictive Postmodifiers to the Head,
(c) in both cases there is a gap inside the S, e.g.:

(128) $\left[_{NP}\text{the man}\left[\left\{\begin{matrix}\text{that}\\ \text{who(m)}\\ \text{Ø}\end{matrix}\right\}\left[_{S}\text{we liked --- so much}\right]\right]\right]$

that, *who(m)* and zero are thus largely interchangeable, except that for stylistic reasons *who(m)* may be preferred. We assume, then, that the complementiser *that* here also links the Head noun and the embedded S. Since in other languages and in Middle English one can also find strings of a *wh*-word followed by *that* (literally, for example:

(129) The dog which that we saw yesterday

and not the reverse), we shall assume that the COMP slot has two positions:

(130)	(a)	+WH	(b)	*that*

COMP is thus reserved for *wh*-elements (a) and for complementisers (b).

To form a relative clause we now have quite a few options. Take the following underlying structure:

(131) The woman $\left[_{\bar{S}}\left[_{\text{COMP}}\text{(a)}\quad\text{(b)}\right]\left[_{S}\text{we invited whom to our party}\right]\right]$

Move *whom* to position (a) in COMP:

(132) The woman whom (b) we invited --- to our party.

We may delete *whom*:

(133) The woman Ø (b) we invited --- to our party.

We may also insert the complementiser *that* at position (b) in COMP:

(134) The woman (a) that we invited --- to our party.

In present-day English, sentences like (129) are ungrammatical. Modern English has a rule that the COMP slot may be filled by one element only, either a *wh*-word or the complementiser *that*.

4.2.6.5 Adverbial Relative and Free Relative Clauses

The relative clauses below (italicised) also contain *wh*-elements. Identify the *wh*-elements, find the gap in each embedded S, and determine the function of the moved *wh*-element:

(135) This is the village *where I spent my youth.*

(136) Did they tell you the reason *why they all left*?

Relative clauses introduced by *where, why, when,* etc. are called **adverbial relative clauses.**

In some cases, the Head noun seems to merge with the *wh*-word or *that* into one element.

(137) $\left\{\begin{array}{l}\text{Any person who}\\\text{Whoever}\end{array}\right\}$ knows him hates him.

(138) I shall give you $\left\{\begin{array}{l}\text{anything that}\\\text{what}\\\text{whatever}\end{array}\right\}$ you want.

Relative clauses like these, which lack a real Head noun, are called *free relative clauses.* In structure these clauses resemble full NPs consisting of an empty Head noun and a postmodifying clause. For example, *whatever you want* may be analysed as follows:

(139) $[_{NP}\emptyset\ [_{\bar{S}}\text{whatever}\ [_{S}\text{you want}\ ---]]]$

4.2.6.6 Non-restrictive Relative Clauses

Consider now the following sentences:

(140) The Pope, who was expected to visit Poland again this summer, decided to go to France instead.

(141) This car, which I bought only two years ago, is already beginning to show signs of disrepair.

Bracket the NPs with relative clauses, and underline the Head nouns.

The postmodifying clauses above do not restrict the reference of the Head noun. Thus, the clause *who was expected to visit Poland again this summer* is not meant to identify the Pope, since the reference is sufficiently clear. Under normal circumstances, there can be hardly any misunderstanding between speaker and hearer about the identity of the referent.

The above relative clauses are said to be **non-restrictive** (see 4.2.6.2). They provide extra, non-essential information, and can be left out without changing or obscuring the reference of the Head.

In non-restrictive relative clauses deletion of the relative pronoun is not possible:

(142) *The Pope, Ø was expected to visit Poland again this summer, ...

Nor does the complementiser *that* normally occur here:

(143) *The Pope, that was expected to visit Poland again this summer, ...

The intonation of non-restrictive clauses is different from that used for restrictive clauses. In print, non-restrictive relative clauses are usually marked off (preceded *and* followed) by commas.

4.2.6.7 Exercises

I Insert a restrictive relative clause into the following (incomplete) sentences. The clauses should postmodify the italicised Head nouns:

(1) The *girl* is my sister
(2) I have never met a *student*
(3) I thought you knew the *woman*
(4) She always enjoys reading *novels*
(5) I never trust *men*
(6) I hate *people*
(7) *Politicians* are liars
(8) The *professor* is now in jail

II Consider the following examples of complex NPs containing restrictive relative clauses:

(1) The man {who(m) / *which / that / Ø} we saw

(2) The book {*who(m) / which / that / Ø} I read last night

(3) The man {who / *whom / *which / that / *Ø} came to dinner

(4) The book {*who(m) / which / that / *Ø} deals with this problem

(5) The man for {whom / *who / *which / *that / *Ø} we are looking

(6) The man {who(m) / *which / that / Ø} we are looking for

(7) The book for {*who(m) / which / *that / *Ø} we are looking

(8) The book {*who(m) / which / that / Ø} we are looking for

On the basis of examples like those above, devise a set of rules which adequately describes the use of *who, whom, which, that* and *zero* in English restrictive relative clauses. Try and formulate your rules in terms of the contrasts [+Human]/[−Human], [+Subject]/[−Subject] and [+ immediately preceded by P]/[− immediately preceded by P].

III Discuss the difference in structure between the two complex NPs in the sentences below (italicised):

(1) We look forward to *the day when we can stop working for that idiot.*
(2) I shall follow you *wherever you go.*

4.2.7 APPOSITIVE CLAUSES

Consider the following sentences containing complex NPs:

(144) The news that John had left his wife came as a shock to us all.

(145) The rumour that the Princess of Wales is pregnant again has not been confirmed by Court officials.

(146) The story that Bill met Anne secretly behind the chemistry building has been made up from beginning to end.

(147) The fact that the Prime Minister was involved in a drugs scandal was an embarrassment to the Government.

(148) The assumption that John is coming back soon seems unfounded.

What is the structure of the above NPs?

Superficially, the complex NPs in the above sentences have the following structure:

Spec	H	Postmodifier $\overline{S}$ (= *that* + S)
the	news	$[_{\overline{S}}$that $[_{S}$John had left his wife$]]$

Analyse (145)–(148) in the same way.

Is the postmodifying clause a relative clause? We have said that relative clauses are preceded by a relative pronoun which binds the gap inside the relative clause, and we have said that the function of linking the Head and the embedded S may also be fulfilled by *that*. For example:

(149) the man {who(m) / Ø / that} you saw --- there

Can you locate similar gaps in (144)–(148)? You will find that the answer is: No. Compare these examples with those in (150)–(154) below:

(150) The news that John told his wife gave her a shock.

(151) The rumour that Anne spread in town was terrible.

(152) The story that Mr Adams wrote for his children has recently been published in a collection.

(153) The news that the Prime Minister gave the reporters did not surprise anyone.

(154) The assumption that he bases his theory on may be false.

In (150)–(154) we find the expected gap in the embedded S, while in (144)–(148) there is no gap. We must conclude, then, that (144)–(148) are not relative clauses. What are they?

Consider the Heads of the Subject NPs in (144)–(148): in some of the examples the Head noun relates to a verb (*report*); in other cases it has something to do with 'messages' (*news, story, . . .*), i.e. communication. In fact, the *that*-clause gives the content of the communication. For (144), for example, the news was: 'John has left his wife'. Paraphrase (145)–(148) in the same way.

Note that *which* cannot replace *that* here, and that *that* fulfils no grammatical function (e.g. Subject or Object) in the clause; moreover, *that* is obligatory here and this use of *that* can also occur before *non-restrictive* clauses (e.g. *Your assumption, that there is no life on other planets, is unfounded*). In all these respects, the *that*-clauses in (144)–(148) differ from relative *that*-clauses. *That*-clauses like those in (144)–(148), which give the content of nouns such as *fact, report, news*, etc., are called **appositive clauses**. Appositive clauses may also be introduced by the complementiser *whether* (e.g. *I have no idea whether they will appreciate our help*).

4.2.7.1 Exercises

I Add a restrictive or non-restrictive appositive clause to the italicised Head Ns below. Then bracket the NPs.

(1) The *belief* was unfounded.
(2) The *fact* speaks for itself.
(3) Her *announcement* distressed him very much.
(4) The *claim* was later shown to be false.
(5) The *theory* is difficult to accept.
(6) He was given a *warning*.

II Identify relative clauses and appositive clauses in the following sentences.

(1) The money that John left his wife came in very useful.
(2) The idea that John has left home for good is depressing.
(3) The theory that men are superior to women is blatantly false.
(4) The fact that Julia is Irish is apparent the moment one sees her.
(5) The story that John told his friends surprised many of them.
(6) Mary herself spread the rumour that she was pregnant.
(7) Where did I put the letter that I received last week?
(8) How did she react to the message that she had inherited a fortune?
(9) He has an intriguing theory that the dinosaurs were wiped out by their young.
(10) I have no idea whether this is true.

Sum up the differences between relative clauses and appositive clauses.

III The NPs in *my neighbour John* are said to be appositive NPs. How would you define an appositive relationship? Is the relationship between the NPs *my neighbour* and *John* restrictive or non-restrictive? And what about *the Prime Minister, Mrs Thatcher*?

4.2.8 REDUCED RELATIVE CLAUSES

(155) The first man to arrive at the place of the crime was our local police officer.

(156) The last man to talk to in such circumstances is your father.

(157) I want a tool to fix the sink with.

(158) We all want a decent place to live in.

(159) The first train to leave from platform 3 is the 6.03 for Reading.

Bracket NPs in these sentences and determine their GF in the sentence. The structure of these NPs is as follows:

Spec	Premod	H	Postmod
the first		man	to arrive at the place of the crime
a	decent	place	to live in

The *to*-constructions above serve as Postmodifiers and can be changed into full relative clauses, e.g.:

(160) The first man who arrived at the place of the crime . . .

The *to*-constructions used in (155)–(159) are called **reduced relative clauses**. Expand (156)–(159) into full relative clauses.

Full relative clauses, introduced by *who*, *which*, etc., are finite. The postmodifying strings in (155)–(159), on the other hand, are non-finite (*to*-infinitive) clauses.

Reduced relative clauses may also have an *–ing* or *–ed* VP:

(161) The train arriving at platform 7 is the 7.03 from Reading.

(162) The guy wearing those odd clothes is Jane's husband.

(163) None of the guests invited by John turned up.

(164) Essays handed in after 1st July will not be marked until the beginning of next term.

The non-finite clauses above are restrictive. Here are two examples of non-restrictive non-finite clauses:

(165) The Pope, warned not to go to Poland, decided to visit France instead.

(166) The Princess of Wales, haunted by the press, found it more and more difficult to lead a normal life.

Let us now consider the structure of reduced relative clauses in more detail. We find that certain syntactic positions which in full relative clauses are usually occupied by lexical material are left empty in reduced relative clauses, i.e. not filled by overt lexical material. Compare, for example, (155) with its full version (155a):

(155) The first man to arrive at the place of the crime ...

(155a) The first man who arrived at the place of the crime ...

The underlying structure of (155a) is as follows:

(a) before *wh*-movement:

(155b) $[_{NP}$ the first man $[_{\bar{S}}$ COMP $[_{S}$ who $[_{VP}$ arrived ...]]]]

(b) after *wh*-movement of the NP/Su:

(155c) $[_{NP}$ the first man $[_{\bar{S}}$ who $[_{S}$ --- $[_{VP}$ arrived ...]]]]

The gap --- is bound by the moved *wh*-word (*who*).

For the reduced clause (155) we shall assume an analogous underlying structure, but instead of a finite VP there is a non-finite VP:

(a) before *wh*-movement:

(155d) $[_{NP}$ the first man $[_{\bar{S}}$ COMP $[_{S_{to}}$ Ø $[_{VP}$ to arrive ...]]]]

(b) after *wh*-movement:

(155e) the first man $[_{\bar{S}}$ $Ø_{COMP}$ $[_{S_{to}}$ --- $[_{VP}$ to arrive ...]]]]

(155) differs only minimally from (155a):

(1) the VP in (155) is non-finite, that in (155a) is finite
(2) the Subject *wh*-word in (155a) is an overt element (*who*), that in (155) is non-overt, i.e. not lexically realised and here indicated by Ø. We assume now that the overt *wh*-word as well as the non-overt element Ø move from the Subject position into COMP, leaving a gap ---.

Now let us consider (156). Here, too, we may try to base the structure of (156) on the analogy with its finite full version:

(156a) The last man that you should talk to in such circumstances ...

It is immediately clear that there is a gap inside both (156) and (156a) and that the preposition *to* is stranded: $[_{PP}$ to ---].

In (156a) the complementiser *that* (in COMP) binds the gap and relates the relative clause to the Head N; in (156) there is no overt element in COMP. Let us thus assume that again there is a non-overt element Ø in COMP.

However there is another problem now. What is the Subject of the relative clause in (156a)? Clearly, it is *you*. In (156) the non-finite relative clause lacks an overt Subject, but we may interpret the Subject as referring, for example, to *you*, as represented in (156b):

(156b) The last man $\left[_{\overline{S}}\text{for}\left[_{S}\textit{you}\text{ to talk to}\right]\right]$

We shall thus have to say that (156) also has a non-overt Subject, which we shall indicate by (   ).

We assume then that before *wh*-movement (156) has the structure:

$$\text{(156c)}\quad \left[_{NP}\ \text{the last man}\ \left[_{\overline{S}}\ \underset{COMP}{\text{for}}\ \left[_{S_{to}}\ (\quad)\ \left[\text{to talk to } \emptyset\right]\right]\right]\right]$$

and that *wh*-movement moves the non-overt element Ø into COMP:

$$\text{(156d)}\quad \left[_{NP}\ \text{the last man}\ \left[_{\overline{S}}\ \underset{COMP}{\emptyset\ \ \text{for}}\ \left[_{S_{to}}\ (\quad)\ \left[\text{to talk to } ---\right]\right]\right]\right]$$

In English, the sequence *for* ... *to* is ungrammatical; *for* must be deleted. Essentially the reduced relative clause in (156) thus has a non-overt Subject as well as a non-overt relative element in COMP (after movement) indicated by Ø, which binds a gap indicated by ---. See Chapter 5.

All these non-overt positions are assumed on the basis of corresponding overt positions in other parallel clauses. Try to analyse (157)–(159) in the same way; you will find that (157) and (158) pattern like (156), while (159) is more like (155).

4.2.8.1 Exercises

I Analyse the following sentences in the same way as sentences (155) and (156) above:

(1) I'm looking for a place to stay over Christmas.
(2) My new pet was the most revolting bird to look at.
(3) This is a difficult problem to solve.
(4) The question for all of us to consider now is whether we can afford such expenses.

II Read the following text carefully. It contains several instances of Complex NPs. Try to identify the following types:

(a) NPs with restrictive relative clauses, e.g.:

The girl who John met on the train last week

(b) NPs with non-restrictive relative clauses, e.g.:

The Pope, who was expected to visit Poland this summer

(c) NPs with oppositive clauses, e.g.:

The news that John and Susan had split up

(d) NPs with reduced relative clauses, e.g.:

The girl wearing the green skirt

In the case of relative clauses locate the gap corresponding to the *wh*-word. What is the GF of the *wh*-phrase?

Text 4.2.8.1

In Ms Segal's article 'Even Accountants Will Buy It', which you published on February 8, Durham is quoted as one of a group of universities who 'expect you to concentrate on one or perhaps two subjects from the day on which you start there until your final exams'.

This is inaccurate and profoundly misleading. Quite apart from the fact that Durham offers the degree of BA in General Studies, which is a three subject degree in all three years, and the BSc in Natural Sciences, involving over three years a minimum of three and a maximum of five subjects, a high proportion of other degree courses offered by Durham make it possible for candidates to include more than two subjects in their degree courses. To give but one further example, candidates taking honours courses in the Social Sciences have to read three different subjects in their first year.

There is considerable flexibility within the Durham system for changes in courses after the end of the first year. Indeed about 20 per cent of candidates graduate with a degree whose title is different from the one for which they first registered on entry.

Adapted from *Guardian*, 22 February 1983, p. 15.

4.2.9 FRONTING

So far we have seen that auxiliaries, tense and *wh*-phrases may be moved leftwards. However, other constituents may also be preposed. For example:

(167) Soon after breakfast Mary Ann brought in The Times.

Soon after breakfast has been fronted: it is a PP/A.

(168) Mary Ann $\left[_{VP}\right.$brought in The Times $\left[_{PP}\right.$ soon after breakfast$\left.\right]\left.\right]$

Compare also:

(169a) I have never before met a man like John.

(169b) Never before have I met a man like John.

Fronting of *never before* in this case triggers SAI.

Particles of phrasal verbs (170) and PPs (171) may also be fronted (see Chapter 6). For example:

(170) He came out.

(171) Out he came.

(171a) He walked into the garage.

(171b) Into the garage he walked.

4.2.9.1 Exercise

Identify fronted constituents in the following text. Restore them to their original position.

Text 4.2.9.1
The next moment, the little man's companion was hitting him with her umbrella. Somebody in the row behind jumped on his back. And in about a quarter of a minute the action had become general. I could see a sort of confused blur, with the voice of the Battler proceeding from the middle of it; commissionaires and others began to arrive, and policemen in bevies, and all was over.

Next day, the Battler was hauled up before the majesty of the law and sentenced to fourteen days in the coop without the option. On the morning of the fifteenth day I was waiting at the prison gates, and out he came, trained to a hair.

Adapted from P.G. Wodehouse, *Lord Emsworth and Others.*

4.3 PASSIVISATION

4.3.1 THE PROCESS

Read the following text. Bracket the major constituents in each sentence, and underline the Head of the VP. Assign GFs.

Text 4.3.1
The eating habits of the Indo-Pakistan sub-continent are influenced by historical and geographical factors. Since the earliest times the sub-continent has been invaded by many tribes from the North. Later on it was occupied by the British. Only recently was the region divided into the two independent countries of India and Pakistan.

The influence of all the different invasions can be found in the culture and the eating habits of the sub-continent. Indian and Pakistani food are very similar, but regional and religious influences can be observed. The consumption of beef is forbidden to the Hindu, and the consumption of pork is not allowed for Muslims.

The art of the presentation of food was also developed in these countries. Silver or gold leaf is often used for decoration. The metal is beaten very fine: it can almost be blown away.

Nowadays Indian food is esteemed all over the world.

Adapted from A. Hosain and S. Pasricha, *Cooking the Indian Way.*

This text contains several instances of passive sentences. Passive sentences have the following pattern:

(1) $[_{S} [_{NP}] [_{VP} \textit{be}\ \text{V}-\textit{ed}\ [_{PP} \text{by} \ldots]]]$

For example:

(2) $[_S[_{NP}$The eating habits of the Indo-Pakistan sub-continent$]$

$[_{VP}$are influenced $[_{PP}$by historical and geographical factors$]]]$

(3) $[_S[_{PP}$Since the earliest times$]$ $[_{NP}$the sub-continent$]$

$[_{VP}$has been invaded$[_{PP}$by many tribes . . .$]]]$

Identify other passive sentences in text 4.3.1.

Normally a **passive** sentence has a corresponding **active** sentence. The active sentence is seen as the underlying structure, from which the passive sentence is derived. The active sentence corresponding to (2), for example, is (4):

(4) $[_S[_{NP}$Historical and geographical factors$]$ $[_{VP}$influence

$[_{NP}$the eating habits of the Indo-Pakistan sub-continent$]]]$

Sentence (4) contains a transitive V (*influence*), which requires as its Complement an NP functioning as Od. The structure of the sentence is: NP/Su[V–NP/Od].

If we compare the passive sentences from text 4.3.1 with their active counterparts, we see that the active strings contain an Object NP. The process of passivisation crucially involves moving the Object NP (Od or Oi) from the active VP into the Subject position. Consider also:

(5a) The gardener takes the newspaper to Mr Ellis.

(5b) The newspaper is taken to Mr Ellis by the gardener.

Bracket the Subject and the Object NP in (5a). Now bracket (5b). If we compare (5a) and (5b), we find that the Object of (5a), *the newspaper*, is moved to the left, and ends up in Subject position in (5b). The Object NP is assumed to leave a gap --- in the underlying active sentence after passivisation. Since this gap is not relevant to our discussion, we shall simplify matters and avoid reference to it here. In order to verify the Subject status of the NP *the newspaper* in (5b) we can apply various tests, including the agreement test (a) and the SAI test (b):

(6a) *The newspapers are* taken . . .

(6b) *Is the newspaper* taken . . .?

The tests confirm that in (5b) *the newspaper* is the NP/Su.

The shift of the Object NP into Subject position is accompanied by another operation: the Subject of the active sentence is removed from its original position and may end up as the Agent *by*-phrase in the passive sentence: *by the gardener* (very often the Agent *by*-phrase is deleted).

In the active sentence (5a) the role of Agent is assigned to the Subject NP. In the passive sentence (5b) the Agent role is assigned to the *by*-phrase.

In addition, passivisation converts *takes* into *is taken*: the auxiliary *be* is added and the verb is changed into a past participle. The change from active to passive verb form may be represented as follows:

(7a) present–take : *takes*

(7b) present–be–taken: *is taken*

Schematically passivisation works as follows:

(8a) $[_S[_{NP}\text{The gardener}][_{VP}\text{takes}[_{NP}\text{the newspaper}][_{PP}\text{to Mr Ellis}]]]$

(8b) $[_S[_{NP}\text{The newspaper}][_{VP}\text{is taken}[_{NP}\text{to Mr Ellis}][_{PP}\textit{by}\text{ the gardener}]]]$

or more abstractly:

(9a) active: $[_S[_{Su}NP_1][_{VP}V\,[_{Od}NP_2]]]$

(9b) passive: $[_S[_{NP_2}][_{VP}\textit{be}\ V\text{–}\textit{ed}\,[_{PP}\textit{by}\,[_{NP_1}]]]]$

4.3.2 THE *BY*-PHRASE

Consider again the last sentence of the first paragraph of text 4.3.1:

(10) Only recently was the region divided into the two independent countries of India and Pakistan.

Only recently is a fronted AdvP, originating in VP. The fronting has given rise to SAI. Compare the word order of (10) with that of (11):

(11) The region was divided into the two independent countries only recently.

Bracket the main constituents of (11) and assign GFs. Try to restore (11) to the active. At first sight, this seems impossible, since there is no *by*-phrase in (11). We get something like (12), which is ungrammatical:

(12) *– – – divided the region into the two independent countries only recently.

The Agent of the action denoted by the verb (*divide*) is not explicitly mentioned, although in this case we know that the 'understood' Agent is probably something like *The British Government*, etc. (cf. the Indian Independence Act, 1947). Sentence (12) requires an explicit Subject (cf. the PS rule: S ⟶ NP–VP), otherwise it will be ungrammatical. If one does not know precisely who the Agent of the activity is, or if it is irrelevant or unnecessary to specify who performed the activity, one may choose to use a passive sentence, since in passives the Agent *by*-phrase is optional. Passivisation allows us to suppress the Agent. Read through text 4.3.1 once more, and determine whether all passive sentences contain an Agent *by*-phrase.

Very often the effect of passivisation is that the text becomes more impersonal and formal. *Agent-less* passives are especially characteristic of the style of official documents, textbooks, scientific articles, instructions, rules, etc. Examples:

(13) You are hereby given leave to enter the United Kingdom for six months.

(14) Bicycles must not be left in front of the building.

(15) Smoking in this room is prohibited.

(16) Contributions are welcomed from linguists in all countries, and not merely from members of the Linguistics Association of Great Britain.

4.3.3 Exercise

Underline the passive sentences in the text below. Are there any Agent *by*-phrases?

Text 4.3.3
Payment information: Granada television rental
This book must be given to the cashier each time that payment is made. The top part of a payment slip is removed and the receipted stub is left in the book. That is the record of your payment.

Postal payments must be made by cheque or postal order. Tear the top part of the next payment slip and send it with your money. If a receipt is required, send this payment book with your money.

The rental rates which are shown in this book include VAT at the rate in operation at the time when the book was issued.

Adapted from *Granada Showroom Payment book*, 1981.

4.4 MOVEMENT TO FOCUS POSITION

4.4.1 *IT*-EXTRAPOSITION

Read the text below. Bracket the *that*-clauses.

Text 4.4.1

It arouses indignation that some night workers at British Leyland's Rover factory in Solihull are in the regular habit of sleeping for a large part of their shift.

But on whom should the indignation be vented? From the beginning of time, it has been accepted that men who are on duty during the night will be tempted to sleep. It is assumed that nothing but the most diligent supervision supported by grave penalties will prevent them from going to sleep.

The fact that it took a newspaper reporter to unveil this particular manifestation of a normal human phenomenon to the Leyland management speaks for itself.

It is said that the erring workers normally finish their assignment by 3 a.m. and that they are not due to clock off until seven. It is possible that management has given them far too little to do or much too long in which to do it. For them to remain alert and idle at their posts for four solid hours each night simply out of piety to Sir Michael Edwardes would argue an almost perverted sense of duty.

Adapted from *Daily Telegraph*, 13 November 1979.

4.4.1.1 *It*-extraposition in Passive Sentences

A very common pattern in the text above is the following:

It + passive verb + *that*-clause.

In the second paragraph, for example, we find:

(1) From the beginning of time, it has been accepted that men who are on duty during the night will be tempted to sleep.

(2) It is assumed that nothing but ... will prevent them from going to sleep.

What is the Subject of (1) and (2)? The Subject of the main clause is obviously *it*, since SAI affects the order of *it* and the auxiliary *has* or *is*:

(3) *Has it* been accepted that ...?

(4) *Is it* assumed that ...?

Since the verb is in the passive (*has been accepted, is assumed*), we should be able to reconstruct the underlying active string. Indeed, the active sentences corresponding to (1) and (2) may be something like:

(5) ... everyone has accepted that men who are on duty during the night will be tempted to sleep.

(6) One assumes that nothing but ... will prevent them from going to sleep.

The choice of the items *everyone* and *one* as underlying Subject NPs in (5) and (6) is fairly arbitrary, of course: some other general NP would also have been possible here. In any case, the Subject NPs of (5) and (6) are absent from the corresponding passives (1) and (2) above.

Bracket the constituents in the main clauses of (5) and (6). What is the GF of the *that*-clause in (5) and (6)? We represent the structure of (5) as follows:

(7) $[_{S}\ldots [_{NP}\text{everyone}] [_{VP}\text{has accepted}$

$[_{\bar{S}}\text{that men who} \ldots \text{will be tempted to sleep}]]]$

The *that*-clause ($\bar{S}$) is a Complement of the V, and functions as Od. Sentence (7) has the same structure as simple sentences such as (8)

(8) $[_{S} [_{NP}\text{Everyone}] [_{VP}\text{has accepted } [_{NP}\text{the fact}]]]$

Pseudo-clefting bears out the analysis of (5), showing that the *that*-clause is integrated in the VP:

(9) What everyone has done is $[_{VP}$accept that men who are on duty

during the night will be tempted to sleep$]$

It is also possible to use the auxiliary *have* as a substitute for the whole VP, as (10) illustrates:

(10) Everyone has accepted that men who are on duty during the night will be tempted to sleep, but John hasn't (accepted that men who ...)

If the *that*-clause is the Od of (5), then under passivisation it should become the Subject of the passive sentence. And this is indeed what happens:

(11) *That men who are on duty during the night will be tempted to sleep* has been accepted (by everyone).

Sentence (11) can be given the following constituent structure:

(11a) $[_{S} [_{NP}\text{That men who are} \ldots \text{will be tempted to sleep}]$

$[_{VP}\text{has been accepted}]]$

However, (11) is not a very elegant sentence; there is something wrong with the balance between Subject and Predicate. The Subject is heavy and the VP following it relatively short. We get rather a lot of information at the beginning of the sentence, while in English the **focus** of attention in a sentence is usually towards the end of the sentence.

It is for this reason that (11) should preferably be converted into (12):

(12) It has been accepted that men who are on duty during the night will be tempted to sleep.

In this section we shall deal with the relations which hold between structures such as (11) and (12) above. Consider again:

(11) That men who ... will be tempted to sleep has been accepted.

(12) It has been accepted that men who ... will be tempted to sleep.

Two main operations are involved in converting (11) into (12):

(a) The Subject clause (with *that*) is shifted rightwards towards the end of the sentence, leaving a gap ---:

(13) --- has been accepted

$\left[_{\bar{S}}\right.$that men who ... will be tempted to sleep$\left.\right]$

(b) *It* is inserted into the vacated Subject position. *It* is a dummy element, functioning as a place-holder for the Subject, and is called the **grammatical** or **anticipatory Subject**, as opposed to the **notional Subject** (the *that*-clause). The anticipatory Subject will be labelled **su**, to distinguish it from 'normal' Subjects (Su).

The structure of sentence (12) may now be summed up as follows: *It*/su [Vpass–$\bar{S}$/Su]. In (12), the moved *that*-clause gives content or meaning to *it*; the two are linked and are said to form a **chain**.

The movement transformation which shifts the *that*-clause rightwards in the sentence is called **extraposition**. The combination of extraposition + *it*-insertion is referred to as it-*extraposition.*

Try to reconstruct the process of *it*-extraposition in (2) above and in other examples of passive sentences with *it*-extraposition in text 4.4.1.

4.4.1.2 *It*-extraposition in Active Sentences

It-extraposition is not confined to passive sentences such as (1) and (2) above. If you read through text 4.4.1 again, you will also find active sentences showing the same process. For example:

(14) It arouses indignation that some night workers ... are in the regular habit of sleeping for a large part of their shift.

If we bracket the sentence constituents, we get the following:

(15) $\left[_{S}\left[_{NP}\text{It}\right]\left[_{VP}\text{arouses}\left[_{NP}\text{indignation}\right]\left[_{\bar{S}}\text{that some night workers}\ldots\right]\right]\right]$

The function of the NP *indignation* is that of Od, as passivisation shows:

(16) $\left[_{NP}\text{Indignation}\right]$ is aroused by (the fact) that some night workers . . .

What is the GF of the *that*-clause? It supplies the content for *it*:

(17) What arouses indignation is $\left[_{\bar{S}}\text{that some night workers}\ldots\text{are in the regular habit of sleeping for a large part of their shift}\right]$

It in (14) is the grammatical Subject, and the *that*-clause the notional Subject. (14) is another instance of an *it*-extraposition pattern. We can, in fact, undo the effect of *it*-extraposition quite easily:

(a) remove *it*:

$\left[_{S}\text{---}\left[_{VP}\text{arouses indignation}\left[_{\bar{S}}\text{that some night workers}\ldots\text{are in the regular habit of sleeping}\ldots\right]\right]\right]$

(b) replace the displaced *that*-clause into its original position:

$\left[_{S}\left[_{\bar{S}}\text{That some night workers}\ldots\text{are in the regular habit of sleeping}\ldots\right]\left[_{VP}\text{arouses indignation}\right]\right]$

Here is another example of *it*-extraposition from the text:

(18) It is possible that management has given them far too little to do.

What is the analysis of sentence (18)? Can you undo the effect of *it*-extraposition (i.e. first remove *it*, then shift the *that*-clause back to its normal position at the beginning of the sentence)?

The effect of *it*-extraposition is that the heavy Subject clause is moved into focus position at the end of the sentence.

4.4.1.3 *It*-extraposition with Non-finite Clauses

So far, we have concentrated on extraposition involving finite Subject clauses. However, *it*-extraposition may also move non-finite clauses. In the last paragraph of the text we find:

(19) $[_S [_{\bar{S}}$For $[_S$them to remain alert and idle at their posts for four solid hours each night simply out of piety to Sir Michael Edwardes$]]$ $[_{VP}$would argue an almost perverted sense of duty$]]$

As we can see, the Subject of this sentence is realised by a non-finite clause ($\bar{S}$). The complementiser in this clause is *for*, and *for* cannot be left out. Sentence (19) has not undergone *it*-extraposition. The effect of *it*-extraposition would be as follows:

(a) extraposition:

$[_S$--- would argue an almost perverted sense of duty $[_{\bar{S}}$for $[_S$them to remain alert and idle for four solid hours each night simply out of piety to Sir Michael Edwardes$]]]$

(b) *it*-insertion:

$[_S$*It* would argue an almost perverted sense of duty $[_{\bar{S}}$for $[_S$them to ...$]]]$

Now apply *it*-extraposition to the following two sentences:

(20) For me to be writing a book on this subject was an irrational act.

(21) Talking to her was great fun.

See also Chapter 5.

4.4.1.4 Exercise

Undo the effect of *it*-extraposition in the following examples.

(1) *It* is a pity that he should have told her that.
(2) *It* would be very unwise to give in at this point.
(3) *It* is generally assumed that Philip is the best candidate.
(4) *It* was revealed last night that the unemployment figures have risen again.
(5) *It* is not quite clear whether the trains will be running on time tomorrow.
(6) *It* will be announced soon who will get the prize.
(7) *It* had never happened to her that she had trusted someone so blindly.
(8) *It* did not occur to me at the time that you might be interested.
(9) Is *it* conceivable that the man was joking?
(10) *It* is expected by most experts that the pound will be devalued.

Note: the non-extraposed versions of some of the sentences above sound rather awkward. In such cases *it*-extraposition is said to be preferable *stylistically*. There are also cases which have no non-extraposed version, i.e. where *it*-extraposition is obligatory. For example:

*That it would be better if she went on her own was thought.

This must become:

It was thought that it would be better if she went on her own.

4.4.1.5 *It*-extraposition in Verbless Clauses

Let us now look at the examples below:

(22) They considered her affair with George very foolish.

(23) The committee found the proposal unacceptable.

Bracket the constituents in the sentences and assign GFs. Both examples may be analysed as follows (cf. 3.4.11.2 for an alternative analysis):

(24) $\mathrm{NP/Su}\left[\mathrm{V}\left[_{\hat{S}/\mathrm{Od}}\mathrm{NP/Su{-}AdjP/Pc}\right]\right]$

In other words: *consider* in (22) and *find* in (23) have as their Direct Object a verbless clause (*her affair with George very foolish* and *the proposal unacceptable*).

The verbless clauses in themselves contain a Subject and a Predicative Complement, but there is no verb to link them. Compare (22) with (25) and (26) below:

(25) They considered *her affair with George to be very foolish.*

(26) They considered *that her affair with George was very foolish.*

Obviously, nothing would prevent the Subject of the verbless clause in (22) from also being realised by a clause, rather than by an NP. For example:

(27) They considered *that she had an affair with George* very foolish.

(28) They considered *for her to have an affair with George* very foolish.

In (27) the Subject of the verbless clause is a finite *that*-clause; in (28) it is non-finite. But again (27) and (28) sound very awkward; they can be improved if we rephrase them as (29) and (30):

(29) They considered *it* very foolish *that she had an affair with George.*

(30) They considered *it* very foolish *for her to have an affair with George.*

(29) and (30) are related to (27) and (28) by *it*-extraposition. In this case, the domain of *it*-extraposition is the verbless clause functioning as Od. The two familiar steps can again be described as follows:

(a) extrapose the Subject clause of the Object clause:

They considered $\left[_{\overline{S}}--- \text{ very foolish } \left[_{\overline{S}}\text{that she} \ldots\right]\right]$

(b) insert *it*:

They considered $\left[_{\overline{S}}\, \textit{it} \text{ very foolish } \left[_{\overline{S}}\text{that she} \ldots\right]\right]$

Or schematically:

U.S.: $NP\left[_{VP}V\left[_{\overline{S}}\left[_{\overline{S}}\right]\left[_{AdjP/Pc}\right]\right]\right]$

(a) $NP\left[_{VP}V\left[_{\overline{S}}---\left[_{AdjP/Pc}\right]\left[_{\overline{S}}\right]\right]\right]$

(b) $NP\left[_{VP}V\left[_{\overline{S}}\,\textit{it}\left[_{AdjP/Pc}\right]\left[_{\overline{S}}\right]\right]\right]$

In (29) and (30), *it* is the filler of the Subject position inside the verbless Object clause. The notional Subject is the extraposed Subject clause. U.S. stands for 'underlying structure' (cf. 4.1).

4.4.1.6 *It*-extraposition with Object Clauses

Consider the following sentence:

(31) Mary called William's behaviour rather odd.

Bracket the constituents in (31) and label them. Assign GFs. If we adopt the analysis proposed in 3.4.6, the following pattern emerges:

(32) NP/Su [V–NP/Od–AdjP/Pc+Ac]

The AdjP realises the GF of Pc+Ac. (cf. 3.4.6). As we have seen, an Od may also be realised by a clause (an Object clause). For example:

(33) We $\left[_{VP}\text{regretted } \left[_{\overline{S}/Od}\text{that she arrived so late}\right]\right]$

Consider now also:

(34) We $\left[_{VP}\text{called } \left[_{\overline{S}/Od}\text{that she arrived so late}\right]\right.$

$\left.\left[_{AdjP/Pc+Ac}\text{very regrettable}\right]\right]$

(34) is, of course, a very clumsy sentence. Its style can be improved if we rearrange it as follows:

(35) We called it very regrettable that she arrived so late.

(34) and (35) have the same meaning. If we compare their structures, we see that (35) is the result of *it*-extraposition. We have again applied the two-step procedure which we have seen before:

(a) extrapose the (Object) clause, i.e. shift it to the right:

(36) We called --- very regrettable $[_{\overline{S}/Od}$ that she arrived so late$]$

(b) insert *it* in the vacated slot:

(37) We called *it* very regrettable $[_{\overline{S}\ Od}$ that she arrived so late$]$

It is the place-holder for the extraposed Object clause: *it* is the grammatical or anticipatory Object of *called*, and the *that*-clause is the notional Object. The grammatical Object is labelled **od**, to distinguish it from 'normal' Objects (Od); cf. also the distinction above between su and Su (4.4.1.1). The structure of (35) may be summed up as follows:

(35a) NP/Su [V–*it*/od–AdjP/Pc+Ac–$\overline{S}$/Od]

However, in 3.4.11.2 and 3.4.11.3, we have pointed out that there are alternative analyses for sentences with so-called complex transitive verbs. One such alternative (cf. 3.4.11.2) is to treat (31) as follows:

(38) Mary $[_{VP}$called $[_{S_{\emptyset}/Od}$ $[_{NP/Su}$William's behaviour$]$ $[_{AdjP/Pc}$rather odd$]]]$

and there is a similar analysis for (34) above:

(39) We $[_{VP}$called $[_{S_{\emptyset}/Od}$ $[_{\overline{S}/Su}$that she arrived so late$]$ $[_{AdjP/Pc}$very regrettable$]]]$

Under such an analysis (35) would be a straightforward example of *it*-extraposition of a Subject clause inside a verbless clause, similar to the cases dealt with in 4.4.1.5:

(40) We $[_{VP}$called $[_{S_{\emptyset}/Od}$ $[_{NP/su}$it$]$ $[_{AdjP/Pc}$very regrettable$]$ $[_{\overline{S}/Su}$that she arrived so late$]]]$

It is the place-holder (su) for the extraposed Subject clause; the domain of *it*-extraposition is $S_{\emptyset}$.

In 3.4.11.3 we have given yet another way of analysing examples such as (31). Rather than treating the AdjP *rather odd* in (31) as merely a phrasal constituent of the entire S, we have proposed that it might be seen as part of a verbless clause:

(41) Mary $[_{VP}$called $[_{NP/Od}$William's behaviour$]$ $[_{S\emptyset}[_{NP/Su}()]$ $[_{AdjP/Pc}$rather odd$]]]$

Again this would have consequences for the analysis of (35), which would then have the following analysis:

(42) We $[_{VP}$called $[_{NP/od}$ it$]$ $[_{S\emptyset}[_{NP/Su}()]$ $[_{AdjP/Pc}$very regrettable$]]$ $[_{\bar{S}/Od}$that she arrived so late$]]$

4.4.2 SUBJECT–VERB INVERSION

Let us consider the following text.

> *Text 4.4.2*
> Blackstable was a fishing village. It consisted of a high street in which were the shops, the bank, the doctor's house, and the houses of two or three coalship owners. Round the little harbour were shabby streets in which lived fishermen and poor people.
> Adapted from W. Somerset Maugham, *Of Human Bondage.*

We shall first look at a simplified version of the last sentence.

(43) Round the little harbour were shabby streets.

In what respect is (43) a 'simplified version' of the last sentence of the text? Bracket and label the constituents in (43). Assign GFs. If you have problems in determining GFs it might be useful to compare (43) with (44) below:

(44) The shabby streets were round the little harbour.

This last sentence has the pattern NP/Su[V–PP/Ac].

The PP *round the little harbour* has been fronted in (43), and the Subject and the Verb have changed places. (43) and (44) are both grammatical. They have the same meaning, and contain identical constituents with identical GFs, but the distribution of these constituents is different. By reorganising the sentence, the author achieves greater emphasis on the Subject NP, since this is now in sentence-final (i.e. focus) position. The rearrangement is a two-step procedure:

(a) the PP/Ac is fronted.
(b) the Subject is moved to the right.

Step (a), the fronting (4.2.9) of the Adverbial Complement, precedes and triggers step (b), the inversion of the Subject and the verb. Step (b) is called **Subject–Verb Inversion**.

Let us return to the original sentence in the text:

(45) Round the little harbour were shabby streets in which lived fishermen and poor people.

What is the Su? Make sure you bracket the full NP/Su. The constituent order of (45) is: Ac–V–Su, which is not a basic pattern (cf. 3.1). If you restore the sentence to its basic pattern, you will get a sentence of the Su–V–Ac type, but with a heavy Subject NP:

(46) $[_{S} [_{NP}$ Shabby streets in which lived fishermen and poor people$]$ $[_{VP}$ were $[_{PP}$ round the little harbour$]]]$

By fronting the PP *round the little harbour* and moving the Subject NP *shabby streets in which lived fishermen and poor people* rightwards, the sentence is made much more balanced.

Let us now look at the postmodifying clause in the Subject NP: *in which lived fishermen and poor people.* The constituent order of this clause is as follows:

(47) $[_{\bar{S}} [_{PP}$ in which$]$ $[_{S} [_{VP}$ lived $[_{NP}$ fishermen and poor people$]]]]$

Is this a basic sentence pattern? If it is not, what arrangements do you think have been made?

Of course, one rearrangement is due to *wh*-movement of *in which* into COMP. A second rearrangement moves the Subject NP *fishermen and poor people* to the right, placing it after the verb *lived* (Subject–Verb Inversion or **SVI**, for short).

We repeat the structure underlying the NP *shabby streets in which lived fishermen and poor people*:

(48) $[_{NP}$ shabby streets $[_{\bar{S}} [_{\substack{COMP\\+WH}}\ ]$ $[_{S}$ fishermen and poor people lived in which$]]]$

The two rearrangements work as follows:

(a) *wh*-movement of *in which* (with pied-piping) results in:

(49) $[_{NP}$ shabby streets $[_{\bar{S}} [_{\substack{COMP\\+WH}}$ in which$]$ $[_{S} [_{NP}$ fishermen and poor people$]$ lived --- $]]]$

This movement is obligatory.

(b) Subject–Verb Inversion produces:

(50) $\left[_{NP} \text{shabby streets} \left[_{\bar{S}} \left[_{\substack{COMP\\+WH}} \text{in which}\right] \left[_{S} \text{--- lived ---} \left[_{NP} \text{fishermen and poor people}\right]\right]\right]\right]$

The inversion is not obligatory.

There is another example of *wh*-movement and SVI in text 4.4.2 above. Can you find it?

SVI often greatly improves the style of a sentence by creating a better balance between the beginning and the end of the sentence. The result is again that a prominent Subject is moved into the focus position at the end of the sentence. It is often called a 'stylistic inversion'.

Like *it*-extraposition, SVI shifts a constituent towards the end of the sentence.

There is an interesting difference between Subject–Verb Inversion and Subject–Aux Inversion. SVI changes the order of Su and V by moving Su rightwards, placing it after V in the VP, whereas SAI reorders Su and aux by moving aux (+ tense) leftwards out of the VP, placing it in front of Su. Compare:

SVI: $\left[_{S}\text{NP/Su}\left[_{VP}\ldots \text{V} \ldots\right]\right] \Rightarrow \left[_{S}\text{---}\ \left[_{VP}\ldots \text{V} \ldots \text{NP/Su}\right]\right]$

SAI: $\left[_{S}\text{NP/Su}\left[_{VP}\text{Aux(+Tns) V} \ldots\right]\right] \Rightarrow \left[_{S}\text{Aux (+Tns) NP/Su}\right.$ $\left.\left[_{VP}\text{V} \ldots\right]\right]$

4.4.3 *THERE*-INSERTION

Consider example (51):

(51) There were three chapels in the village.

Bracket the constituents and identify the Subject. You will find that there are two constituents which seem to be likely candidates for Subject status:

(a) the word *there*, which seems to occupy the Subject position, as is confirmed by Subject-Aux Inversion:

(52) Were there three chapels in the village?

(b) the NP *three chapels*. Support for this can be found in the fact that this NP and the verb have agreement. Compare:

(53) There was one small chapel in the village.

Has this sentence then got two Subjects? If we look at it more carefully, we find that it corresponds to a more basic pattern:

(54) Three chapels were in the village.

This is an Su[V–Ac] sentence. Bracket the constituents and label them. (51) and (54) can be related by a movement operation, which shifts the Subject NP in (54) rightwards (SVI) to the position after *be*:

(55) --- were three chapels in the village.

Into the vacated slot we then insert a dummy element: *there*. *There*-insertion in (55) gives us (51) above. Like *it*, *there* serves to announce that the notional Subject is to follow. *There*-sentences, also called **existential sentences**, are often used to introduce new elements into the discourse, as the following text illustrates:

Text 4.4.3

There was a university in New England where the students operated a bank of term papers and other homework assignments. There were papers for every need: there were papers for an A grade, papers for a B and papers for a C.

In this university there was also a student who had spent the weekend on pursuits other than homework; he went to the bank. He drew out a paper for C, retyped it, and handed his work in. In due course he received it back with comments in red ink and they were as follows: 'I wrote this paper myself twenty years ago. I always thought it worth an A, and now I am glad to give it one'.

Adapted from Christian Brann, *Pass the Port.*

There-insertion is usually only possible with indefinite Subjects and the verb used is normally *be* (either the lexical verb *be*, or one of the auxiliary uses of *be*):

lexical verb *be*:

(56) A mouse is in the kitchen.⟶There is a mouse in the kitchen.

Especially with the lexical verb *be* the versions with *there* sound far better than those without *there*.

progressive *be*:

(57) A man is waiting for you.⟶There is a man waiting for you.

passive *be*:

(58) Some money has been stolen.⟶There has been some money stolen.

Try to perform *there*-insertion on the sentences below:

(59) Three more people may have been in the wreck.

(60) Has anyone been to see her?

(61) Five children have been killed.

(62) How much money has been stolen?

There-insertion is also possible with a small number of other verbs, which usually relate to the idea of 'being', 'coming into being', 'existing', etc. Consider how *there*-insertion has operated in the following:

(63) There will arise a lot of confusion after the death of the President.

(64) There came a brief spell of beautiful weather.

(65) There appeared another picture on the large screen.

(66) There exist two copies of this medieval manuscript.

(67) There occurred another accident the next day.

(68) After independence there followed a period of great political unrest.

4.4.4 EXTRAPOSITION FROM NP

A further method of balancing the sentence is by extraposition from an NP. In the sections above we have seen that heavy Subjects may be moved towards sentence-final position. For example:

(69) It is a scandal that they have allowed this practice for so long.

(70) In this area live fishermen, painters, ironmongers, coalminers, and unskilled workers.

The tendency to move heavy constituents to the right is very general in English. We shall give a few more examples below. Consider, for example, (71) and (72):

(71a) Did you see that man with those funny clothes yesterday?

(71b) Did you see that man yesterday with those funny clothes?

(72a) A new book by Professor Winters which deals with the suppression of women in the fifteenth century has just appeared.

(72b) A new book by Professor Winters has just appeared which deals with the suppression of women in the fifteenth century.

Bracket NPs in the (a)-sentences and assign GFs. Now compare the (a)-

sentences and their (b)-variants. In the (b)-sentences part of the NP has been moved to the right: in (71b) the operation affects a postmodifying PP, in (72b) it affects a postmodifying clause. Such a movement is optional, and helps to create a better balance in the sentence.

Moving constituents out of an NP is also called **extraposition**, more specifically **extraposition from NP**. If we look at the effect of this operation in the (b)-sentences, we see that it splits up the NP into two parts:

(73) $\left[_{NP}\right.$that man ... $\left[_{PP}\right.$with those funny clothes$\left.\right]\left.\right]$

The PP *with those funny clothes* is not an independent constituent: it cannot be the focus element in a cleft sentence, for example. We can thus say that NPs may be **discontinuous**: their components may be separated by intervening material.

Identify discontinuous NPs in the sentences below. Restore each sentence to its original order with the Postmodifier immediately following the Head of the NP. Label the intervening constituents.

(74) I received an anonymous letter last week which rather shocked me.

(75) There lives a man round the corner who was born in South Africa.

(76) Did you hear the news the other day that unemployment benefits are going to be cut by 10 per cent?

(77) A man came into our shop last week who told us he was Napoleon's great-grandson.

To determine GFs in sentences such as (74)–(77), it is always best to restore the sentence to its basic word order first, since separated components of a constituent really make up only one constituent, with one GF. In (74), for example, the Object NP in the basic pattern is:

(78) $\left[_{NP}\right.$an anonymous letter which rather shocked me$\left.\right]$

4.4.5 HEAVY OBJECT-SHIFT

Now consider (79a) and (79b):

(79a) You will give him a sleeping tablet every night.

(79b) You will give him every night two sleeping tablets, a cup of hot chocolate, and a glass of brandy.

Bracket the constituents, and assign GFs.

Sentence (79a) has the following pattern: NP/Su [V–NP/Oi–NP/Od–NP/A]. (79b) is very similar, but the Direct Object NP has now been shifted rightwards to sentence-final position. Again this is a stylistic movement. The NP/Od in (b) is rather long and heavy, and it is exactly such long and heavy Object NPs which tend to be moved rightwards. Here is another example from P.G. Wodehouse, *Lord Emsworth and Others*:

(80) Poskitt was a man who brought to the tee the tactics which in his youth had won him such fame as a hammer thrower.

In the following examples, too, the Od has been shifted rightwards. Bracket the Direct Object NP. Note that if you replace the heavy NP by a short one (e.g. a pronoun), there is no need to extrapose it to the end of the sentence.

(81) The butler recalled to my mind the occasion when my aunt had left the house in her nightgown.

(82) They have scheduled for this month three plays and two musicals.

(83) She added to the mixture a teaspoon of sugar, two drops of almond essence and a hint of rum.

4.4.6 SUMMING UP

We have identified various types of rightward movement, whereby an important/heavy constituent gets moved towards the end of the sentence. We have dealt with the following cases:

(a) *it*-extraposition (4.4.1), e.g.:

It was a scandal *that there were three chapels in the High Street.*

(b) Subject–Verb Inversion (4.4.2), e.g.:

Round the little harbour *were shabby streets* in which *lived fishermen and poor people.*

(c) *there*-insertion (4.4.3), e.g.:

There were *three chapels* in the village.

(d) extraposition from NP (4.4.4), e.g.:

There is a man at the door *who sells encyclopedias.*

(e) heavy Object-shift (4.4.5), e.g.:

The patient should be given every day *three sleeping tablets and two injections.*

Write two more examples for each of the five types of movement just mentioned. Reconstruct the underlying basic pattern for each example above and for the examples which you have devised yourself.

Read text 4.4.6 (cf. 4.4.2). It is a good example of how rightward movement operations may be used by authors to achieve certain effects. Identify the rightward movements.

Text 4.4.6
Blackstable was a fishing village. It consisted of a high street in which were the shops, the bank, the doctor's house, and the houses of two or three coalship owners: round the little harbour were shabby streets in which lived fishermen and poor people; but since they went to chapel they were of no account. When Mrs. Carey passed the dissenting ministers in the street she stepped over to the other side to avoid meeting them, but if there was not time for this fixed her eyes on the pavement. It was a scandal to which the Vicar had never resigned himself that there were three chapels in the High Street: he could not help feeling that the law should have stepped in to prevent their erection.

W.Somerset Maugham, *Of Human Bondage.*

4.5 CLEFTING AND PSEUDO-CLEFTING

4.5.1 CLEFTING

Clefting, as we have noted, is a device which is used to focus on a particular constituent in the sentence. The process of clefting involves extracting a constituent from its basic position in the sentence and putting it in a more prominent position (cf. 1.3.2). Consider the ways in which clefting could be applied to sentence (1):

(1) Jane gave this book to Bill on Saturday.

The cleft versions of (1) include the following:

(2) It was *on Saturday* that Jane gave this book to Bill.

(3) It was *to Bill* that Jane gave this book on Saturday.

(4) It was *this book* that/which Jane gave to Bill on Saturday.

(5) It was *Jane* that/who gave this book to Bill on Saturday.

We could extend sentence (1) by adding an Adjunct clause. For example:

(6) Jane gave this book to Bill on Saturday because it was his birthday.

If we take the *because*-clause as the focus element, (6) becomes (7):

(7) It was *because it was his birthday* that Jane gave this book to Bill on Saturday.

The focus element may be either an NP ((4) and (5)), a PP ((2) and (3)) or an Adjunct clause ((7)). As the examples show, the focus element is surrounded by: *It is/was ... that/who/which*-clause. Although these *that/who/which*-clauses are very similar in appearance to relative clauses (4.2.6), they are not quite the same. One difference is that normal relative clauses usually serve to postmodify Heads of NPs, i.e. Ns, not PPs or Adjunct clauses. As we have seen, the relative clauses in cleft sentences can 'postmodify' PPs and Adjunct clauses. Another difference is that in the common type of relative clauses the *that/who/which*-element cannot be left out if it is the Subject of the clause, but in cleft sentences *that, who,* or *which* can be omitted in colloquial style if it is the Subject of the clause. Compare:

(8a) The girl who gave the book to Bill is my sister.

(7b) *The girl gave the book to Bill is my sister.

(9a) It is Jane who gave the book to Bill.

(9b) It is Jane Ø gave the book to Bill.

See also 4.2.6.3.

The text below illustrates the use of cleft sentences. Identify the cleft sentences in the text. Try to rewrite the text without the cleft sentences.

Text 4.5.1

Yet no one can claim that since then Labour's difficulties have diminished — in fact they have increased and multiplied. It was Mr. Foot who presided over, and in fact partly precipitated, the defection of 30 Labour MPs to the SDP — the biggest split in Labour's history since 1931; it was Mr. Foot who tried and failed to include Mr. Benn in a unity encampment of the party — a failure of such dimensions that just over 12 months ago he escaped by the merest hair's breadth from having him foisted on him as his own deputy; it is Mr. Foot who, having stated last autumn that there would be something 'inconsistent' about active Militant Tendancy supporters standing as Labour candidates, now gives every indication of acquiescing in eight or nine of them doing exactly that.

Observer, 27 February 1983.

4.5.2 PSEUDO-CLEFTING

Clefting is a useful way of making clear what you are focusing on, but it is not possible, for example, to make the verb the Head of a cleft construction. However, there is an alternative way of focusing on constituents, which is applicable to verbs and their Complements. For example:

(10) What Jane did was give the book to Bill on Saturday.

(11) What the waiter did was open the beer-tins first.

We focus on the VP *give the book to Bill on Saturday*, or *open the beer-tins first* by putting it sentence-finally and placing the string: *what NP/Su did was* ... before it. This process is called **pseudo-clefting**. Some more examples:

(12) What Bill will do is *have a quick shower before he leaves.*

(13) What Anne did was *open the box and take out the gun.*

(14) What I am doing is *trying to clear up this mess.*

Pseudo-clefting is not only used for focusing on the VP as a whole. Other constituents can also be focused on by pseudo-clefting. For example:

(15a) I need a cigarette and a drink most at this time of the day.

(15b) *What I need most at this time of the day* is *a cigarette and a drink.*

What... day in (15b) is a free relative clause (4.2.6.5) functioning as Subject. It may also be a Complement (Pc):

(15c) A cigarette and a drink is *what I need most at this time of the day.*

4.6 SUBSTITUTION BY PRO-FORMS

We have seen that constituents as a whole may at times be replaced by substitute forms, also called **pro-forms**. Consider:

(1) Bill's sister announced the news of her marriage the day before yesterday.

In this sentence the NP *Bill's sister* may be replaced by *she*; *the news of her marriage* by *it*; *the day before yesterday* by *then*;

(2) $\Big[_{S}\Big[\text{She}\Big]\Big[_{VP}\text{announced}\Big[\text{it}\Big]\Big[\text{then}\Big]\Big]\Big]$

She and *it* are personal pronouns (cf. 2.4.2.2); *then* is an adverb replacing a time Adjunct. *She, it* and *then* are examples of pro-forms.

Interrogative pronouns (*who, what, which*) and interrogative adverbs (such as *when, where, why, how*) are also used to replace constituents. Take, for example:

(3) What did Bill's sister announce the day before yesterday?

The answer to this *wh*-question may be: 'The news of her marriage'. The formation of such questions has been discussed in 4.2.4. We have seen that *wh*-pronouns also serve to introduce relative clauses (clauses which postmodify the Head of an NP), as in:

(4) The girl who announced the news was Jane.

This occurrence of *who* is also a pro-form.

Read text 4.6 below carefully. Identify all the pro-forms and try to decide what constituent each pro-form is meant to replace.

Text 4.6

'You pawned your aunt's brooch?'

'Yes.'

'And that endeared you to her?'

'I will explain all that later. Meanwhile, let me begin at the beginning. Have you ever run across a man named Joe the Lawyer?'

'No.'

'Stout fellow with a face like a haggis.'

'I've never met him.'

'Endeavour not to do so, Corky. I hate to speak ill of my fellow man, but Joe the Lawyer is not honest.'

'What does he do? Pawn people's brooches?'

Ukridge adjusted the ginger-beer wire that held his pince-nez to his flapping ears and looked wounded.

'This is scarcely the tone I like to hear in an old friend, Corky. When I reach that point in my story, you will see that my pawning of Aunt Julia's brooch was a perfectly normal, straightforward matter of business. How else could I have bought half the dog?'

'Half what dog?'

'Didn't I tell you about the dog?'

'No.'

'I must have done. It's the nub of the whole affair.'

'Well, you didn't.'

P.G. Wodehouse, *Lord Emsworth and Others.*

Another important replacive device which may be used to avoid repetition is the string *do so*, as in:

(5) Mary bought her wedding dress in London and *so did* Jane.

The string *do so* substitutes for the VP *bought her wedding dress in London.* If the VP contains auxiliaries, these may also be used as substitutes for the entire VP:

(6) Mary may buy her wedding dress in London and $\left\{\begin{array}{l}\text{Jane } \textit{may too} \\ \textit{so may } \text{Jane}\end{array}\right\}$.

(7) Susan may already have left and $\left\{\begin{array}{l}\text{Anne } \textit{may have too} \\ \textit{so may } \text{Anne}\end{array}\right\}$.

Find replacive uses of *do* or of other auxiliaries in text 4.6.

It is, of course, possible to rewrite the text above, supplying for each pro-form the elements it replaces. However, this would make the text repetitious and over-explicit: there would be a great deal of redundant information. It is a matter of economy to use substitute forms for elements or information already known to the reader or hearer.

4.7 ELLIPSIS

It is not just pro-forms that are used to economise in language. For example, speakers often reduce redundancy by *leaving out* superfluous information, i.e. information which can easily be recovered from the situation or the context. This phenomenon is called **ellipsis**. Elliptical sentences depend for their interpretation on what precedes them in discourse. Thus, in:

(1) A: When did Susan leave? B: *At two o'clock.*

We may assume that in the 'response sentence' (italicised) the string *Susan left* has been omitted. In the sections below we shall look at some examples of ellipsis in English.

4.7.1 SUBJECT DELETION

Consider the following sentence:

(2) Ukridge adjusted the ginger-beer wire that held his pince-nez to his flapping ears and looked wounded.

The sentence is compound-complex: it contains two coordinated clauses, the second of which is *looked wounded*, but this is incomplete as it stands: *looked wounded* is a VP without NP/Su. Can you supply the missing Subject? Intuitively, we know that the Subject of *looked wounded* must be *Ukridge*, or *he*: ... *and* **he** *looked wounded.*

It is characteristic of clauses coordinated by *and*, *or* and *but* that the Subject of the second clause may be deleted if it is co-referential to the Subject of the first clause (cf. 2.2.2). Other examples are:

(3) John sat down and (he) told us the news.

(4) Susan will sing a song or (she) will play the piano.

(5) Bill arrived at eight but (he) had to leave immediately.

4.7.2 VERB GAPPING AND BACKWARD GAPPING

In 4.7.1 we have seen how the second of two identical Subject NPs may be deleted in coordinate clauses. Similarly, a verb may be omitted if it is identical with a preceding verb:

(6) John *was eating* cornflakes and Mary *was eating* porridge.

In (6) *was eating* is repeated, but it may be deleted:

(7) John was eating cornflakes and Mary --- porridge.

This kind of deletion is called **verb gapping**. Note that you can only gap over adjacent clauses:

(8) John *was writing* an essay, Bill *was reading* a novel and Anne a short story.

In (8) the gapped V in the third clause must be *was reading*; it cannot be *was writing.*

Let us look at another example with such parallelisms:

(9) John liked the film about Gandhi and Mary disliked the film about Gandhi.

Here the V differs, but the NP/Od is identical: *the film about Ghandi.* We can replace (9) by (10):

(10) John liked, and Mary disliked, the film about Gandhi.

Sentence (10) is an example of gapping in reverse: the NP/Od is deleted in the first clause in anticipation of the identical NP/Od in the second clause. This process is called **backward gapping**. Further examples:

(11) Mary wrote, and Susan typed out, the essay.

(12) Jim earned, and his wife spent, the money.

(13) Mary bought, and Peter immediately sold, the shares.

Apart from reducing redundancies (identical Object NPs), the process of backward gapping also throws light on the contrast between the verbs in the clauses. The process of gapping is not sentence-bound: its domain is not restricted to one clause/sentence, but also involves the immediate context: it is discourse-bound.

4.7.3 OTHER EXAMPLES

Consider:

'You pawned your aunt's brooch?'
'Yes'

Here *Yes* is a reply to the question 'You pawned your aunt's brooch?'. *Yes* means 'Yes, I pawned my aunt's brooch'. Read through text 4.6 once more and observe that *Yes* and *No* answers always relate to entire sentences in the preceding context.

Let us now look at the string:

(14) Stout fellow with a face like a haggis.

This is an NP (cf. text 4.6 above). What is its structure? If we try to fit this NP into the frame characteristic of NPs, we shall find that it contains no determiner. Compare it, for example, with:

(15) The handsome policeman with the sun-glasses.

(16)

Spec	Premod	Head	Postmod
Det	AdjP	N	PP
The ?	handsome stout	policeman fellow	with the sun-glasses with a face like a haggis

Since *fellow* is a singular countable N, we expect there to be a determiner. For example:

(17) *There is stout fellow with a beard in the other room.

The determiner has been ellipted in (14): we can reinsert it quite easily:

(18) A stout fellow with a face like a haggis.

In text 4.6 the NP (without a Det) is used as a sentence, beginning with a capital letter and ending with a full stop. This is, of course, not in line with what we have said about the structure of sentences: our PS rules prescribe very rigidly: S ⟶ NP–VP and NP ⟶ Det–N.

How do we reconcile these rules with the example? Again we shall want to say that the Subject NP and the verbal part of VP have been ellipted. We interpret the NP as if it had the following underlying structure:

(19) (He is a) stout fellow with a face like a haggis.

5

NON-FINITE CLAUSES: RAISING AND CONTROL

5.1 INTRODUCTION

In the preceding chapters we have seen that sentences may be embedded inside other sentences. In (1), for example, there is an Object clause ($\overline{S}$) inside an S:

(1) $\left[_{S}\left[_{NP}\text{The Vicar}\right]\left[_{VP}\text{said}\left[_{\overline{S}}\text{that}\right.\right.\right.$

$\left.\left.\left.\left.\left[_{S}\text{evil communications corrupted good manners}\right]\right]\right]\right]$

In (1) $\overline{S}$ is a finite clause. However, subordinate clauses are not always finite. Compare (2a) and (2b):

(2a) The Vicar believed *that evil communications corrupted good manners.*

(2b) The Vicar believed *evil communications to corrupt good manners.*

In (2a) there is a finite subordinate clause, as in (1). In (2b) the subordinate clause is non-finite: its VP contains a *to*-infinitive. The function of Object may also be realised by a clause containing a VP with a bare infinitive, an *–ing* participle or an *–ed* participle:

(3) I heard *Mary sing carols.*

(4) I heard *Mary singing carols.*

(5) They found *their house occupied by squatters.*

Finally, an Object clause may also be verbless: in such cases there is a predicate relationship between the clause elements:

(6) I consider *him guilty of this crime.*

In this chapter we shall look more carefully at the structure of sentences with subordinate non-finite clauses.

5.2 FINITE AND NON-FINITE CLAUSES

5.2.1 INTRODUCTION

Read text 5.2.1. Identify the complex sentences. Draw up a list of complex sentences with *finite* Object clauses, and one of sentences with *non-finite* Object clauses.

> *Text 5.2.1*
> It became clear to me that I wanted to write a book based on my childhood in Bombay. If you want to write books about your childhood, you must develop some sort of stratagem. I decided to take a child's view of the world.
>
> The book shows how children believe they are responsible for everything in their lives. I wanted to recount my childhood in that way. But I did not wish the book to become a family saga. Of course, there is always the problem of verisimilitude: everyone thinks that you are writing straight from life. They all believe your parents were really like that. In fact, the house I lived in was like the house in the book. The clock tower is still there; the servant with the leprosy curse really existed. But people do not believe these things to be real. They are thought to be acts of imagination.
>
> I used memory and showed that memory works. But I got one thing wrong in the book; and I wish I had not got it wrong: that was the Dyer incident. I wrote that Dyer commanded only white troops. In fact, there were Indian troops too. General Dyer told his troops to fire on an unarmed crowd in the streets.
>
> I did not intend the book to be taken as an oracle book either. In fact, people feel like that about the book, however. The political parts of the book were intended to reveal many things which had been falsified. There seemed to exist a conspiracy in the country. People preferred very much for these things to be forgotten.
>
> The process of writing was very consuming. Sometimes I thought that I was mad. It was such an irrational act for me to be writing a book on this subject. Most of the time I thought it would not be published.
>
> Adapted from *Vogue*, December 1982.

5.2.2 FINITE SUBORDINATE CLAUSES

Text 5.2.1 above contains the following sentence:

(1) The book shows how children believe they are responsible for everything in their lives.

Bracket the main constituents in (1). Is the sentence simple, compound or complex? What is the Od of *shows*? In (1) the Od is realised by a *wh*-clause. The *wh*-element *how* occurs in COMP. The subordinate clause itself is also complex: it contains another Object clause: the Od of *believe* is:

(2) [$_{\bar{S}}$(that) [$_{S}$they are responsible for everything in their lives]]

The structure of sentence (1) may be represented as in (2) or (3):

(2)

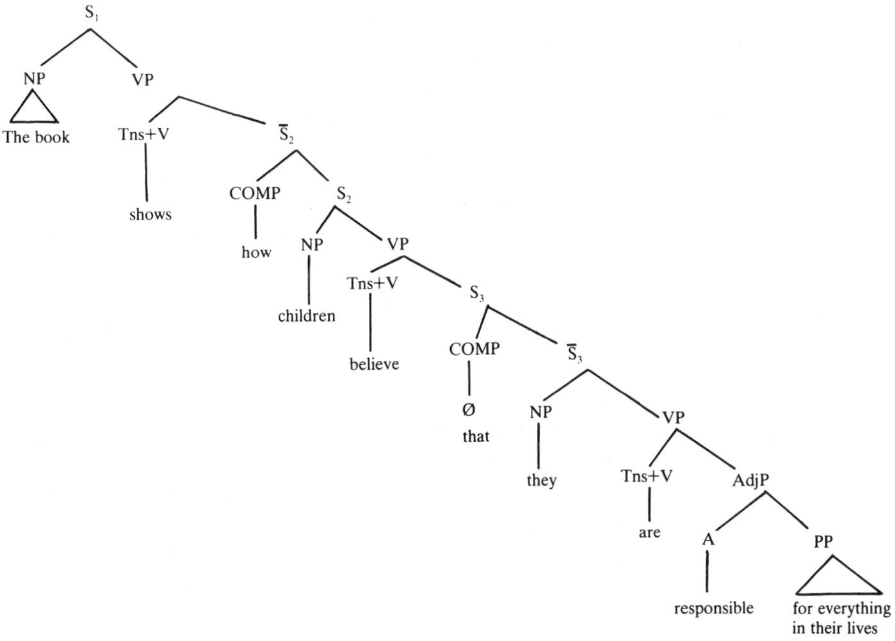

(3) [$_{S_1}$The book [$_{VP}$shows [$_{\bar{S}_2}$how [$_{S_2}$children [$_{VP}$believe [$_{\bar{S}_3}$(that) [$_{S_3}$they [$_{VP}$are responsible for everything in their lives]]]]]]]]

Going from top to bottom in tree diagram (2) you will find three S nodes:

(a) the main clause: S_1
(b) the first Object clause: of *shows*: $\bar{S}_2$
(c) the second Object clause: of *believe*: $\bar{S}_3$.

Analyse the following sentences from text 5.2.1 in the same way as (1) above: use a tree diagram (cf. (2)) and labelled brackets (cf. (3)):

(4) Everyone thinks that you are writing straight from life.

(5) They all believe your parents were really like that.

(6) ... and (I) showed that memory works.

(7) ... and I wish I had not got it wrong.

(8) I wrote that Dyer commanded only white troops.

(9) Sometimes I thought that I was mad.

(10) Most of the time I thought it would not be published.

What sentences (4)–(10) have in common is that the superordinate verb in each case (*show*, *believe*, *think*, *wish*, etc.) takes a finite clause as Od. Finite clauses always have an explicit Subject. We also see that the subordinator *that* may sometimes be deleted (cf. (1), (5), (7), (10)).

5.2.3 NON-FINITE SUBORDINATE CLAUSES WITH LEXICAL SUBJECTS

Now compare (11a) and (11b):

(11a) But I did not wish (that) the book should become a family saga.

(11b) But I did not wish (for) the book to become a family saga.

Bracket the main constituents in (11a) and (11b). Notice that *wish* takes a clause as its Od in both examples, but in (11a) the Object clause is finite (cf. 5.2.2), while in (11b) it is non-finite. In (12a) and (12b) we show how the sentences in (11) should be bracketed:

(12a) $\Big[_{S}\Big[_{NP}\ \text{I}\Big]\Big[_{VP}\ \text{did not wish}\ \Big[_{\bar{S}}\begin{Bmatrix}\text{that}\\ \emptyset\end{Bmatrix}\Big[_{S}\ \text{the book should become a family saga}\Big]\Big]\Big]\Big]$

(12b) $\Big[_{S}\Big[_{NP}\ \text{I}\Big]\Big[_{VP}\ \text{did not wish}\ \Big[_{\bar{S}}\begin{Bmatrix}\text{for}\\ \emptyset\end{Bmatrix}\Big[_{S}\ \text{the book to become a family saga}\Big]\Big]\Big]\Big]$

The subordinate clauses in (12a) and (12b) differ in several respects:

(a) The finite subordinate clause in (12a) is introduced by the complementiser *that* in COMP. *That* is optional (cf. Ø). The non-finite subordinate clause in (12b) is introduced by the complementiser *for*, which is optional.
(b) The VP of (12a) is finite; that of (12b) is non-finite.
(c) If we insert a pronoun in the Subject position of an embedded finite clause, the pronoun will take the Subject form:

(13a) I did not wish that *they/she/he/it* should ...

But if we use a pronoun as the Subject of a non-finite clause, the pronoun will take the Object-form:

(13b) I did not wish (for) *them/him/her/it* to ...

By analogy, *the book* in (12a) is assumed to be in the Subject form, and *the book* in (12b) in the Object form.

Analyse the following sentences, all taken from text 5.2.1, in the same way as (11b) above, using both the tree diagram representation and the labelled brackets notation:

(14) People preferred very much for these things to be forgotten.

(15) I did not intend the book to be taken as an oracle.

(16) But people do not believe these things to be real.

Replace the non-finite clauses by their finite counterparts.

The complementiser *for* in (14) is obligatory, while it is optional in (15): *for* may be inserted. However, the non-finite Object clause in (16) cannot take *for*:

(16a) *But people do not believe for these things to be real.

On the basis of these examples we can draw the following conclusions:

(a) Some verbs, like *prefer*, take non-finite clauses with the complementiser *for*; others, such as *believe*, take non-finite clauses without *for*. In the latter case the COMP of the non-finite clause is empty:

(16b) But people do not believe $\left[_{\bar{S}}\left[_{S}\text{these things to be real}\right]\right]$

(b) The complementiser *for* may be deleted if it is immediately preceded by a V such as *prefer*. If *prefer* (or a similar V allowing *for*) is separated from the complementiser by intervening material (for example by an Adjunct), then *for* is no longer deletable (cf. (14) above).

The non-finite clauses discussed above all occur as Complements of Vs; they are all Object clauses. Non-finite clauses may also be Subjects:

(17a) For me to be writing a book on this subject was an irrational act.

(17b) It was an irrational act for me to be writing a book on this subject.

In (17a) the non-finite clause is the Su; in (17b) it is an extraposed Su, linked to the Subject position by *it* (su) (cf. Chapter 4).

In (17) the non-finite clauses are again introduced by *for* in COMP, but *for* is not deletable here.

(18a) *Me to be writing a book on this subject was an irrational act.

(18b) *It was an irrational act me to be writing a book on this subject.

5.2.4 NON-FINITE CLAUSES WITHOUT LEXICAL SUBJECTS

Now consider (19a) and (19b) below. What is the difference between them?

(19a) I did not wish (for) the book to become a family saga.

(19b) I did not wish to write a family saga.

Both clauses have an embedded Object clause, and in each case the embedded clause is non-finite. In (19a) the Subject of the embedded clause is lexically realised by an NP, *the book*; the complementiser *for* is optional. In (19b), on the other hand, the embedded clause lacks an overt Subject. The Subject position is not lexically filled, and we shall indicate this by parentheses ( ). Furthermore, the COMP in (19b) must not be filled by *for*:

(19c) *I did not wish for to write a family saga.

The structure of (19b) is indicated in (20):

(20) I did not wish $[_{\bar{S}} [_{S} ( ) [_{VP}$ to write a family saga$]]]$

What does (19b) mean? Of course, it means 'I did not wish that I should write a family saga'. ( ) in (20) is to be interpreted as 'I'. We shall say that the non-lexical Subject position ( ) is **controlled** by the Subject of the higher clause. We return to control in 5.4.

It is not just non-finite Object clauses that may be lacking an overt lexical Subject. Subject clauses, too, may have a non-realised Subject:

(21a) To be writing a book on this subject was irrational.

(21b) It was irrational to be writing a book on this subject.

5.2.5 *FOR ... TO* FILTER

Compare (21a) and (21b) with (17a) and (17b). Observe that there is no overt Subject in the embedded clauses of (21a) and (21b), while there is one in the embedded clauses of (17a) and (17b). We assign the Subject clause of (21a) the following structure:

(22) $[_{\bar{S}} Ø [_{S} ( ) [_{VP}$ to be writing a book on this subject$]]]$

As in (19b), the complementiser *for* is not allowed to occur here. In other words, the string $[_{COMP}$for ( ) to] is not allowed in English: it must be filtered out. The complementiser *for* must not immediately precede *to*.

The rule which disallows the string *for ... to* is more general than shown above. Take, for example, the sentence:

(23a) You wished for which book to become a success?

If *wh*-movement applies to this sentence we arrive at (23b):

(23b) *Which book did you wish for --- to become a success?

but (23b) is ungrammatical, since it contains the string *for* ... *to*; *for* must be deleted:

(23c) Which book did you wish to become a success?

See also 4.2.8.

5.3 RAISING

5.3.1 RAISING WITH PASSIVE VERBS

Consider (1a) and (1b):

(1a) I intended (for) the political parts of the book to reveal many things.

(1b) The political parts of the book were intended to reveal many things.

The higher clause in (1a) is active (*I intended*); that in (1b) is passive (*were intended*). In (1a) the NP *the political parts of the book* appears as the Su of the embedded S:

(2) $[_{S}$I intended $[_{\bar{S}}[_{S}[_{NP}$the political parts of the book$][_{VP}\ldots$

In (1b) the NP *the political parts of the book* is the NP/Su of the higher clause: it is the Subject of *were intended* (apply the tests for Subject-hood described in 3.3.1 to verify this claim)

Furthermore, it would seem that the embedded S in (1b), *to reveal many things*, lacks an overt Subject. (1b) is the passive counterpart of (1a). Passivisation results in the suppression of the original Subject of *intend* (I), and the leftward movement of the Su of the embedded non-finite clause (*the political parts of the book*), which is now placed in the Su-position of the higher clause, leaving a gap at its original position:

(3a) $[_{S}$I $[_{VP}$intended $[_{\bar{S}}[_{S}$the political parts of the books to reveal many things$]]]]$

(3b) $[_{S}[_{NP}$The political parts of the book$][_{VP}$were intended $[_{\bar{S}}[_{S}$--- to reveal many things$]]]]$

Again *for* must not be present in (3b), since this would result in a string *for* ... *to*.

Let us look more closely at the properties of the NP *the political parts of the book* in (3b). We have seen that it is the grammatical Subject of the higher passive verb (*were intended*). Secondly, it is also related to the Subject position in the embedded clause: we claim that passivisation triggers movement of the NP/Su out of the embedded clause into the higher clause, leaving a gap ---. We shall say that the NP/Su of the higher clause **binds** the Subject position (more specifically the gap) in the lower clause, in the same way that an antecedent NP binds a reflexive pronoun (cf. 2.4.2.2). The operation of moving a Subject out of a non-finite clause into the Subject position of the next clause up is called **raising**.

Let us return once more to (3b) above and consider one further problem. We know that the function of the NP *the political parts of the book* is that of Su of the higher clause. Now what is the function of the embedded non-finite S: $[_S$--- *to reveal many things*]? It is obviously not the Subject of *were intended*, though it is related to the Subject by the gap ---. Structurally the non-finite clause appears in the position of a Verb Complement, parallel to an Object clause (cf. (3a)). It might thus be justified to treat the clause as a 'retained' Object clause: the non-finite clause is a remnant of the original Object clause. Passivisation in this case does not affect the whole Object clause, but only the Subject of the Object clause, leaving the rest of the clause in its original position following the verb in the higher clause.

The passives of verbs such as *intend*, *think*, *expect*, *say* etc. all trigger raising of a NP/Su from an embedded non-finite S, as can be seen in the following examples:

(4) They are thought to be acts of the imagination.

(5) John is expected to be back soon.

(6) They are said to be leaving at dawn.

(7) Anne was found to be guilty of high treason.

(8) This was felt to be the only solution.

(9) She was considered to be the best player in the team.

(10) Mary was seen to steal the money.

Use dashes --- to mark the original position of the Subject NPs in (4)–(10) above.

It is very important to observe that the gap left after movement cannot be filled by another lexical element. Compare the examples in (11) and (12):

(11a) The political parts of the book were intended --- to reveal many things.

(11b) *The political parts of the book were intended various chapters to reveal many things.

(12a) Who did the terrorists assassinate ---?

(12b) *Who did the terrorists assassinate the ambassador? (Cf. 4.2.4.1)

Compare also (13a) and (13b):

(13a) A conspiracy was believed to exist in the country.

(13b) There was believed to exist a conspiracy in the country.

In (13a) the Subject position of the main clause is occupied by the NP *a conspiracy.* As in the examples discussed above, this Subject NP has been raised out of the embedded clause, leaving a gap:

(14a) $\left[_{NP}\text{A conspiracy}\right]$ was believed $\left[_{\bar{S}}\left[_{S}--- \left[_{VP}\text{to exist in the country}\right]\right]\right]$

In (13b) the GF of Su in the main clause is realised by *there.* We shall assume, again, that *there* originates in the lower clause as the Subject of *exist,* and has been moved into the main clause Subject position:

(14b) There was believed $\left[_{\bar{S}}\left[_{S}\text{---to exist a conspiracy in the country}\right]\right]$

There binds the gap (---) in the subordinate clause. We have seen before (4.4.3) that *there* can only function as the Subject of existential sentences. In (14b) we see that such a Subject of a non-finite existential sentence may also be raised.

So far we have concentrated on raising from non-finite clauses with *to*-infinitives. The process also applies, however, to clauses with participles in *−ing* and *−ed,* and to verbless clauses (cf. 5.1):

(15) Mary was heard singing carols.

(16) Their house was found occupied by squatters.

(17) He was considered innocent.

Mark the vacated Subject position in the subordinate clauses in (15), (16) and (17) by ---.

5.3.2 RAISING WITH INTRANSITIVE VERBS AND WITH ADJECTIVES

In 5.3.1 we have given examples of raising triggered by passive raising verbs:

(18) John is believed $\left[_{\overline{S}}\left[_{S}---\right.\right.$ to have left already$\left.\left.\right]\right]$

The pattern in (18) can also be found with non-passive, intransitive verbs:

(19) John seems to have disappeared.

(19) corresponds to (20):

(20) It seems that John has disappeared.

In (20) *John* is the Subject of the embedded finite clause *that John has disappeared. It*-extraposition is obligatory here: **That John has disappeared seems.*

In (19) we also want to relate *John* to the Subject position of the subordinate non-finite clause. This can be done if we assume (as in (18)) that the NP *John* originates as the Subject of the subordinate clause and is then raised to the Subject position of the main clause:

(19a) $---$ seems $\left[_{\overline{S}}\left[_{S}\right.\right.$John to have disappeared$\left.\left.\right]\right]$

(19b) John seems $---$ to have disappeared.

Some comments are necessary here.

(a) the embedded clause must not be introduced by the complementiser *for*, because this would give rise to the sequence *for* ... *to*. (Cf. 5.2.5 above.)
(b) (19a) as it stands could not take *it* as an anticipatory NP/su. If *seems* takes a non-finite clause, *it*-extraposition is impossible and raising is obligatory. Conversely, if *seems* takes a finite clause, raising is not possible and *it*-extraposition is obligatory (cf. (20) above).
(c) As in the case of passive raising verbs (5.3.1), the vacated Subject position of the non-finite clause accompanying *seems* cannot be filled by lexical material:

(21) *John seems Bill to have disappeared.

Other verbs which behave like *seem* are *appear*, *happen*, *turn out* (a phrasal verb, cf. Chapter 6).

(22) John appeared/happened/turned out to have left already.

Again we may ask what the GF is of the non-finite S accompanying *seem* in (19). On the one hand it is like a Subject clause, in that it parallels a finite extraposed $\overline{S}$/su (cf. (20)). On the other hand it is not the NP/Su of *seem*, since the Subject position of this V is occupied by an NP (*John* in (19)), which has been raised out of the non-finite clause. Again, we might call $---$ *to have disappeared* a 'retained' clause; in this case, it is the remainder of the original non-finite Subject clause, from which the NP/Su has been moved.

Certain adjectives in English may also trigger raising. For example:

(23) John is likely --- to propose to Mary.

Here *John* is the grammatical Subject of *is likely*, which binds the Subject position of the subordinate non-finite clause. The clause is interpreted as 'John will propose to Mary'.

Identify raising adjectives in the examples below:

(24) John is certain to propose to her tomorrow.

(25) The weather is unlikely to remain stable for long.

Rewrite each sentence with a finite clause and *it*-extraposition.

These raising adjectives have as their underlying Subject a non-finite clause (e.g. *John to propose to Mary*): what is likely is 'that John will propose to Mary'. In (23), for example, *John* has been raised out of the non-finite clause into main clause Subject position. As with raising verbs, it is impossible to have another Subject NP in the gap after raising. For example:

(26) *John is likely Bill to propose to Mary.

5.3.3 SUMMING UP

We have seen that raising verbs and raising adjectives share the following general properties:

(a) Raising only applies to the NP/Su of non-finite clauses.
(b) There is a gap after the V or Adj, which cannot be filled by a lexical NP:

(27) They seem/are likely/are said --- to have left.

(28) *They seem/are/likely/are said the children to have left.

The gap is bound by the Subject NP of the main clause.

(c) There is usually a paraphrase with a finite clause and *it*-extraposition:

(29) It seems/is likely/is said $\left[_{\bar{S}}\text{that they have left}\right]$

(d) In raising patterns the Subject *there* may be separated from the existential verb it goes with by raising:

there raising $\left\{\begin{matrix}\text{verb}\\ \text{adj}\end{matrix}\right\}$ --- to be/exist/ ...

(30) There seem/are likely --- to be many children with reading problems.

5.3.4 EXERCISES

I Identify raising operations in the examples below. Locate the gap in the subordinate clause. Rewrite each sentence as a sentence containing *it* and an extraposed finite Subject clause. For example:

John is likely to vote against this scheme.
John is likely --- to vote against this scheme.
It is likely that John will vote against this scheme.

(1) Two men are reported to have attacked an elderly widow in Bath.
(2) They are said to have been carrying guns.
(3) They were thought to be in their mid-thirties, wearing blue jeans and leather jackets.
(4) One of them is thought to have been involved in the assault of a 22-year-old girl last week.
(5) They appear to have taken no money from their victim.
(6) They are unlikely to remain in the area.
(7) They are expected to travel North in a red Jaguar.
(8) These men are certain to be found soon.
(9) Two police officers are believed to be involved in the search.

II Describe the process by which the following three sentences are derived:

(1) There is believed to exist a conspiracy in the country.
(2) There seems to exist a conspiracy in the country.
(3) There is likely to exist a conspiracy in the country.

III Discuss the syntax of the following sentences, taken from one issue of the *Guardian* (25 April 1983). Identify the raised NP and locate the gap in the subordinate clause. Is it always possible to rewrite the sentences as sentences containing *it* and an extraposed finite clause?

(1) The sale is bound to provoke a fresh controversy.
(2) The courts tended to accept too easily the licence holder's defence that he did not know the customer was a minor.
(3) The Government is understood to be considering amalgamating the existing nuclear bodies under the chairmanship of Sir Walter.
(4) Mr. Stott was thought to have won by about 10 votes.

IV Analyse the following sentences:

(1) I was kept waiting for hours.
(2) His election was considered disastrous for the country.
(3) All the seats were found occupied.

5.4 CONTROL

5.4.1 NON-LEXICAL SUBJECTS

In 5.2.4 we have seen examples like the following:

(1) I did not wish to write a family saga.

We have already pointed out that such sentences contain a non-finite

Object clause, whose Subject is not lexically filled. We have adopted the following convention for marking such non-lexically realised Subject positions:

(2) I did not wish $\left[_{\bar{S}} \left[_{S}(\quad) \left[_{VP}\text{to write a family saga}\right]\right]\right]$

We have also seen that non-finite subordinate clauses may have a lexical Subject.

(3) I did not wish $\left[_{\bar{S}}\text{(for)} \left[_{S}\text{the book to become a family saga}\right]\right]$

The complementiser *for* is allowed in (3), but it is disallowed in (2), because the string *for . . . to* is not grammatical in Standard English.

In (1), but not in (3), an NP outside the subordinate clause controls the Subject position in the subordinate clause. The non-lexical Subject is controlled by the main clause Su/NP (*I*): ( ) is interpreted as 'I'.

Reflexivisation can be used to support the analysis proposed here. Consider, for example:

(4) I want $\left[_{\bar{S}} \left[_{S}(\quad) \text{ to enjoy myself}\right]\right]$

Myself is a reflexive pronoun and must be bound within its clause (cf. 2.4.2.2). We assume that in (4) *myself* is bound inside the subordinate clause by ( ), the non-lexical Subject, which in turn is controlled by the higher Subject *I*. This may be represented as follows:

(5) I want $\left[_{\bar{S}}(\quad) \text{ to enjoy myself}\right]$

Compare (5) with (6):

(6) I want $\left[_{\bar{S}}\text{you to enjoy } \begin{Bmatrix}\text{yourself} \\ \text{*myself}\end{Bmatrix}\right]$

5.4.2 CONTROL VS RAISING

It is important to realise that the controller NP in (5) above is both the underlying and the surface Subject of *want*; it is not the case that *I* has been moved into that Subject position by a raising transformation: *want, decide, wish, hope* are **control verbs**, not raising verbs.

In order to verify this claim, let us compare sentences like (1) above with raising patterns. We have seen (5.3.2) that intransitive raising verbs (*seem, appear*, etc.) may appear in the string:

NP–*seem* --- *to*–infinitive, where --- cannot be filled by a lexical NP:

(7a) They seem --- to have left.

(7b) *They seem *the children* to have left.

Secondly, raising verbs usually have a paraphrase with a finite clause and *it*-extraposition:

(8a) They seem to have left.

(8b) *It* seems *that they have left.*

And, thirdly, in *there*-sentences the Subject *there* may be separated from its existential verb (*be, exist,* etc.). This can be accounted for by assuming that *there* has been raised, and has thus been moved away from the existential verb. For example:

(9) *There* seem --- to be many children with reading problems.

Let us see what happens if we apply the same three tests to the string: NP–*want*–( )–*to*–infinitive, where the empty Subject position ( ) is controlled by the Subject NP.

In the first place, we often have the option here of filling or not filling the empty Subject slot:

(10) I want $\left\{ \begin{matrix} (\ \ ) \\ \text{you} \end{matrix} \right\}$ to leave

A lexical Subject NP may occur in the subordinate non-finite clause.

Secondly, there is no paraphrase with *it*-extraposition:

(11a) I want to go.

(11b) *It wants that I should go.

And thirdly, there are no sequences like:

(12) **There* want ( ) to be many children with reading problems.

Table 5.4.2 sums up the results of these tests. The first column gives the way in which the tests work for raising verbs like *seem*, the second shows the results of applying the tests to control patterns with verbs such as *want*:

Table 5.4.2

		Raising	*Control*
(a)	lexical Subject in non-finite clause	no	yes
(b)	*it*-extraposition paraphrase	yes	no
(c)	*there* V *to* . . .	yes	no

What raising and control have in common is that both apply to non-finite clauses: raising operates *from* non-finite clauses, and control *into* non-finite clauses. Only non-finite clauses may lack an overt NP/Su (indicated by --- or ( )).

5.4.3 SUBJECT AND OBJECT CONTROL

(13) He promised her to mow the lawn.

(14) General Dyer told his troops to fire on an unarmed crowd in the streets.

Both sentences have the pattern Su [V–Oi–Od], unlike sentence (1), which has the pattern Su [V–Od]. What is the difference between (13) and (14)? In (13) the non-lexical Subject position in the subordinate clause is controlled by the Subject NP *He*, not by the NP/Oi *her*, whereas in (14) it is the NP/Oi *his troops* which is the controller, not the NP/Su *General Dyer*. (13) and (14) may thus be bracketed as follows:

(15) $[_{S}[_{NP}\text{He}][_{VP}\text{promised }[_{NP}\text{her}][_{\bar{S}}(\quad)\text{ to mow the lawn}]]]$

(16) $[_{S}[_{NP}\text{General Dyer}][_{VP}\text{told }[_{NP}\text{his troops}][_{\bar{S}}(\quad)\text{ to fire on an unarmed crowd in the streets}]]]$

The type of verb in the main clause determines whether the NP/Su or the NP/Oi will be the controller. Verbs like *promise* have Subject control, whereas verbs like *tell, order, ask, force, persuade, allow, encourage* have Object control. Here are some examples of control patterns like (16):

(17) He persuaded her to buy some more books.

(18) The boys did not allow the girls to take part in the game.

(19) We encouraged them to try again.

(20) They asked him to resign.

Identify the controlled Subject position in these sentences, and the controller.

Sentences like (17)–(20) can be passivised: the NP/Oi (*her, the girls, them, him*) can be made the NP/Su of the passive sentence. Taking (17) as an example, the passivisation process may be described as follows:

(21) $[_{S}[_{NP}\text{He}][_{VP}\text{persuaded }[_{NP}\text{her}][_{\bar{S}}(\quad)\text{ to buy some more books}]]]$

Passivisation moves the NP/Oi *her*, and leaves the subordinate clause unaffected:

(22) $$[_S [_{NP} \text{She}] [_{VP} \text{was persuaded} --- [_{\bar{S}} (\quad) \text{ to buy some more books}]]]$$

We still have a control structure here, but now the Subject *she* controls the Subject position of the subordinate clause.

5.4.4 INDEFINITE CONTROL

English also has control patterns which have no overt controller. Take, for example:

(23) $$\left\{\begin{array}{l}\text{To write}\\ \text{Writing}\end{array}\right\} \text{ a book on this subject was an irrational act.}$$

The Subject of the non-finite subordinate clause is empty. We analyse (23) as follows:

(24) $$[_{\bar{S}} [_S (\quad) \left\{\begin{array}{l}\text{To write}\\ \text{Writing}\end{array}\right\} \text{ a book on this subject}]]$$

was an irrational act.

The controller in this case might be somebody mentioned in the context, or someone unknown or indefinite. We call this **indefinite control**. Other examples of indefinite control are:

(25) Is ( ) to say No to nuclear weapons a defence policy?

(26) Oxbridge's grip on the top ranks of the civil service should be broken by ( ) encouraging students at provincial universities ( ) to come forward as potential mandarins.

The second control site in (26), unlike the first, is not a case of indefinite control. What is the controller of that second control site?

As we have seen (3.4.11), non-finite clauses may have functions other than Od or Su. They may, for example, be Adjuncts or Modifiers:

(27) I want to go to Paris *to buy some new clothes.*

(28) He received a letter *ordering him to leave the country.*

Both these non-finite clauses lack an overt lexical Subject NP: the empty Subject position in (27) is controlled by *I*, and that in (28) by *a letter.*

5.4.5 CONTROL ADJECTIVES

There are also control adjectives in English, not just control verbs. These adjectives are followed by non-finite clauses with controlled Subject positions:

(29) I am *eager* $\left[_{\overline{S}}\left[_{S}(\quad)\right.\right.$ to come to your party$\left.\left.\right]\right]$

(30) He is *reluctant* $\left[_{\overline{S}}\left[_{S}(\quad)\right.\right.$ to tell her the truth$\left.\left.\right]\right]$

By applying the three tests mentioned earlier, we can determine that (29) and (30) are control patterns, not raising patterns. For example:

(31) I am eager for Mary to be at the party too.

(32) *It is eager that I should come to your party.

(33) *There is eager to be a party next weekend.

Other examples of control adjectives are:

(34) He is *anxious* ( ) to make his new business a financial success.

(35) We are *delighted* ( ) to send you our pamphlets.

(36) She is *afraid* of ( ) hurting his feelings.

5.4.6 EXERCISES

I Consider the following control sentences, and insert round brackets in the right position:

(1) I wish to go immediately.
(2) I intend to write another novel soon.
(3) We prefer to leave now.
(4) I hope to see you again soon.
(5) The prisoner demanded to see his wife.
(6) I need a knife to cut the bread with.
(7) I promise to return these books to you before the end of this month.
(8) I'll try to catch the first train to Amsterdam.
(9) I find that I have brought into my new circle the very person I planned to exclude.
(10) It would never be right to use, or to threaten to use, these weapons, or indeed any other weapons of mass destruction.
(11) Licensing judges should be able to grant a licence permitting adults to take their children into a specified room in licensed premises until 8 p.m. to be served non-alcoholic drinks.
(12) Mr Livingstone has urged council workers to adopt a radical approach in defending their jobs.
(13) Mrs Thatcher demonstrated once again yesterday her determination to keep the Government on its present course and, if possible, her intention to secure a second term.
(14) Further evidence emerged yesterday of the Government's continued attempts in the disarmament propaganda war to bring senior churchmen on its side.

(15) Faced with the British ultimatum and seeking to cut their losses through further delays in price fixing, ministers were preparing for final negotiations last night.

II Consider the following patterns:

(1) He believes Mary to be a spy.
(2) He prefers Mary to leave.
(3) He asked Mary to leave.
(4) He promised Mary to leave.

(5) Mary $\left\{\begin{array}{l}\text{appears}\\ \text{is believed}\end{array}\right\}$ to be a spy.

(6) Mary wants to leave.

Analyse these sentences and indicate the differences between them. Which are control patterns and which are raising patterns?

III Text 5.4.6 contains a number of non-finite clauses, most of which contain no overt Subject NP. Identify such clauses; decide whether they are instances of raising patterns ---, or of control patterns (   ). Other gaps left behind by moved elements are also marked by dashes ---. Remember that non-finite constructions may also be reduced Relative clauses. Assign GFs to the non-finite clauses.

Text 5.4.6

I was invited to present the prizes at a girls' school. It is always difficult to think of something to say on such occasions.

The girls happened to come up in age groups, and eventually the head girl came up to collect the several prizes she had won. She turned out to be a nice looking girl of about seventeen. I wondered what to say to her. Suddenly I thought that, as this was her last term at school, it would be appropriate to ask her:

'And what do you plan to do when you leave school?'

She looked at me very coyly and said:

'Well, I did intend to go straight home.'

Adapted from Christian Brann, *Pass the Port.*

6

REANALYSIS: A PROBLEM OF BRACKETING

6.1 INTRODUCTION

It sometimes happens that a single word or string of words may be analysed in two ways. We have seen (2.4.3.4), for example, that the elements *be* and *have* are structurally ambiguous, in that they may behave like lexical verbs or like auxiliaries. Another instance of double structure in English is that of V–Od strings like *kick the bucket*, which in their literal sense can regularly occur in the passive (*The bucket was kicked*), but not when they are used in their idiomatic sense (**The bucket was kicked by the old man* = *The old man died*). It appears that *kick the bucket*, as an idiom, is no longer a V–Od string, but has been restructured into just a composite intransitive verb. A well-known example of ambiguous patterning is also that of strings such as *depend on*, *look at*, *give in to* and others, which may be structurally interpreted as intransitive verbs followed by a PP, or alternatively as transitive verbs followed by a Direct Object.

These kinds of structural ambiguity result from the process of **reanalysis** (also called 'restructuring'). Reanalysis changes the structure of a string of elements, so that before and after reanalysis the string will pattern differently.

In this chapter we shall compare the properties of verb+preposition strings with those of some other multi-word verbs, and examine the indeterminacy of their structure.

6.2 PREPOSITIONS AND PARTICLES

Read text 6.2. It is a fragment from *Of Human Bondage* which we have looked at before. The sentences have been numbered here for ease of reference.

Text 6.2 (= text 1.2.4)

(1) Soon after breakfast Mary Ann *brought in The Times.*

(2) Mr. Carey shared it with two neighbours.

(3) He had it from ten till one, when the gardener took it over to Mr. Ellis at the Limes, with whom it remained till seven; then it was taken to Miss Brooks at the Manor House, who, since she

got it late, had the advantage of keeping it.

(4) In summer Mrs. Carey, when she was making jam, often asked her for a copy to cover the pots with.

(5) When the Vicar *settled down* to his paper,

(5b) his wife *put on her bonnet*

(5c) and *went out* to do the shopping.

Adapted from W. Somerset Maugham, *Of Human Bondage.*

For the purpose of our discussion we here present skeleton versions of the sentences (1) and (5) above:

(1) Mary *brought in The Times* after breakfast.

(5a) The Vicar *settled down* to his paper.

(5b) His wife *put on her bonnet.*

(5c) She *went out.*

In each of the sentences above, the lexical verb is followed by another element that is closely linked with the verb: *in, down, on, out.* The question is: what is the status of *in, down,* etc.? Are they prepositions which take a Prepositional Complement (as in: *in the vicarage*); do these elements belong to the V, or are they perhaps independent units?

Take example (1) above. This may be bracketed as follows:

(6) $[_{S}[_{NP}\text{Mary Ann}]\ [_{VP}\text{brought in The Times}\ [_{PP}\text{after breakfast}]]]$

There can be no doubt about *after breakfast.* It is a genuine PP: it consists of a preposition *after* and its Complement NP *breakfast.* Together the P+NP make up one phrase, a PP. *After breakfast* is an optional element (an Adverbial Adjunct; cf. Chapter 3).

There seem to be three possible ways of bracketing the remainder of the VP *brought in The Times*:

(7a) $[_{VP}[_{V}\text{brought}]\ [_{?PP}\text{in The Times}]]$

(7b) $[_{VP}[_{?V}\text{brought in}]\ [_{NP}\text{The Times}]]$

(7c) $[_{VP}[_{V}\text{brought}]\ [_{?}\text{in}]\ [_{NP}\text{The Times}]]$

According to (7a) *in* is a P, taking *The Times* as its Complement. According to (7b) *in* is somehow part of the verb itself; *brought* and *in* seem to make up one unit with word-like properties. In (7c) *in* is independent of both *brought* and of *The Times.* The three alternatives may be represented by the following tree diagrams:

(8a)

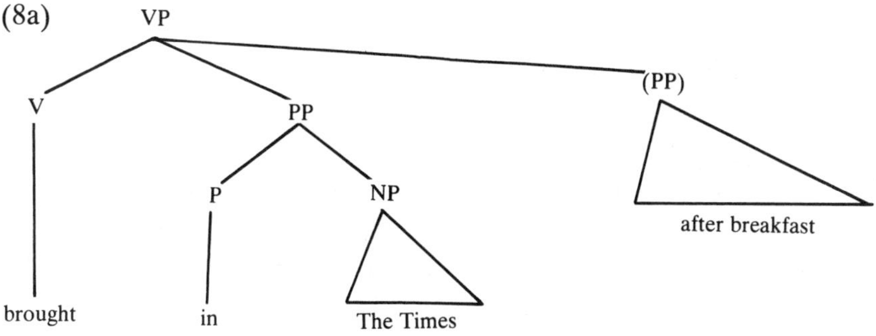

(8b)

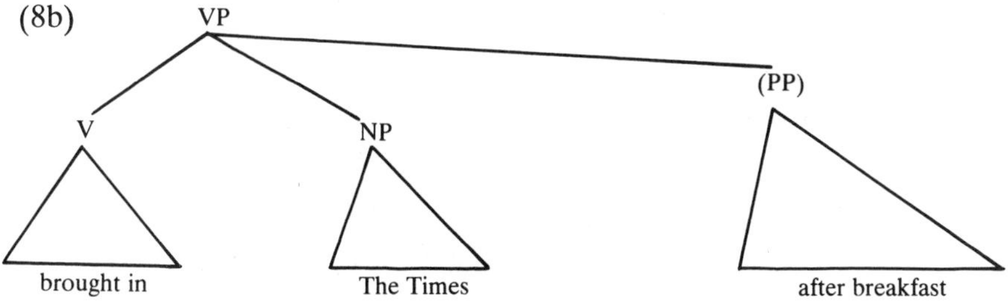

(8c)

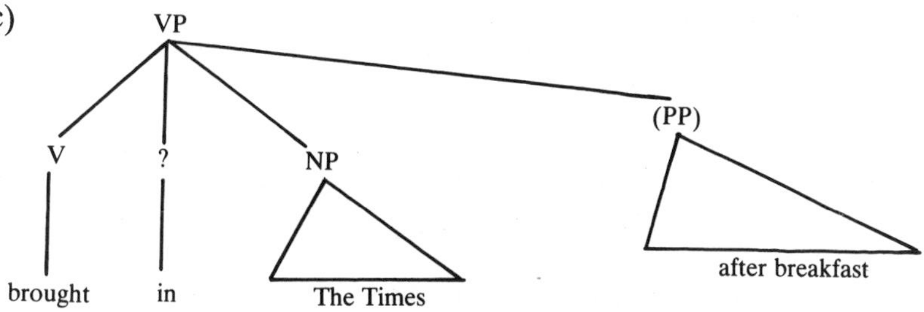

Let us consider the behaviour of *after breakfast,* the optional PP (the brackets around the PP in (8a)–(8c) mark its optionality). What are the properties of this PP?

(I) We can front the PP quite easily:

After breakfast Mary Ann brought in The Times.

(II) The PP may serve as the focus element X in a cleft sentence:

It was *after breakfast* that Mary Ann brought in The Times.

(III) The PP may be replaced by an appropriate Adjunct, here a time Adjunct (*then*):

Mary Ann brought in The Times *then*.

(IV) The PP may be questioned by a *wh*-item like *when, where* or *at what time*:

When did Mary Ann bring in The Times?

At what time did Mary Ann bring in The Times?

(V) The PP may be separated from the rest of the sentence by an Adjunct (Adjuncts can only be inserted between major constituents; they thus mark constituent boundaries):

Mary Ann brought in The Times, as usual, after breakfast.

Tests (I)–(V) show that *after* and *breakfast* make up one constituent. The two elements cannot be separated or inverted, as the following ungrammatical sentences show (tests (VI)–(VIII)):

(VI) **Breakfast* Mary Ann brought in The Times *after.*
(VII) *It was *breakfast* that Mary brought in The Times *after.*
(VIII) *Mary Ann brought in The Times *breakfast after.*

These three examples show that in this case neither fronting of just the NP, nor clefting with the NP as X, nor changing the word order is possible.

Let us now turn to the sequence *in The Times.* Analysis (8a) above suggests that *in+The Times* make up a PP, just like *after breakfast.* If the analysis were correct, we would expect some degree of similarity between the two PPs. Notice, however, what happens if we apply the tests (I)–(V) to *in The Times*:

(I) *in+The Times* cannot be fronted together:

**In The Times* Mary Ann brought after breakfast.

(II) Neither can *in+The Times* serve as X in a cleft sentence:

*It was *in The Times* that Mary Ann brought after breakfast.

(III) *in+The Times* cannot be replaced by *then* or *there*:

*Mary Ann brought {then / there} after breakfast.

(IV) *in+The Times* cannot be questioned by a *wh*-word:

{* *When* / * *Where*} did Mary Ann bring after breakfast.

Nor do we get:

{ **In what* / **In what newspaper* } did Mary Ann bring?

(V) *in+The Times* cannot be separated from the rest of the sentence by an Adjunct:

*Mary Ann brought, as usual, in The Times after breakfast.

Tests (I)–(V) indicate that *in* and *The Times* are not one constituent. If they are not one constituent, it should be easy to separate the elements or to change the word order. This is indeed confirmed by the following sentences, all of which are grammatical (tests (VI)–(VIII)):

(VI) *The Times* Mary Ann brought *in.*

{ *What newspaper* / *What* } did Mary Ann bring *in*?

(VII) It was *The Times* that Mary Ann brought *in.*
(VIII) Mary Ann brought *The Times in* after breakfast.

Note, incidentally, that *in* must normally appear in the position on the right of the Object NP if the NP is a personal pronoun:

Mary Ann brought it in.

*Mary Ann brought in it.

Compare this with:

Mary Ann brought in The Times after it.

*Mary Ann brought in The Times it after.

Summing up the tests, we see that *after+breakfast* and *in+The Times* pattern differently in the sentences:

Tests		*after+breakfast*	*in+The Times*
(I)	Front together	yes	no
(II)	Cleft together	yes	no
(III)	Replace together	yes	no
(IV)	Question together	yes	no
(V)	Adjunct insertion	yes	no
(VI)	Front NP	no	yes
(VII)	Cleft NP	no	yes
(VIII)	Change order	no	yes

The tests show that analysis (8a) above must be wrong: *in The Times* is not a PP.

We are now left with the choice of treating *in* as a **particle** which goes with *bring* (8b), or as a totally independent constituent (8c). As far as the meaning of the sentence is concerned *bring in* is felt to be a lexical unit, meaning something like 'deliver'. Is there any formal support for this intuition? In other words: do *bring* and *in* behave at all as if they were one constituent? To see this, let us first consider the following sentences:

(9) John reads The Times and Susan reads the Guardian.

We have two coordinated clauses here, each with the verb *read*. In English, there is an operation called **gapping**, which deletes the second occurrence of a lexical verb in a coordinated pattern:

(10) John reads The Times and Susan / / / / / / / the Guardian.

There is a gap at the place of the deletion. Note that PPs are left intact if the verb is gapped.

(11) Mary came *after breakfast* and Bill came *after tea.*

(12) Mary came *after breakfast* and Bill / / / / *after tea.*

After tea is a PP and is not involved in gapping of V:

(13) *Mary came *after breakfast* and Bill / / / / / / / / / / / / / / / / *tea.*

Consider now:

(14) Mary Ann brought in The Times and Philip brought in the Guardian.

If we apply verb gapping here, we must also delete *in*, not just *brought*:

(15) Mary Ann brought in The Times and Bill / / / / / / / / / / / / / / the Guardian.

The following sentence is ungrammatical:

(16) *Mary Ann brought in The Times and Philip / / / / / / / / / / in the Guardian.

This means then that *in* is not totally independent: it is tightly linked with *bring*. Together *bring* and *in* act as if they were one lexical verb. This suggests that tree diagram (8b) above is the best alternative. We shall say that *bring* and *in* make up one lexical unit, consisting of a verb *bring* and a particle *in*. *Bring in* is a **phrasal verb**, which behaves like an ordinary transitive verb. We propose the following bracketing.

(17) $[_{S} [_{NP}\text{Mary Ann}] \; [_{VP} \; [_{V}\text{brought in}] \; [_{NP}\text{The Times}]$
$[_{PP}\text{after breakfast}]]]$

In text 6.1 above, sentence (5b) also contains a phrasal verb: *put on.* The analysis of that sentence is as follows:

(18) $[_S [_{NP} \text{His wife}] [_{VP} [_V \text{put on}] [_{NP} \text{her bonnet}]]]$

Now take sentence (5a): *The Vicar settled down to his paper.* Bracket the VP. Inside the VP you will find that V (*settle*) is followed by *down.* This string is again a phrasal verb, but this time there is no NP as Complement inside the VP:

(19) $[_S [_{NP} \text{The Vicar}] [_{VP} [_V \text{settled down}] [_{PP} \text{to his paper}]]]$

However, *settle down* requires the PP *to his paper* for the meaning intended here (PP/Ac). *The Vicar settled down* does not mean quite the same. Another instance of a phrasal verb can be found in (5c): *She went out.*

The phrasal verbs *bring in* and *put up* are transitive, and *settle down* and *go out* are intransitive. The phrasal verb *hand over* in:

(20) She handed over the paper to the Vicar.

is ditransitive.

Try verb gapping in coordinated structures with *put on, settle down, go out,* and *hand over* to show that they constitute one unit. For example:

(21a) Mrs Carey put on her bonnet and Mr Carey put on his hat.

(21b) Mrs Carey put on her bonnet and Mr Carey ///// his hat.

Other examples of phrasal verbs are: *sit down, take off, switch on, look up, call off, call up, write down, bring up, give back, give in,* etc.

6.2.1 EXERCISES

I In the following examples you find coordinated structures containing sentences with identical verbs, but not all of them are phrasal verbs. Use the verb gapping test to determine which of the following sentences contain phrasal verbs.

(1) Mary threw out her old books and Bill threw out his old records.
(2) Mary ate the cake and Bill ate the pudding.
(3) The policeman took down my address and his assistant took down the registration number of my car.
(4) I am going to Madeira and Joe is going to Venice.
(5) The left wing of the party won over the women voters, the right wing won over the men.
(6) Joan voted for the Liberals and Bill voted for the Conservatives.
(7) Sue travelled back on Thursday and Bill travelled back on Friday.
(8) We can put up three more guests, and my parents can put up two.
(9) Bill gave up alcohol and his father gave up smoking.
(10) My father has just resigned from the British Academy and my brother has just resigned from the Social Sciences Research Council.

II Identify phrasal verbs and one-word verbs with PPs in the following text:

Text 6.2.1
Poaching eggs
Use a medium size pan. Pour in boiling water to a depth of 1 inch. Add wine, which speeds up coagulation. Break each egg into a cup. Bring the water to a gentle simmer. Slide in the eggs one by one. Poach for three minutes. Lift out the eggs with a spoon and serve them with baked potatoes.

III We have seen that there is a set of tests available which can help us decide the structure of strings such as *after+breakfast* and *in+The Times*. Bracket VPs in the following sentences and indicate their structure. Using the eight tests given above ((I)–(VIII)) try to decide, in particular, on the structure of the italicised strings. You will see that some of these strings have an indeterminate structure. Under certain tests they behave as if they are constituents and under others they behave as if they are not. Try passivising the sentences.

(1) Mary Ann arrived *after breakfast.*
(2) She picked *up the newspaper.*
(3) The Vicar did everything *for Philip.*
(4) The Vicar prayed *for peace.*
(5) The Vicar was looking *for a new assistant.*
(6) The students filled *in the forms.*
(7) Most people hope *for nuclear disarmament.*
(8) He found her address *in the directory.*
(9) Mary lives *on the third floor.*
(10) The Vicar can rely *on Mary Ann.*

6.3 PREPOSITIONAL VERBS

In this section we shall deal with strings like *pray for*, *look for*, *hope for* and *rely on* (cf. sentences (4), (5), (7) and (10) of Exercise III in 6.2.1).

Let us compare the verbs in the following three examples:

(1) Mary Ann arrived after breakfast.

(2) She brought in The Times.

(3) The Vicar can rely on Mary Ann.

We have seen that *after* in (1) goes with *breakfast* rather than with *arrived* and we have established that *in* in (2) structures with *brought* rather than with *The Times* (cf. the tests in 6.2 above).

(1) corresponds to the structure (see (8a) in 6.2):

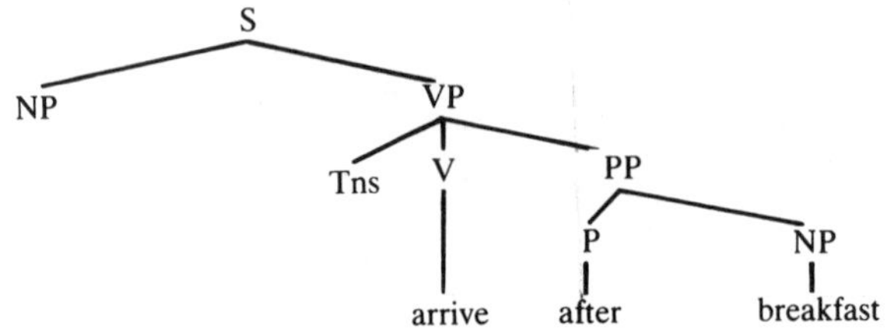

(2) has the structure (see (8b) in 6.2):

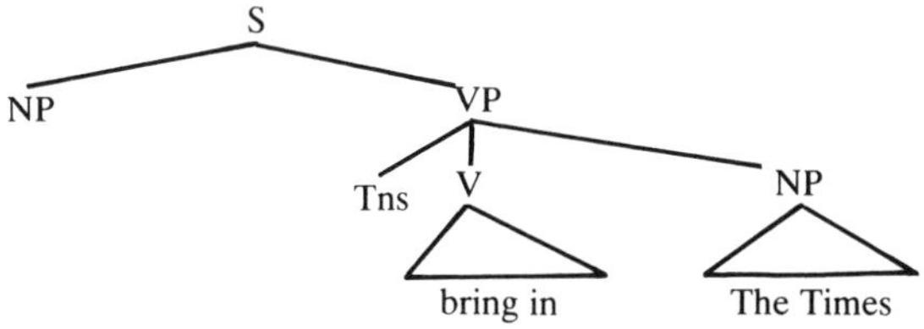

In some respects *rely+on* behaves like *arrive*, whereas in other respects it behaves like *bring in*. To see this, let us apply tests (I)–(VIII) as well as the verb gapping test to (3) (these tests have been applied above to distinguish between V+PP strings and phrasal verbs):

(I) and (VI) Both *on Mary Ann* (PP) and *Mary Ann* (NP) can be fronted:

(4a) *On Mary Ann* the Vicar can rely.

(4b) *Mary Ann* the Vicar can rely on.

(II) and (VII) Both *on Mary Ann* and *Mary Ann* may serve as the focus element X in a cleft sentence:

(5a) It is *on Mary Ann* that the Vicar can rely.

(5b) It is *Mary Ann* that the Vicar can rely on.

(III) *On Mary Ann* cannot be replaced by the pro-form *then* or *there* (but *Mary Ann* can be replaced by *her*):

(6a) *The Vicar can rely *then/there*

(6b) The Vicar can rely on *her*.

(IV) *On Mary Ann* cannot be questioned by a *wh*-item like *when* or *where* (but *Mary Ann* can be questioned by *who(m)*):

(7a) * *When/where* can the Vicar rely?

(7b) *Who(m)* can the Vicar rely on?

(V) *On Mary Ann* may be separated from the rest of the sentence by an Adjunct:

(8a) The Vicar can rely whole-heartedly on Mary Ann.

(8b) *The Vicar can rely on whole-heartedly Mary Ann.

(VIII) The word order of *on Mary Ann* cannot be changed into *Mary Ann on*:

(9) *The Vicar can rely *Mary Ann on.*

Verb gapping gives the following result:

(10a) The Vicar can rely on Mary Ann and Mrs. Carey can rely on Philip.

(10b) The Vicar can rely on Mary Ann and Mrs. Carey ///// on Philip.

(10c) *The Vicar can rely on Mary Ann and Mrs. Carey ////// Philip.

The conclusion is that the structure of the VP with *rely on* is difficult to determine: according to certain tests the string *rely on*–NP is like a one-word verb followed by a PP (cf. tests I, II, VIII and gapping), whereas according to other tests it is like a two-word verb followed by an NP (cf. tests III, IV, VI, VII). In other words, the structure of such V–P–VP strings is indeterminate; it may be either (11a) or (11b) below:

(11a) $\left[_{VP}\left[_{V}\text{rely}\right]\left[_{PP}\text{on NP}\right]\right]$

(11b) $\left[_{VP}\left[_{V}\text{rely on}\right]\left[\text{NP}\right]\right]$

The duality of the structure of *rely on* . . . may be captured by combining two structures into one. Thus, the structures represented by (11a) and (11b) are combined in tree diagram (11c):

(11c)

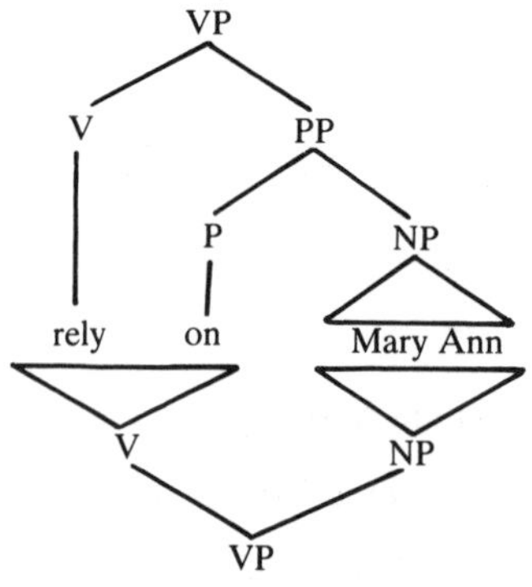

Traditionally, strings such as *rely* + *on* are called **prepositional verbs**. They share grammatical characteristics with V + PP strings as well as with phrasal verbs. Other examples of prepositional verbs are: *look at, look for, look after, call on, call for, deal with, account for, stare at, wait for,* etc.

In so far as prepositional verbs are two-word verbs they resemble (transitive) phrasal verbs such as *bring in, call up,* etc. One important characteristic which they share is that both types of verb allow passivisation:

(12a) Mary Ann brought in The Times.

(12b) The Times was brought in by Mary Ann.

(13a) The Vicar can rely on Mary Ann.

(13b) Mary Ann can be relied on by the Vicar.

Moreover, both types of verb allow *wh*-question formation with *what* or *who* (not *when* or *where*, as we have seen). For example:

(12c) What did Mary Ann bring in?

(13c) Who can the Vicar rely on?

However, there are also some important differences. One point, as we have seen, is that the particle of a phrasal verb may be placed *before* or *after* the NP, whereas the preposition of the prepositional verb can only occur *before* the NP (test VIII above).

Compare (12a) and (13a) with (12d) and (13d):

(12d) Mary Ann brought The Times in.

(13d) *The Vicar can rely Mary Ann on.

This is one reason why we have called *in* a particle in cases like (12d), and *on* a preposition. Another difference, as we have seen, between prepositional verbs and phrasal verbs is that it is usually fairly easy to insert an Adverbial Adjunct immediately before the preposition, but not immediately before the particle. Compare:

(12e) *Mary Ann brought early in The Times.

(13e) The Vicar can rely whole-heartedly on Mary Ann.

A third difference is that in relative clauses the particle of the phrasal verb must not precede the relative pronoun, whereas the preposition of the prepositional verb may, but need not, precede the relative pronoun. Compare:

(12f) The newspaper which Mary Ann brought in ---.

(12g) *The newspaper in which Mary Ann brought ---.

(13f) The girl who(m) the Vicar can rely on ---.

(13g) The girl on whom the Vicar can rely ---.

6.3.1 EXERCISE

Which of the sentences below contain phrasal verbs and which prepositional verbs?

(1) No one can *account for* William's extraordinary behaviour.

(2) The Ministry *turned down* our proposal.
(3) You can always *rely on* Philip.
(4) The boys *waited* patiently *for* their mothers.
(5) You will have to *allow for* a slight loss of quality in the process.
(6) Dorothy's mother will *look after* the baby while she is away.
(7) No one had *reckoned with* William's opposition to the plan.
(8) He *looked up* all the difficult words in his dictionary.
(9) Mrs. Carey *put on* her nicest dress.
(10) They could *think of* no better solution.

6.4 PHRASAL-PREPOSITIONAL VERBS AND PREPOSITIONAL IDIOMS

Phrasal-prepositional verbs are combinations of phrasal verbs and prepositional verbs. Examples are: *catch up with, come up with, cut down on, give in to, keep up with, look down on, put up with*, etc. Like phrasal and prepositional verbs, they may undergo passivisation. For example:

(1a) We have put up with William's rude behaviour too long.

(1b) William's rude behaviour has been put up with too long.

We assume that the VP of (1a) has the same dual structure as (3) in 6.3 above (cf. (11c)):

(2)

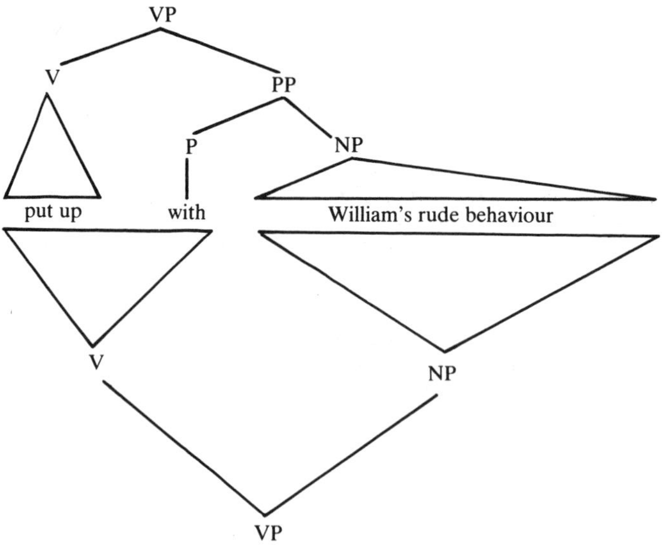

English also has so-called **prepositional idioms**. They consist of a verb followed by an NP and a preposition. Examples are: *make mention of, make use of, pay attention to, take advantage of, set fire to*, etc. These idioms often allow two passives, as a result of their dual structure, as follows:

(3a) Everyone took advantage of her goodness.

(3b) Advantage was taken of her goodness.

(3c) Her goodness was taken advantage of.

What is the structure of the VP *take advantage of her goodness*? Where, in particular, do the NP *advantage* and the preposition *of* belong? The structure of this string might be (4a), (4b) or (4c):

(4a) $[_{VP}[_{V}\text{took}]\ [_{NP}\text{advantage}]\ [_{PP}\text{of her goodness}]]$

(4b) $[_{VP}[_{V}\text{took advantage}]\ [_{PP}\text{of her goodness}]]$

(4c) $[_{VP}[_{V}\text{took advantage of}]\ [_{NP}\text{her goodness}]]$

As with prepositional verbs and phrasal-prepositional verbs, the various tests support analysis (4a), or (4b), or (4c). So, again, the structure of the VP is indeterminate. Try some of the tests (fronting, clefting, *wh*-question formation, verb gapping, etc.) to see whether you agree with our conclusion that there is support for all three analyses.

6.4.1 EXERCISE

Identify prepositional idioms in the following examples. Can you passivise them? Is it always possible to have two passives? Consider the behaviour of the strings if you apply the tests discussed above (6.2):

(1) Her mother took care of the baby.
(2) The students paid no attention to the professor's warning.
(3) The children made fun of the old lady.
(4) You cannot keep pace with all the recent developments in the theory.
(5) The government ought to put an end to crimes of this nature.
(6) Terrorists set fire to the embassy building.
(7) We must never lose sight of the ideals of this enterprise.
(8) This firm makes use of the latest printing techniques.
(9) The police kept close tabs on the student leaders.
(10) The conference took place in a large country house.

7
LEVELS OF STRUCTURE

7.1 INTRODUCTION

In the previous chapters we have looked at constituents at various levels: we have introduced **clausal constituents** (the sentence/clause); we have discussed **phrasal categories**, i.e. NP, VP, AdjP, PP, AdvP; and we have discussed **lexical categories** such as N, V, Adj, P, Adv. Phrasal categories were directly related to lexical categories in that we argued that each phrasal category has as its Head a lexical category; for example: an NP has an N as its Head. Phrasal categories are sometimes said to be **projections** of lexical categories.

Below we repeat the phrasal categories. We have italicised the lexical category functioning as the Head:

(1) *Noun phrase:*

Det	$AdjP_1$ $AdjP_2$	*N*	PP_1 PP_2
these	nice French	students	of English from Paris

(2) *Verb phrase:*

Tns	*V*	NP	NP
Past	buy	a car	last week

(3) *Prepositional phrase:*

AdvP	*P*	NP
soon	after	her arrival

(4) *Adjective phrase:*

AdvP	*Adj*	PP
extremely	worried	about the future

(5) *Adverb phrase:*

AdvP	*Adv*
very	cleverly

We have also shown how the constituents inside the phrase have different GFs: phrases can be described by the following schema:

(6)

$$\text{XP} \rightarrow \text{Spec–X–} \begin{Bmatrix} \text{Mod} \\ \text{A} \end{Bmatrix}$$

Identify the categories realising Spec, Mod and A in the examples above.

In this chapter we shall look more closely at the internal structure of phrases.

7.2 NOUN PHRASES

7.2.1 FLAT STRUCTURES AND LAYERED STRUCTURES

In 2.4.2.5 we have described NPs according to the following diagram:

(1) *NP*:

Category	Det	AdjP_1	AdjP_2	N	PP_1	PP_2
GF	Spec	Mod (Premodifier)		Head	Mod (Postmodifier)	
	these	nice	French	students	of English	from Paris

A diagram such as (1) seems to suggest that if we were to use a tree diagram representation, the structure of the NP would look as follows:

(2)

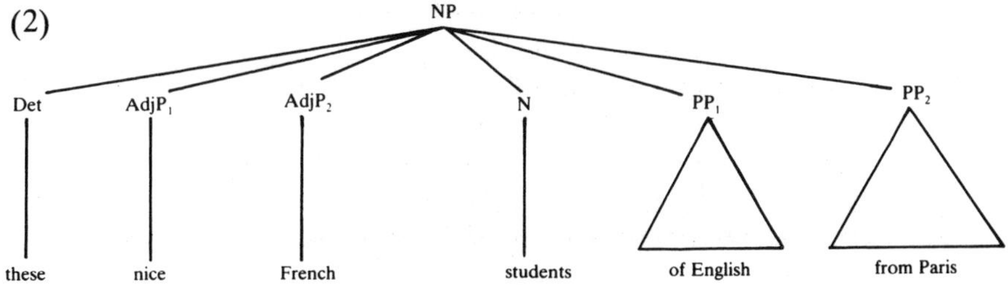

In other words, the structure looks 'flat'; NPs are made to look as if they are just strings of elements with various GFs. Tree diagram (2) suggests that the N *students* takes four Modifiers:

(a) $AdjP_1$ *nice*
(b) $AdjP_2$ *French*
(c) PP_1 *of English*
(d) PP_2 *from Paris*

and that all four Modifiers are of equal rank. However, semantically (i.e. with respect to meaning) such a representation is clearly inadequate, since the NP *these nice French students of English from Paris* does not mean that these students were (a) nice, and (b) French, and (c) of English and (d) from Paris. Rather, the NP means that these students were (a) students of English, (b) that 'these students of English' were French, (c) that 'these French students of English' were from Paris, and that (d) 'these French students of English from Paris' were nice.

There is thus an internal hierarchy among the Modifiers; *of English*, for example, is much more closely associated with the N *students*, than *French*: the string *students of English* is one unit, which is modified by *French*. In its turn, the string *French students of English* is modified by *from Paris*, and finally the string *French students of English from Paris* is modified by *nice*.

This hierarchy is confirmed by the fact that the order of $AdjP_1$ and $AdjP_2$ and that of PP_1 and PP_2 is fairly fixed:

(3) ?These French nice students of English from Paris.

(4) *These nice French students from Paris of English.

(5) *These French nice students from Paris of English.

Using labelled bracketing we arrive at the following build-up:

(6) $$\left[_{NP}\text{these} \left[_{XP_1}\text{nice} \left[_{XP_2}\left[_{XP_3}\text{French} \left[_{XP_4}\text{students of English}\right]\right] \text{from Paris}\right]\right]\right]$$

or in a tree diagram representation:

(7)

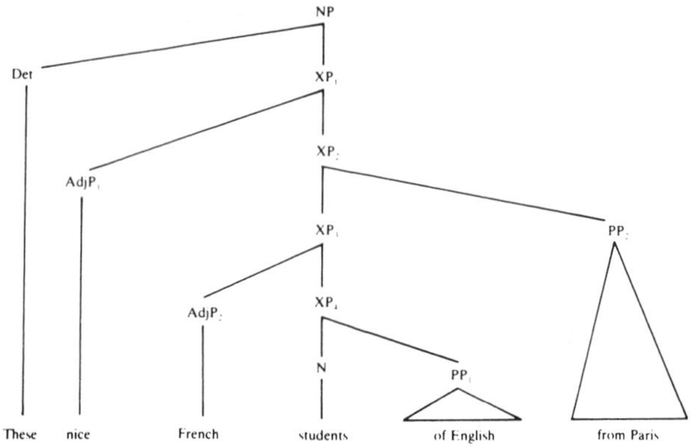

The diagram in (7) is layered: inside the NP we have levels of structure, indicated provisionally by XP_1, etc.

7.2.2 ONE-SUBSTITUTION

Is there any further motivation to support a hierarchical structure such as that in (6) and (7)?

Remember that one type of argument put forward for constituent structure is that of substitution: pro-forms substitute for constituents. In English there is one type of substitution which typically may affect constituents internal to NPs, called ***one*-substitution**.

Consider, for example, (8a) and (8b):

(8a) these nice French students and those nice English ones.

(8b) these nice French students and those awful ones.

In (8a) *ones* stands for *students*, an N. Obviously, lexical categories are constituents (i.e. units) at some level; they are the minimal constituents of syntax. In (8b), on the other hand, *ones* stands for *French students*, i.e. the sequence [AdjP–N]. Since *one*-substitution affects this string, it may also be considered a constituent.

Provisionally, we may say that *one* substitutes for either a Head N, or a Head N and one or more Modifiers.

As (8b) shows, *one*-substitution may, but need not, affect AdjPs. Similarly, *one*-substitution may, but need not, affect PPs (with one major exception which we shall come to immediately):

(9) these nice students from France and those awful ones from Italy (*ones* = students).

Let us return once more to the example in (1), renumbered here as (10):

(10) These nice French students of English from Paris.

One-substitution, as we have seen, may affect constituents at more than one level in the representation. For example, if (10) is conjoined with (10a)–(10d) below, we find that in each case *one(s)* refers to a constituent at a different level (cf. (7) above):

(10a) and those ones (*ones*: nice French students of English from Paris $= XP_1$)

(10b) and those awful ones (*ones*: French students of English from Paris $= XP_2$)

(10c) and those interesting ones from Boulogne (*ones*: French students of English $= XP_3$)

(10d) and those exciting Italian ones (*ones*: students of English $= XP_4$)

(10a)–(10d) show that the level which *one*-substitution affects is not fixed. However, consider the ungrammatical (10e):

(10e) *and the exciting Greek ones of mathematics from Athens.

In the last example *ones* is meant to replace only the Head N *students*, leaving the PP_1 unaffected. This apparently is impossible: PP_1 must be affected by *one*-substitution. However, it would not be correct to claim that the first PP after the Head N is always affected by *one*-substitution either:

(11)	the students	from Paris	in the white shirts
	and		
	the ones	from Greece	in the blue shirts.

In (11) *ones* only affects the Head N *students.*

On the basis of the examples above it seems that *one*-substitution affects the Head N and optionally one or more of any modifiers in the NP, but also that it obligatorily affects constituents of a certain kind such as PP_1 in (10).

If we return once more to the example we see that PP_1 *of English* in fact is not an ordinary Postmodifier. PP_1 rather acts like a Complement. The NP *students of English* corresponds to the VP *study English*, where *English* is a complement of V. Like Vs, Ns also may take a Complement, and this Complement (here realised by a PP) is much more closely linked to the N than the Modifiers. Unlike Verb Complements, however, Noun Complements are syntactically optional.

7.2.3 LAYERING

On the basis of *one*-substitution we may assume that there are good grounds for distinguishing two types of PP after the Head N: (1) the ordinary Postmodifiers, (2) the Complement-like elements which are closely linked to the N, like subcategorised categories in VP. *One*-substitution obligatorily affects the Head N and any Complement-like element. *One*-substitution may, but need not, involve further Premodifiers and Postmodifiers.

The unit consisting of a Head N and its Complements (XP_4 above) is often indicated as $\overline{N}$ (N-bar) or N′ (N-prime). $\overline{N}$ is the first **projection** of N. $\overline{N}$ may further combine with other Modifiers and finally with Det/Spec to form higher levels of structure indicated by $\overline{\overline{N}}$. The structure provisionally posited in (7), may now be represented as follows:

(12)

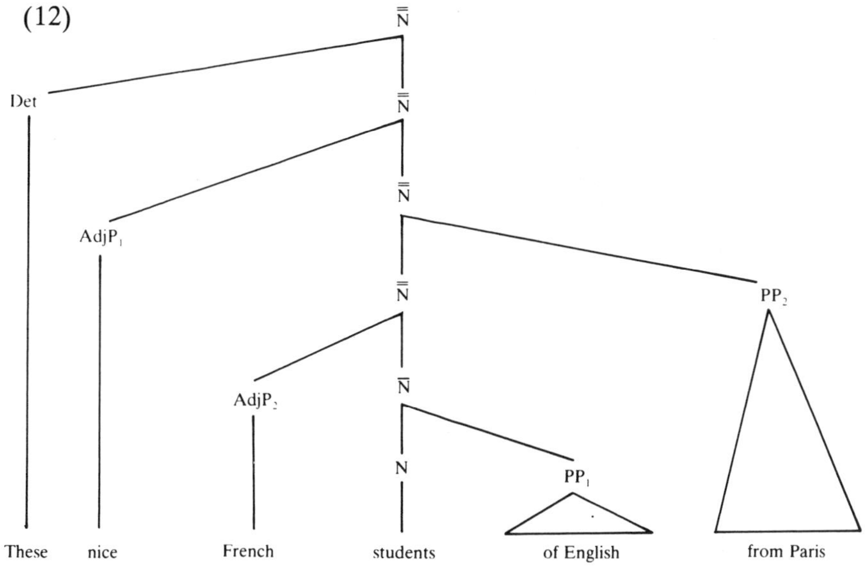

$\bar{N}$ and $\bar{\bar{N}}$ are projections of N; the highest $\bar{\bar{N}}$ is called the **maximal projection**; other levels between N and the maximal projection are called **intermediate projections**.

Tree diagram (12) can be converted into a labelled bracketing:

(13) $\left[_{\bar{\bar{N}}}\right.$these $\left[_{\bar{\bar{N}}}\right.$nice $\left[_{\bar{\bar{N}}}\right.$ $\left[_{\bar{\bar{N}}}\right.$French $\left[_{\bar{N}}\right.$students of English$\left.\right]\left.\right]$ from Paris$\left.\right]\left.\right]\left.\right]$

7.2.4 ONE-WORD PHRASES

Of course, not all NPs have Premodifiers or Postmodifiers, or N-Complements. However, we have shown (2.4.2.3) that single-word phrases (*chocolate*, *milk*, etc.) are also to be treated as NPs. These one-word phrases can thus also be given a layered structure:

(14)

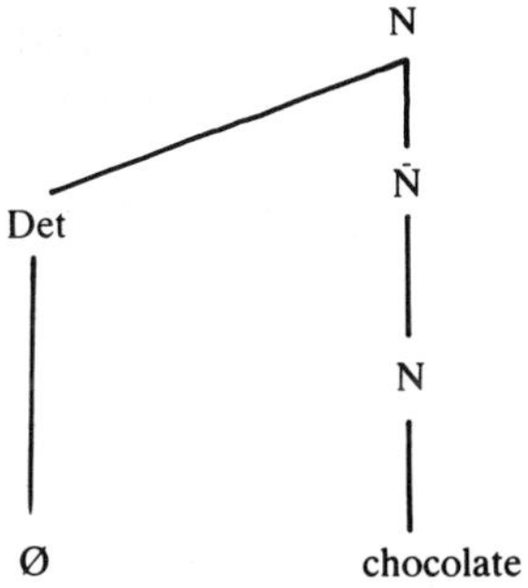

7.3 VERB PHRASES

7.3.1 LAYERING IN VPS

The suggestion put forward for layering NPs can be extended to VPs. Here again we distinguish between the level comprising the Head and its Complements ($\overline{V}$) and higher projections comprising $\overline{V}$ and any optional Adjunct phrases ($\overline{\overline{V}}$). For example, the VP *bought a car last week* has the following structure:

(1)

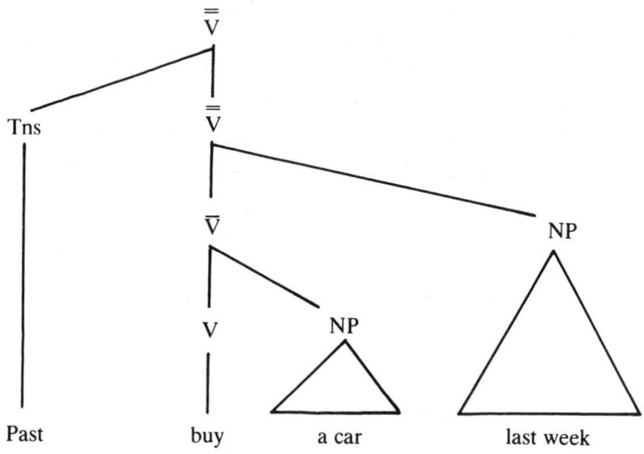

or in labelled bracketing:

(2) $[_{\overline{\overline{V}}}\text{Past}\ [_{\overline{\overline{V}}}\ [_{\overline{V}}\text{buy a car}]\ \text{last week}]]$

7.3.2 FORMAL EVIDENCE

Is there any formal evidence to support the structure above? With respect to NPs we used *one*-substitution as evidence for internal layering; for VPs we may, by analogy, use *do-so* substitution to confirm the structure. Again *do-so* substitution minimally affects the V + Complement(s). Consider:

(3) John bought a car last week and Mary did so the week before. (*did so*: bought a car)

(4) John bought a car last week and Mary did so too. (*did so*: bought a car last week)

(5) *John bought a car last week and Mary did so a motor bike the week before. (*did so: bought)

7.4 PREPOSITIONAL PHRASES

By analogy, the distinction between levels of projection in NP and VP can also be extended to PPs. Again we might distinguish the level of P + Complement (i.e. $\bar{P}$) from a higher level of projection in which further Adjuncts or Modifiers are included ($\bar{\bar{P}}$). Take, for example, the PP in (1):

(1) $\left[_{\bar{\bar{P}}}\text{further} \left[_{\bar{P}}\text{into the room}\right] \text{than Bill}\right]$

as in *George ventured further into the room than Bill.*

In (1) *the room* is the Prepc, *into* is the Head P, and the discontinuous string *further ... than Bill* may be taken as a reduced form of *further ... than Bill ventured*, with ellipsis of *ventured.*

If we take *further* as a Specifier preceding P, then *than Bill* is directly linked to this Spec, and is clearly less inherently linked to P than the NP *the room* is. We might present the internal structure of the PP as follows:

(2)

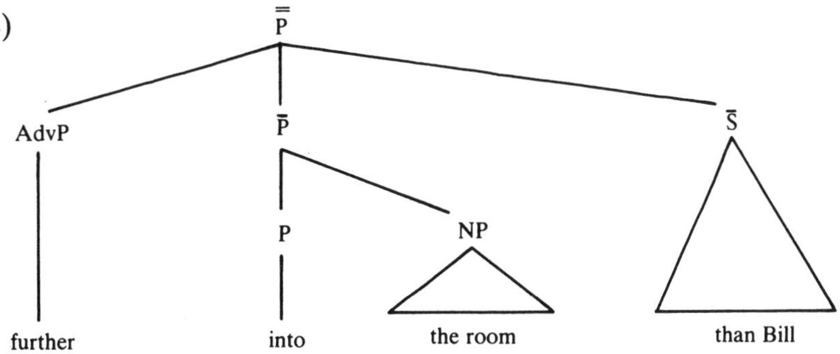

The tree diagram is meant to suggest that *further* and *than Bill* form a discontinuous unit, and are to be interpreted together.

7.5 ADJECTIVE PHRASES

7.5.1 COMPLEMENTS OF ADJS

We have seen that Adjs, like Vs, take Complements. Unlike V-Complements, Adj-Complements in English cannot be NPs, but must be realised by PPs or Ss. For example:

(1a) *aware the danger

(1b) aware of the danger

(1c) aware that she was in danger

(2a) *afraid nuclear war

(2b) afraid of nuclear war

(2c) afraid that they might start a nuclear war

The Adjs above can be said to subcategorise for a PP introduced by some P, or for an $\overline{\text{S}}$. Again we might consider Adj + subcategorised PP as $\overline{\text{Adj}}$, and treat further Modifiers or Specifiers as $\overline{\overline{\text{Adj}}}$-elements.

In the AdjPs below the $\overline{\text{Adj}}$ is italicised, and further elements are $\overline{\overline{\text{Adj}}}$-elements:

(3) sufficiently *aware of the danger* to do something

(4) as *afraid of nuclear war* as her father

The structure may be represented in a tree diagram (simplified):

(5)

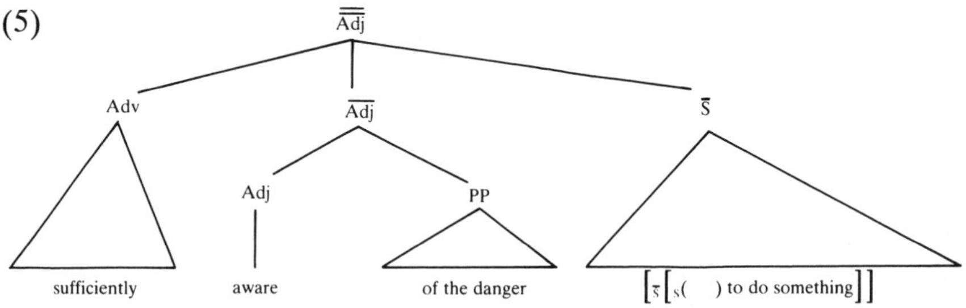

Note that the non-finite clause lacks a lexical Subject and also lacks the complementiser *for*: ( ) is a Subject controlled by some other element in S. For example:

(6) Mary was sufficiently aware of the danger ( ) to do something.

7.5.2 DISCONTINUOUS STRINGS

In 7.5.1 above we have introduced discontinuous strings in AdjPs. These are elements which belong together, but which are separated by intervening material. In the following examples such discontinuous strings are italicised:

(7) He is *too* nice *to do such a thing.*

(8) Susan is *more* ambitious *than her brother.*

(9) This boy is *less* intelligent *than his younger sister.*

AdjPs may be split up by the N they modify:

(10) He is *too nice* a man *to do such a thing.*

(11) You will not find a *more ambitious* girl *than Susan.*

In the examples above the AdjPs are separated by the Head N. In English it is not possible to place an Adj together with its Complement or Postmodifiers before a Head N:

(12) *He is a *too nice to do such a thing* man.

(13) *You will not find *a more ambitious than Susan* girl.

However, it is possible to find the full AdjP as a Postmodifier:

(14) He is a man *too nice to do such a thing.*

(15) You will not find a girl *more ambitious than Susan.*

7.6 ADVERB PHRASES

It would be difficult to extend the analysis proposed here to AdvPs since, as we have seen in 2.4.6, they lack a Complement.

7.7 SUMMING UP: LAYERED STRUCTURE

In Chapter 3 we have suggested that one way of talking about phrasal categories is to set up a general schema in which XP stands for any category of the phrasal level, and X for the lexical Head of the phrase:

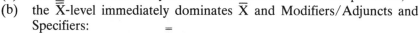

$$\boxed{XP \rightarrow Spec\text{–}X\text{–} \begin{Bmatrix} Mod \\ Adj \end{Bmatrix}}$$

We see now that the schema might be expanded and refined by introducing the bar notation for intermediate projections: phrases have different projections:

(a) the $\bar{X}$-level immediately dominates Heads and their Complements;
(b) the $\bar{\bar{X}}$-level immediately dominates $\bar{X}$ and Modifiers/Adjuncts and Specifiers:

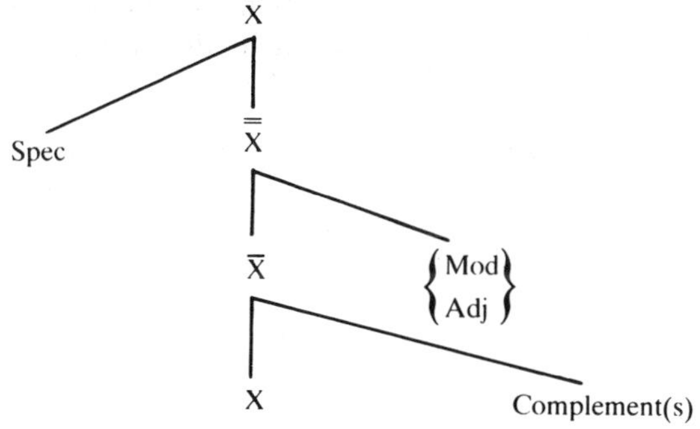

Or in PS rules:

(a) $\overline{\overline{X}} \rightarrow \text{(Spec)}-\overline{X}-\left(\begin{Bmatrix}\text{Mod}\\ \text{Adj}\end{Bmatrix}\right)$

(b) $\overline{X} \rightarrow$ X–Complement(s).

7.8 EXERCISE

Discuss the structure of the phrases below.

(1) John's unexpectedly severe criticism of the play
(2) the recent attacks on Beirut by Israel
(3) the review of the play by that famous author from France which appeared in the Sunday Times
(4) Rembrandt's famous painting of Saskia
(5) the man with a scar who came to dinner last week
(6) the best Dutch classical music of the seventeenth century
(7) sufficiently aware of the problem to advise us what to do
(8) waiting for his wife in the hotel lounge after the reception
(9) too excited about the trip to remember to take his passport
(10) the American invasion of peaceful Grenada in the autumn of 1983

INDEX

£13-99

A MODERN COURSE IN ENGLISH SYNTAX

HERMAN WEKKER AND
LILIANE HAEGEMAN

ROUTLEDGE
London • New York

First published in 1985
by Croom Helm Ltd

Reprinted in 1989, 1991, 1992
by Routledge
11 New Fetter Lane, London EC4P 4EE
29 West 35th Street, New York, NY 10001

Printed and bound in Great Britain
by Billing and Sons Ltd, Worcester

British Library Cataloguing in Publication Data

Wekker, Herman
A modern course in English syntax.
1. English language—Syntax
I. Title II.Haegeman, Liliane
425 PE1361

Library of Congress Cataloging in Publication Data

Wekker, Herman.
A modern course in English syntax.

1.English language—Syntax. I.Haegeman. Liliane M.V. II.Title
PE1361.W37 1985 428.2 85-13994

ISBN 0-415-03684-4